A COOKBOOK CELEBRATING THE CUISINE OF THE PACIFIC NORTHWEST

Oregon Hazelnut Country

THE FOOD, THE DRINK, THE SPIRIT

~ written and illustrated by ~

JAN ROBERTS-DOMINGUEZ

Published by HMB, Hazelnut Marketing Board

21595 Dolores Way, N.E.
Aurora, Oregon 97002
www.oregonhazelnuts.org

Printed by B&B Print Source, Tigard, Oregon, United States of America.

Library of Congress Cataloging-in-Publication Data

Roberts-Dominguez, Jan.

Oregon Hazelnut Country/ written and illustrated by Jan Roberts-Dominguez

p.   cm.

Includes index.

ISBN 978-0-615-41545-1

FIRST EDITION

Editor: Steve Dominguez

Book Design by Joanne McLennan

Watercolor Illustrations by Jan Roberts-Dominguez

Food and Cover Photographs by Karl Maasdam

Food Styling by Jan Roberts-Dominguez

Recipe Editor: Sharon Maasdam

Index by Steve Dominguez

For Steve, of course.

Wise partner, best friend, and delightful husband.

Next summer, stars and mountains.

TABLE OF CONTENTS

ACKNOWLEDGEMENTS

Book editing is thankless work. If you goof, everybody blames you. If you do your job, the author gets the credit. So to my editor, Steve Dominguez, I owe a huge debt of gratitude for working so tirelessly to maintain my style, tone, continuity within and around each recipe and thought, dealing with my long recipe titles, and making me look pretty smart. He's knowledgeable, curious, sensitive, caring, creative, generous, dogged, uncompromising and lately, chronically hungry. Okay, he is my husband. But when he's sitting in his office, working on my copy, he definitely has his editor's hat on. He simply won't settle for anything short of whatever level of perfection he feels we can achieve on a given project. Only once did he complain: "How come you put so many words in this book?"

Hearty thanks to my publisher, the Hazelnut Marketing Board. When they took on this project, they remained committed to making it the best book possible at every turn during its creation. In particular, thank you to the promotion committee: Chairman Mike Klein of Hazelnut Growers Bargaining Association, Compton Chase-Lansdale of Hazelnut Growers of Oregon, Daryl Kihs of Blue Diamond, and hazelnut grower Peter McDonald. Thanks for being so accessible, reasonable, and dedicated to supporting the creative process. Thanks also to Lonna Severson, HMB's assistant manager, for maintaining a sense of calm and control as the project evolved, following through with whatever administrative task needed doing "yesterday," and always doing it with good humor.

And most especially, a huge thank you to the amazing HMB manager Polly Owen, who got the ball rolling by suggesting this book would be a wise undertaking, and for keeping us all moving forward. I've never before enjoyed a book project so thoroughly from start to finish, and it's due, in great part, to Polly.

To our book designer and art director, Joanne McLennan, special thanks for bringing such panache and creativity to the project. Book designers are under-appreciated by everyone who doesn't know how important they are. But without them, a book is just words and pictures on paper. Nothing sings. Nothing sets the tone and communicates at the level the author envisions. In a nutshell, it's about creating the look of every single page in the book. Choosing typefaces and sizes, colors on the page, the arrangements of text, which art to use and where, and having the intuition to know when white space is artistic and when it's a place where a juicy little illustration would work better. All must be done without impairing the clarity of the text or rendering it inefficient to use, this being an instructional work. An artfully designed book compels the reader to keep turning pages. And Joanne did it with enthusiasm and grace. She also brought her valuable eye for design to our photo shoots, ever-vigilant for the best shot, helped with choosing and interfacing with the printer, and formatted the manuscript into a press-ready digital file.

Thanks to Sharon Maasdam, who edited my recipes at The Oregonian's FOODday section for two decades, for letting me pull her out of retirement for this book. And a huge thank you to Mary Bozza for her many hours of thorough and thoughtful proofing.

To Karl Maasdam of Karl Maasdam Photography, I'm especially grateful for his patience, and a delightful run of fun and deliciously beautiful food shoots. Another uncompromising artist, Karl's eye and sense of composition and lighting instilled confidence during a phase that could have been painfully white knuckle-ish. Instead, we were all just sad when it was over. At least we had something to eat in those moments.

Many more people helped to bring this book to life. I will always be grateful to them for their kindness in sharing their thoughts and expertise. Beyond the value of their inputs, their involvement is now the stuff of many fond memories. Heartfelt thanks to:

Ryan Gardner of Visual People Design for his technical assistance during our photo shoots, and for providing an extra pair of photographer's eyes and right-brain thinking.

The Oregon artists who entrusted me with their art for use in the photo shoots: Steve Aulerich, Ted Ernst, Sandy Stegna, Karen Miller, Debra Shapiro, Andre Shapiro, Jan Maitland, Linda Heisserman, Laura G. Berman, Lee Kitzman, Natalie Warrens, Bruce Coblentz, and Dale Donovan.

The hazelnut processors who have helped build this industry. There are about 20 of them who handle the bulk of the harvest. Within the hazelnut handler community, six companies have grown into entities that handle about 85% of the total hazelnut production. During the writing of this book, all have kept me well-supplied with information and hazelnuts. So special thanks to Pat Ehli and his team at P.J. Ehli Company in Albany; the group at Hazelnut Growers of Oregon and Westnut, LLC, in Cornelius; the folks at Blue Diamond in Salem; the Newberg based George family and their crew at George Packing Company who keep two plants in the Willamette Valley very busy; the Mitchell family of Willamette Filbert Growers in Newberg; and Jeff Kenagy and his associates at Northwest Hazelnut Company in Hubbard. Special thanks to Daryl Kihs at Blue Diamond for his patience and insight while touring me through my very first hazelnut processing plant at the height of harvest. And

a very special thank you to Pat Ehli of P.J. Ehli Company, for being tour guide and chief information officer of his amazing high-precision facility; and for all of the post-harvest brain-picking sessions.

The research team at Oregon State University's hazelnut breeding program, headed by plant breeder Dr. Shawn Mehlenbacher, which was there at every turn, responding to all my needs, from impromptu tours of their test fields during a critical phase of research, to vetting my technical writings about the work. Thanks to Senior Research Assistant David Smith, who spent hours with me going through the research activities month by month and touring their campus greenhouse. Also many thanks to Senior Research Assistant Becky McCluskey, for her quick and knowledgeable input whenever I sent some technical copy her way for review.

Dr. Mehlenbacher's predecessors in the breeding program, Dr. Maxine Thompson and Dr. Harry Lagerstedt, who generously shared their knowledge and experience, as did OSU Extension Horticulturists Jeff Olsen of Yamhill County and Ross Penhallegon of Lane County.

Hazelnut grower Dave Buchanan, who granted my wish that he write a hazelnut poem for the book. His beautiful poem, "A Living Legacy," captures the essence of filbert orchard stewardship. Dave also gave generously of his time and wisdom in relaying his philosophies regarding sustainable agriculture. You've earned a lifetime supply of hazelnut caramels, my friend. But you have to share them with your wife, because Margy helped me with her philosophizing and insight on growing hazelnuts, cooking with hazelnuts, and sharing her passion for making a living off the land and welcoming all visitors to the Buchanan Century Farm.

Hazelnut grower Wayne Chambers, for whom sufficient words of thanks can't be found for the energy and love he has given to the hazelnut industry, while actively avoiding the limelight. Wayne and his wife, Joann, have always been a champion of my creative spirit, encouraging me through action and deed. They were there as usual for this project.

Rob and Sally Hilles of Hazelnut Hill, who generously shared their time and knowledge.

Barb and Fritz Foulke of Freddy Guys Hazelnuts, who sent me out into their orchard on a Gator, shared recipes, and sent me some of the earliest production of their wonderful toasted hazelnut oil that was literally "hot off the press."

David and Suzanne Cutsforth, who provided special delivery of some essential Southern Oregon vino, and helped in tracking down my group of food prop artists.

Caron and Paul Klopping, for hosting a wacky band of hazelnut potluckers to launch the project in delectable style; and to their lively guests: John and Debbie Griesmeyer, Rob Thurston and Jan Maitland Thurston, Dave and Margy Buchanan, Pam and Dan Bottom, Joanne and Seaton McLennan, Trudi Timpone, Debbie and Bill Lauer, Shari and Karl Maasdam, Carol and Tim Murphy, Deb and Bruce Bynum, thanks for being good sports.

Albany pilot Ron Terhaar for our flight over the Willamette Valley which provided me a fresh perspective for creating my Willamette River painting. It also refreshed my appreciation for the scale of the local agricultural enterprise.

NOAA biologist Dan Bottom for his fisheries expertise. Dave Buchanan helped with this also, since he is a fisheries biologist too, in addition to growing nuts and wine grapes and owning a winery. I don't know what it is about hazelnuts, but they sure attract energetic people to the industry.

Maggie Crawford of Grand Vines Wine Shop and Bistro in Salem for her overall wine savvy as well as her thoughts on pairing port with nuts. Also to Louise Chelifoux for her tireless taste-testing expertise, and Patrick Magee of Burst's Chocolates for fielding questions and product evaluation.

All the winery folk who were so generous with their time and tastings, particularly Mary Olson at Airlie Winery; Joe Wright and Claire Magee at Belle Vallee; Jolee Wallace at Del Rio Vineyards and Winery; Tom Huggins and Ann Batson at Eola Hills Wine Cellars; Amanda Sever at Harris Bridge Vineyard; PK McCoy and Dai Crisp at Lumos; Nancy Elwer at Mary's Peak Winery; Marcia and Charlie Gilson at Pheasant Court Winery; Tabatha Compton at Spindrift Cellars; and Margy and Dave Buchanan at Tyee Wine Cellars. I have a magnum full of gratitude for you.

Rogue Ale and Spirits president, Brett Joyce, for his generous time and tastings.

Mother Peach's Caramels founder Cheri Swoboda for talking caramels with me, and Sheri Albin for accepting my assignment to adapt and test her peanut brittle recipe using Oregon hazelnuts.

Chef Merlyn Baker, owner of Foley's Station in La Grande, for sharing three of his treasured restaurant specialties.

Sandy and Don Powell of Garland Nursery, for providing insight on the impact that nurseries such as theirs had on the growth of the hazelnut industry when it was in its infancy.

Hugs and kisses to Lily Dominguez for her brilliant discovery about skinning hazelnuts, and to Lily and her sister Anna for their enthusiastic participation in the testing of my hazelnut caramels, and for being such fantastic grandchildren.

And finally, to my parents, Margaret and Will Roberts, for their steadfast support, and all the delicious foods and adventures they provided in my youth that formed the foundation for my lifelong passions...thank you so much. I love you!

~ Jan Roberts-Dominguez

A LIVING LEGACY

We created an orchard of filberts, hazelnuts
Hand shoveling and planting in wet winters
Nurturing fragile solitary whips to survive
Drought and competition from mice, grass, deer

When the trees were young and vigorous
We walked hand in hand to the secret center
Spread a blanket and picnicked with wine
Sheltered by a mosaic of sun and shady green leaves
Light breezes caressed our cheeks

Thirty five years later, our orchard is mature
Summer sun seldom reaches the fecund floor
Stout mossy trunks with a thick leaf canopy
Produce tasty, wholesome hazelnuts and family income
Plus living habitat for wild birds and mammals

Some folks need to move mountains to be happy
We sit back and watch trees grow
Immerse ourselves in seasons and rhythms
Listen to the gentle ground-plunking of falling nuts
Our gift of life to the future

David V. Buchanan
Buchanan Family Century Farm

PROLOGUE

This was my last year of graduate school at Oregon State University and I was researching a paper on hazelnuts. Or, as they were called then, filberts. I discovered that Homer Twedt would be the farmer most likely to provide strong background material for my topic. He was one of the many growers in the area.

When I arrived at his north Corvallis farm, he asked me if I'd ever seen a filbert tree close up. I hadn't.

"Well, let's go for a ride, then," he said.

I climbed up into his old Ford pick-up and off we went, windows down, a welcome breeze blowing orchard dust through the cab. It was late August and the fist-sized clusters of nuts had swollen to maturity, their grass-green husks punctuating the dimness around us.

As we bumped along between the rows of trees, the gnarled old branches were bending down to scrape the roof of the truck. Although a good 27 feet separated the trunks, a dusty-green canopy filtered the afternoon sun.

Somewhere toward the center of his orchard, Homer cut the engine. We sat in the stillness. In every direction, trees marched away in stately order, silent and strong. Deep in my bones I sensed that this place provided a level of peace and pride that I couldn't begin to comprehend. Nor could I visualize how everything would change so drastically in just a few short weeks. Harvest was that close. And throughout the Willamette Valley, all the growers were readying their equipment. Bringing in the totes. Keeping an eye on the weather.

All I could do was sit there and enjoy the summer breeze and speculate on what it must be like to raise such a treasured crop.

CHAPTER 1

Setting the Table

WE'RE A LUCKY LOT HERE IN OREGON

OUR WILD LANDS ARE VAST AND COLORFUL, with looks that carry through fertile river valleys and ancient green forests, up snowy peaks atop mountain ranges, across high arid rangelands and down into grand basins to the east, and finally up into yet more mountains. And then there's the tamed land, just as inspirational in its own way, in the incredible variety and quality of its harvests.

When a friend of mine moved from Utah to Corvallis on the west side of the state, the first thing she did was turn her backyard into one big garden. She was determined to "Eat from the source" in her retirement years. Of course, when she relayed this goal to her son his response was: "But Mom, you moved to the Willamette Valley. Isn't that sort of like cheating?"

And it's true. We live in a horticultural paradise. This northwest Oregon valley, 150 miles in length, north to south, and 60 miles across at its widest point, is cradled in the arms of two water-rich mountain ranges. It bears the name of the river all that water generates, flowing north through some of the richest farm land in the world to its journey's end at the mighty Columbia River.

One of the many joys of living here is the anticipation of local seasonal foods. The first rhubarb and peas of spring are followed by the fabulous Oregon strawberry in early June. Summer brings more berries—elegant raspberries, a jumble of blueberries (more varieties than you would ever imagine!), Marionberries, Loganberries, sweet cherries, peaches, apricots, melons, juicy new-crop garlic, sweet corn, onions, and two months of non-stop heirloom tomatoes.

As autumn's short-but-golden days tantalize, the farmers' markets still yield plenty of juicy bounty, from flavorful plums, crisp apples, potent storage onions, and thick-fleshed squash, to succulent pears.

We grow great hops here too. Enough to support a vibrant craft beer industry that dazzles the rest of the country and encourages a band of researchers at Oregon State University to continue to develop new and even better varieties.

And then there's the wine. World class wine. The Willamette Valley is Oregon's largest wine region, with over 200 wineries within a varied appellation that is actually comprised of six sub-appellations—Chehalem Mountains, Dundee Hills, Eola-Amity Hills, McMinnville, Ribbon Ridge and Yamhill Carlton. Thanks to David Lett, who against the advice of his California wine industry friends traveled north from California and made the first planting of Pinot Noir in 1965, this fertile valley has become known as one of the premier Pinot Noir producing regions in the world.

Actually, this is just a taste of the abundance unleashed upon us each year. Altogether it's an amazing journey that won't slow down until the fields are finally nudged into dormancy by cooling autumn weather, and the grapes come off the vines. It is only then, like a beautiful parting gift, that the hazelnut trees release their bounty, fully packaged to last the long winter.

This book is mostly about that last harvest of golden nuts and its incredible potential to enhance one's personal cuisine. In Europe, with its vast and ancient hazelnut industry, this would be old news. One might think it odd that this commodity is so little understood and so underutilized in an America heavily influenced by a European immigrant heritage. We've even had a hard time settling on a name for it, with candidates too disparate for song. Think "You say tomato, and I say tomahto, You say potato, and I say potahto," and then try to work in "You say filbert, and I say hazelnut." See what I mean? Hazelnut is currently in vogue, but many growers still say they grow filberts and sell hazelnuts. In this book, I'll stick with hazelnut, since you and I are on the buying end. But don't be surprised if a few filberts leak into the story.

Anyway, the fact is that until the mid-20th century, commercial production of hazelnuts in North America was not very significant, and this may explain how they more or less dropped out of our cuisine. Now, even though some of the best hazelnuts in the world are being grown in large numbers in Oregon, most of that crop is exported because the product is more of an enigma than the incredible resource it should be to American cooks.

"Food is the handshake between rural and urban communities, the thing most closely shared among all Oregonians."

Peg Herring, Editor,
"Oregon's Agricultural Progress,"
Fall, 2009, Vol. 55, No. 2,
Oregon State University.

A Prophecy Fulfilled

"Following about a dozen filbert trees planted by Mr. A.A. Quanberg of Vancouver, Washington, I believe the next 300 in the Northwest were planted by me.

"Twenty years ago, of the few people who knew filberts were being grown here, not to exceed half a dozen had reason to hope that it would eventually become an important minor industry. I was one of them. At the 1914 meeting of the Oregon State Horticultural Society I delivered the first address on filberts ever delivered in the Northwest and aside from some possible local reference in some newspaper (if such a reference was ever made), I think it was the first time the public was reminded of the possibilities of filbert culture.

"Based on the previous record of my groves which I gave in that address I had the temerity to say: 'I fully believe that in time the filbert groves of the Willamette Valley will rival the famous groves of Naples, Sicily or Terragona.'

"Uninfluenced by the prevalent opinion that the hope I then voiced was only a pipe dream, I continued to broadcast my views through many addresses and newspaper articles, some of which were given much publicity. In later years I was ably seconded by others of the same opinion and due to our united efforts it is now conceded that instead of a pipe dream it has become a reality that as fine filbert groves as there are in the world are now in the Willamette Valley—a dream come true."

George A. Dorris, excerpt from the 1934 publication
"Filbert Nursery Stock, Grown by the Tip System,"
by George A. And Ben F. Dorris, Springfield, Oregon.

So let us begin at the beginning and shed a little light on this gift from nature, to demystify it from cultivation to kitchen to table. It is a story worth the telling.

HAZELNUTS IN OREGON

EVERY BIG THING BEGINS WITH A PERSON, an idea and a dream. For the Oregon hazelnut industry, that person was George Dorris. His idea was that the Willamette Valley was the perfect place to grow hazelnut trees. His dream, that it would one day become the hazelnut-growing capital of America. So in 1905 he purchased 200 filbert trees from Portland nurseryman J.B. Pilkington and made the first commercial planting. All five acres were the Barcelona variety, which remains the predominant variety in Oregon orchards today.

Dorris kick-started the realization of his dream through the sale of nuts to another innovative upstart company, Meier & Frank. The Meier & Frank Company, in turn, sold Dorris' filberts in 10-pound bags directly to consumers. Everybody concerned was happy. And well fed! Other Oregon farmers soon came to believe that this was a crop to bank on, and were willing to dedicate acre upon acre to orchards. But trees were in such short supply that Dorris was moved to set up the first hazelnut nursery, which, in its 40 year span, produced an average of

70,000 trees per year. Today over 650 growers produce over 99.9 percent of the domestic hazelnut crop, up to 49,000 tons and averaging 35,000 tons, in Oregon's fertile and climatically temperate Willamette Valley. Up until just a few years ago, more than half of the trees in use originated as Dorris Ranch nursery stock.

Of course, Dorris wasn't the only early believer. In a 1921 article in The Oregon Statesman, nut and fruit orchard development expert Knight Pearcy made a case for a strong hazelnut industry in the mid-Willamette Valley: "The filbert is a nut that offers even more than does the walnut to the planter in this favored section with the "mistland" climate. It comes into commercial bearing the fifth year, under proper conditions. It bears prolifically; requires a minimum of labor to produce and to harvest; is not injured by rains at harvest or by frosts at blossom time; is comparatively non-perishable; and is not as exacting as to soil conditions and location as is the walnut. There is at present American consumption of about twenty million pounds, a demand created without a

dollar's worth of advertising, and yet there is no other section of America that can grow the nut commercially.

"Before the war the filbert brought the grower 15 to 18 cents per pound and went up to 35 cents in 1919. George Dorris, the veteran grower at Eugene, says that a number one planting should produce as follows: 500 to 1000 pounds per acre at five years; 1000 to 1500 pounds at six years; 2000 to 3000 pounds at eight years; 3000 to 4000 at ten and 4000 to 5000 at 12 years. Reduce these yields, all of which are attainable, by 50 percent and still they offer splendid returns on that investment."

Another early grower was Ferd Groner. In 1880, at the age of 17, Ferd helped his family build a grand Victorian-style house, one brick at a time. The historic estate still stands where Scholls Ferry Road and River Road intersect about 20 miles southwest of Portland. After taking over the family business at age 28, when his father died, Ferd soon built a farming empire around hay and walnuts. Somewhere along the way he also put in a hazelnut orchard, which grew to 200 acres. It wasn't until 1943,

when he was 80, that Ferd decided he needed some help with the orchard. His ad in the Oregonian was answered by Andrew Loughridge, who had a wife and infant son to support and needed the work. To the questions posed by Ferd, "Do you smoke? Do you drink?" Andy was able to answer in the negative. Ferd took a shine to him and even invited the family to move into living quarters on the lower level of his brick mansion.

The Loughridge family lived in the main house for about a year before moving to another house on the estate. A few short years after that, Ferd died. In his will, he bequeathed half of the hazelnut orchard—100 acres!—to Andy. And so, for the next 60 years, Andy grew hazelnuts.

It was a life that suited a man with such a strong work ethic, with the consistency of its year-round demands. His barn-like red nut dryer, with its iconic cupola, drew customers from near and far. Others came to Loughridge Farm to buy his nuts. And after Andy filled up their bags and weighed them, he always topped off the purchase with a few extras—just in case there were some bad ones.

Up to the age of 89, he was still farming the entire orchard on his own, with only one hired hand. Then he leased out all but 5 acres, which he kept working. In November of 2005, at the age of 94, Andy suffered a debilitating stroke. That previous October, however, he had participated in the harvest one last time. He'd raked the end rows in the orchard, run the sweeper, and even driven the tractor pulling the harvester that picked up the wind-rowed nuts. Before his death, he was told that the price for nuts had hit a new high, $1 a pound. His eyes lit up: "I'll have to tell the bank to get a bigger box to put my money in."

The Good Old Days....

THINGS WERE A LOT DIFFERENT after harvest when hazelnut growers David and Wayne Chambers were just starting out. David's wife Darlene has vivid recollections: "We washed all our own nuts after harvest, outside in big galvanized buckets, with the hose. And then we had to spread them out on screens with a fan to dry."

Dave and his brother Wayne built special drying racks, she added, "and we had them drying all over the place. In our basements and garages...nuts everywhere. And then we'd crack them all by hand."

But at one point, she said, "Dave's little light bulb went on and he said, 'you know, our grandfather used to have a nut cracker. An electric nutcracker. I'll bet you that thing is still down there in the barn somewhere.'

"So he went down to the old barn, dug around and sure enough found the darn thing. And it was just a little machine that you could adjust the width on so you could crack different types and sizes of nuts. And it worked great, except that the big ones would get squished and the little ones would fall through.

"So then David built a sorter," laughed Darlene. "I'm not kidding! Out of parts of other things, like a leaf blower, he made a grader and a little track. So the smaller nuts would fall through and the big ones kept going. It had a little chute that squeezed down smaller, smaller, smaller...and sorted them into little boxes. It was so cool, because then he could adjust the cracking machine and crack them by size.

"Well, I think back to all that work we did. We washed the nuts by hand and it was always cold, freezing weather and your hands were cold and you were cold. Hey we were young, right? And now, after harvest, we just haul them up the road to Pat Ehli's plant, and then we buy them back, all washed, dried, cracked, graded, and sorted."

HOW ITS DONE TODAY

THESE DAYS, HAZELNUT GROWERS can't necessarily count on $1 per pound, but they do get to put in the same hard work as always. Briefly, it goes like this: Hazelnuts bloom in January with tiny red flowers gleaning pollen from large yellow catkins. Trees leaf out in spring and the fruits mature over the summer, falling to the ground of their own accord in mid-September to early November. Along the way the orchards are meticulously cared for and groomed. Once the nuts are on the ground, they are mechanically swept into long windrows, and then scooped up with a tractor-drawn harvester and poured into large totes. The totes are typically delivered to a "handler", which is a business specializing in cleaning, drying, bleaching, grading, inspecting, and packing whole and shelled nuts for distribution. Some also roast kernels and even produce value-added products such as retail-packaged nuts or confections.

A few farmers undertake the whole process from tree to retail, which takes a real love for the business. Here is how Kathy Beutler who farms near Salem, OR describes it: "First off, I am a city girl who moved to the farm about 15 years ago. My husband Neil and I have 60 acres of Casina hazelnuts, in addition to a cleaning and drying operation. Over the years, I have never tired of the cycles I see in the orchard. The catkins in January, with their yellow pollen, the small red blossoms

The Oregon Nut Bill

Twenty years ago, Richard Fritz was getting a little razzing from his friends for his association with a certified nut. The Oregon hazelnut. At the time, Fritz was assistant director of the Oregon State Department of Agriculture, overseeing the Agricultural Development and Marketing Division. His goal? Find unusual and creative ways to help Oregon producers move their product.

So when Karen Lobb sought his support for her campaign to make the Oregon hazelnut the official state nut, he got on board. The state that had pioneered measures such as mandatory deposits on bottles and cans would become the first state in the nation to have an official nut.

Back in 1988, when Lobb was Promotion Manager for the Hazelnut Marketing Board, she figured what better way to raise public awareness for one of Oregon's oldest and dearest commodities? She made her case, pointing out that the hazelnut was big business for Oregon, annually pumping millions of dollars into the state's economy. Even though Washington and British Columbia were also in the hazelnut business, Oregon had already established itself as the leader in production, accounting for 98 percent of the nation's supply (now it's pushing 99.9 percent.) Ultimately, the Legislature agreed to make it official:

THE OFFICIAL STATE NUT
65th Oregon Legislative Assembly—1989 Regular Session
Senate Concurrent Resolution 5

Whereas the hazelnut (Corylus avellana) is a nutritious, healthful food, useable in many different and delicious forms; and

Whereas Oregon produces 98 percent of the nation's supply of hazelnuts; and

Whereas hazelnut production contributes significantly to the Oregon economy, ranging from $12.3 to $38.3 million annually, depending on the year; and

Whereas an estimated 19,700 tons of hazelnuts were harvested in Oregon in 1987; and

Whereas there are more than 1,100 growers and handlers of hazelnuts in the state; now,

Therefore, be it Resolved by the Legislative Assembly of the State of Oregon:

The hazelnut is recognized as and hereby is proclaimed to be the official Oregon nut.

hardly visible, the tinges of green as the leaves unfold in the spring. As summer progresses, nuts appear in tiny clusters and then suddenly there they are and the branches are bending to the land. As harvest approaches the nuts are turning brown and falling to the ground, but in the tree you see the green tight catkins for next year. As fall comes upon us the nuts are swept up into tidy rows to be picked up by the harvester as the leaves on Casinas turn to yellow, gold and rust. Soon the leaves provide a colorful carpet for the orchard and the catkins for next year are hanging on bare branches ready to start the cycle again."

"Hazelnut trees bloom in the middle of winter and the wind carries their pollen from yellow catkins to tiny red flowers. The nuts don't begin forming until June but, like New Year's resolutions, the promises that produce the harvest ahead are made today.

So here is my first New Year's resolution for 2010: think like an Oregon hazelnut grower."

Alison Dennis, Director of Sustainable Programs,
Burgerville Corporation,
December 31, 2009.

HOW TO BUILD A BETTER NUT

ON THE SURFACE, THE HAZELNUT INDUSTRY is still trees standing in orchards. But that, and hard work, is where resemblance to the old days and ways ends. Things are better now. Of course, better is a relative term. Especially when you're talking about something that's already near-perfect by world standards. But the industry is always trying to find ways to improve. So, for example, what would be the dream harvest characteristics for this nut? For the grower, it would be one that ripens and drops from its frilly pod on the same day as the rest of the nuts in the orchard. Then there would be no agonizing over how long to wait before harvesting. And they'd only have to sweep through the orchard one time. And while we're at it, let's arrange for hazelnuts to drop comfortably in advance of the mid-autumn rains. Mud is such a downer when you're trying desperately not to leave a single nut behind. Finally, since we're dream-spinning here, let's also shoot for ways to assure a predictable harvest from year to year, rather than yields that are high one year and less the next.

The interesting thing is that Oregon growers invest in their dreams to bring them to life. It's this kind of forward thinking that makes the Oregon Hazelnut Industry so progressive. I've seen it over and over as I've gotten to know these people. They're a special breed. As a group, they're continuously seeking to arm themselves with the kind of information that will foster safe and responsible cultivation of this special nut, and with new varieties that are naturally resistant to disease and exhibit high quality kernel characteristics, high yield, and performance in a wider variety of soils. To these ends, Oregon State University and the hazelnut industry maintain a vibrant partnership that has spanned almost 40 years. It's been a patient, successful journey, with much promise for continued success.

The OSU breeding program began under the direction of C.E. Schuster in the mid-1920's. With the joint support of OSU's Agricultural Experiment Station and the U.S. Department of Agriculture, Schuster began the quest for disease resistance, focusing most determinedly on the Barcelona variety of hazelnut, due to its many excellent characteristics.

When Maxine Thompson took over the reins from Schuster in 1969, she concentrated on improvements that would be particularly beneficial for the kernel market and would generate a premium price on the world exchange. During her seventeen year tenure she produced several crosses that were eventually released as named varieties.

In the mid-1980's, Dr. Shawn Mehlenbacher arrived to carry on the breeding program. In a time-consuming, and sometimes mind-numbing process, Mehlenbacher, along with his highly capable team, make 25 to 50 crosses each year. This generates about 8000 seedlings, every one of which ulti-mately gets evaluated by Mehlenbacher, and most don't make the cut to stay in the program. In fact, the phrase amongst the research team is "We grow 'em to throw 'em."

Building on the work of his predecessors, Mehlenbacher and his team were finally able to release a new variety named Lewis in 1997, followed by Clark in 1999, and Santiam in 2004. All have excellent cultural and physical characteristics. Santiam, in particular, offers a unique level of disease resistance for a hazelnut that is early-maturing and high-yielding with a shell that is satisfyingly thin and a kernel that is as lovely as the Barcelona's when it comes to flavor, size, and shape.

During Shawn's remaining years at Oregon State, he'll continue to fine-tune the quality of his crosses. He travels the world collecting hazelnut seed for his breeding program from varieties that present ideal traits in kernel and inshell quality. His program is, in fact, the envy of the hazelnut world.

QUEST FOR SUSTAINABILITY

ALISON DENNIS, DIRCTOR OF SUSTAINABLE PROGRAMS at Burgerville Corporation, brings a refreshing perspective to the concept of practicing agriculture with a conscience: "This morning, I was reminded of some wisdom an Oregon hazelnut grower shared with me...: 'Cared for sustainably, a hazelnut tree can be productive for as long as a hundred years, so hazelnut growers tend to make decisions from a hundred year perspective.'

"Imagine the future that is possible when we all make decisions in our work and lives from a hundred year perspective, like the 650 hazelnut farming families in Oregon."

Clearly, anyone thinking of assuring a small tree a century of productive life is thinking in terms of sustainable techniques. Issues of soil maintenance, pest control, disease control and resistance, and impacts on surrounding ecosystems are all germane to the industry. Many growers are employing more selective and prescriptive measures to keep their orchards at peak performance and health. New approaches such as use of pheromones in insect management are being investigated. Innovations in orchard geometry and pollination science are improving yield. And, of course, the aforementioned breeding program is highly relevant. This isn't the place to get into the weeds of sustainability science, but for its sheer perfection I will leave you with one triumph from the industry.

Unlike Europe, the Willamette Valley once had a problem with filbert aphids. An OSU graduate student in entomology, Russell Messing, decided to cross the pond to find out why, and ultimately returned with some little wasps. Not just any wasps, said Oregon hazelnut grower David Buchanan. "A special little wasp that was a preda-

A Breeder's Life

"I loved when the hazelnuts were getting ripe. I loved walking up and down and looking at all of the variabilities. Every seedling is different. You make crosses. You cross this one with that because one has certain characteristics you want, the other has other characteristics. And then you wait and see what the seedlings are gonna look like. And walking up and down those rows as the nuts ripen, seeing all the variability—'Oh, that one is really good!'—it's exciting. A breeder's life is fascinating.

"I remember when the faculty was agitating for more money, or unionizing or whatnot, and my associate, Jim Baggett, turned to me at a meeting. He said: 'I don't know why they pay me so much money to do what I like to do so well anyway, let alone agitating for more money.'

"I said, 'I feel the same way. This is my joy.'"

Dr. Maxine Thompson, hazelnut plant breeder at OSU from 1965 to 1987; on being asked what one of her favorite parts of her job was.

tor for the filbert aphid. He released this wasp in three Willamette Valley hazelnut orchards, and one of those orchards was mine." said Buchanan.

"Unfortunately, we didn't notice any response to the release. No discernable population of wasps was established, and no reduction in hazelnut aphids was noticed. Messing eventually headed further west, to Hawaii, certain that he had failed.

"Six years later," Buchanan said, "I noticed this tiny little winged bug. Smaller than, say, a sugar ant. I didn't know what it was at first. Then I real-

ized that it was the wasp that Russell had tried to establish here." "It's true," said OSU senior research assistant David Smith. "After a number of years, this wasp became established in Oregon hazelnut orchards and became, literally, a textbook example for biological control of an insect pest. His work changed the face of pest management in Oregon hazelnuts... We love bugs that eat bugs!"

NUTRITION

WE ARE FORTUNATE TO LIVE IN AN ERA in which the nutritional characteristics of foods are well known, as is the importance to health of a balanced diet. However, I have to say that most of us could do a better job of maintaining that balance over time, and cutting back on foods that offer only "empty calories". In one sense, that is what this book is about, because whatever you do with hazelnuts, you can rest assured that you are dealing with a naturally healthful, richly nutritious commodity. In fact, their remarkable nutritional profile alone is reason enough to work them into your personal cuisine.

Among all nuts, hazelnuts are one of the lowest in saturated fat, and an excellent source of monounsaturated fats, considered to be "good fats." Beyond that, hazelnuts are a good source of vitamins E and K, B vitamins (hazelnuts are tops among tree nuts in folate), magnesium, copper, manganese, and fiber.

With ever-growing appreciation of the benefits of antioxidants, it's good to know that all nuts are excellent sources, with hazelnuts being the best. They are, in fact, on a par with dark chocolate and Concord grape juice, which are considered to be among the world's superfoods when it comes to antioxidant content. Imagine a snack of chocolate covered hazelnuts with a glass of Concord grape juice. What a trifecta!

Fitting the pieces together

"The most excitement is looking at all the genetic diversity available to develop new varieties. Seeing how the pieces fit. There's so much potential. And it's exciting from the perspective of the discipline and knowing that everything you do will have an impact, which makes it so personally rewarding.

"Another really good part for me is working with such good people. Growers are supportive of the research. They share with each other, which I find amazing. They're so welcoming of other points of view. And they're patient. Plant breeding is a slow process."

Dr. Shawn Mehlenbacher, OSU Professor and Head of the OSU Hazelnut Breeding Program, taking a break during harvest and reflecting on the rewards of his profession.

From Farm to Fork

A Year in the Life of the Oregon Hazelnut Industry
Growing and Improving the Best Hazelnuts in the World

WINTER

Barring ice storms, though, the main excitement in the winter orchard is the
miracle of reproduction. You see, in the deep of winter, at a time when all other
orchard crops are dormant, hazelnut trees are very much awake. Catching a ride
on chill winds flowing through the orchard, pollen from prolific yellow
catkins finds its way to tiny red flowers. So, even as the grower trims and prunes,
the trees are setting themselves up for new growth and nut production.

From Farm to Fork

A Year in the Life of the Oregon Hazelnut Industry
Growing and Improving the Best Hazelnuts in the World

WINTER IN THE ORCHARD

Let's start off slow, shall we? It's January in the Willamette Valley, and the frenetic pace that drives a hazelnut grower around harvest time is months and months away. There's plenty to be done in the orchard, but there's also, for once, more time to do it.

Leaves have dropped, revealing each tree's true form. It's an opportunity to evaluate the orchard's growth and health. This is the time to prune, since nuts grow on new wood, and the old has to be trimmed away. It's also the time to plant new trees. It's an ongoing process, pulling old trees from the orchard in favor of new varieties. Or adding new pollenizers that might improve yield or quality.

WINTER IN THE BREEDING PROGRAM

Things aren't quite so mellow over at Oregon State University in Corvallis, Oregon where plant breeder Dr. Shawn Mehlenbacher is the mastermind and driving force behind the hazelnut breeding program. He's up to his eyeballs in research in the lab and physical labor at the OSU research farm. As of 2010, there are about 100 selections in six trials that are being evaluated for their potential as new cultivars, including 40 that were planted in the spring of 2009. Because it takes almost two decades to develop a new cultivar, it's crucial to choose each cross wisely. Each choice represents a tiny, hopeful step forward in the search for the perfect hazelnut.

At the OSU research farm, 25-50 young trees have been selected to be a part of the year's cross-pollination trial. Each one of these trees has some desired traits that Mehlenbacher wants to carry forward into the next generation. That will happen by pollination with another tree that has its own set of good traits. To accomplish this, first, half of the selected trees need pruning so they can be fitted with 8- by 8-foot wood-framed cages that are covered in white polyethylene plastic. The cages will isolate the trees inside from the ambient pollen stream that will soon flow by on air currents. Next, Senior Faculty Research Assistants Becky McCluskey, David Smith, and crew emasculate each enclosed tree by cutting off all its pollen-laden catkins. Then, in February, while the trees are in bloom, the team—armed with a collection of pollens that

Mehlenbacher has chosen from the other half of the trial trees—enters the pollination cages and applies the selected pollen by hand, one flower at a time, to anywhere from 400 to 2000 flowers per tree. "Busy little bees," says Smith of their activity.

Every five days throughout the season McCluskey makes the rounds at the farm taking notes on the pollen shed and flower emergence behavior of 100 trees. She also collects pollen from fat yellow catkins to test in the search for better pollenizer varieties. At the same time, Mehlenbacher is trekking out to the research farm two and three times each week to collect flowers from literally hundreds of hazelnut limbs that have been tucked away in pollen-proof bags. Hazelnuts have evolved a complicated mechanism that ensures lots of diversity and survival in the species. Shawn spends long days looking through a microscope at hand-pollinated flowers to determine the specific reaction for each new tree. "There's about a three week period when it is really crazy with pollen shedding and flowers at optimum quality, and we just go, go, go," says McCluskey. "While the vegetable and fruit researchers are working away indoors, we're getting cold toes and plenty of fresh air." A hazelnut tree's living cycle waits for no scientist.

When the pollen shed is complete, winter pruning in the research orchard begins in earnest. McCluskey, Smith and Mehlenbacher sort trees for advanced selection trials that will be planted when the weather improves in April.

In early March, Smith pulls the collection of hybrid seeds from the last harvest from their cold, dark, damp storage facility. This is, literally, the fruit of last year's crosses. As the nuts warm to ambient temperatures, their internal clocks say "Spring has come!" Within a week, they're sprouting and Smith starts planting them out in the greenhouse. There are about 8000 to handle but only half will ultimately make it to the farm for field planting. The rest get tossed, thanks to a disease resistance screening test that can be done when the trees are a mere 4-6 inches tall.

When the entire campus pauses to celebrate the end of Winter term, the team takes a breather, says McCluskey, seeking sunnier climes "to thaw out for a week."

SPRING

Bud swell—it's a tiny moment signaling a crushing cascade of events. As Uncle Ray says: "You need to get it all done, and all done right in the spring, and then the whole season will follow in an orderly manner. Mess up one spring job and you'll pay for it all down the line."

Barb Foulke, Freddy Guys Hazelnuts,
Monmouth, Oregon, describing spring in the orchard.

From Farm to Fork

A Year in the Life of the Oregon Hazelnut Industry
Growing and Improving the Best Hazelnuts in the World

SPRING IN THE ORCHARD

Tender green buds, enticed by warming sunlight bathing naked branches, begin to swell. Leaves emerge and the entire scene, when viewed from afar, is a delicate blur of spring green on winter grey. It's time to crank up activities in the orchard.

Mowing needs to be done. But before that, the orchard needs tidying up, policing up all the fallen wood and orchard debris. The tractor is run up and down each row, dragging along a wide steel beam that flattens and grooms the ground. Then it's time to fertilize, which means performing detailed leaf and soil analysis first. If an orchard tests low for boron levels, then this is the time to add that as well. Studies have shown that boron helps with nut set.

In late Spring growers have to be thinking about sun scald, which can be particularly hard on young trees that haven't developed a wide enough canopy to protect their trunks. Trunk collars or tree paints need to be applied, particularly on the south and southwest sides of the trees. Pest and disease management practices are put in motion as needed to keep trees healthy.

By early June, the orchard is fully clothed in leaves. Young shoots have sprung up several feet. Along the branches, the immature nuts are showing themselves and fertilization is about to take place. Pollination, of course, was way back in January. That's the quirky side of this plant.

SPRING IN THE BREEDING PROGRAM

Over on the research farm, as the trees begin to leaf out and it's determined that the last late-shedding pollen is gone, the polyethylene cages isolating cross-breeding test trees can be slit open to let the wind blow through. Once the trees are acclimated to their fresh environment, the cages come down.

Transplanting in the greenhouse, grafting, planting field trials, and DNA extractions on 2400 to 3000 plants that are analyzed for genetic markers of disease resistance occupy the team.

This is not genetic engineering. Rather, the information acquired helps direct the choices of cultivars for the cross-breeding program, eliminating many false steps.

SUMMER

On hot summer days, sunlight filters down through the branches, landing in golden puddles on the orchard floor. It's a cool and comfortable environment for all winged and earth-bound creatures.

From Farm to Fork

A Year in the Life of the Oregon Hazelnut Industry
Growing and Improving the Best Hazelnuts in the World

SUMMER IN THE ORCHARD

While other Willamette Valley crops—the blueberries, strawberries, Marionberries, raspberries, peaches, apricots, salad greens, tomatoes, and herbs—are in the throes of harvest, the hazelnut orchard is biding its time. After the intense activities of spring, the necessities of June, July and even early August, seem almost lackadaisical.

In a healthy, mature orchard, the overhead canopy is full and thick. Growers occasionally tractor along between the shady rows with their water tanks, giving the baby trees a much-needed drink. The mature trees get along just fine with their deeper roots. On hot summer days, sunlight filters down through the branches, landing in golden puddles on the orchard floor. It's a cool and comfortable environment. Stand still and identify the trills and coos of the many songbirds sheltering among the branches. You may spot some little nut thieves plying their trade. They don't have it as easy as you might think. Listen for the occasional screech from red-tailed hawks working the edges for squirrels. A cooper's hawk might glide close overhead, working the canopy for jays. Owls keep up the watch at night right inside the orchard. Integrated pest management sometimes just comes naturally, with talons.

Of course, summer is also the time for vigilance against insect pests. There is growing regard in the industry for restrained management, which depends on careful monitoring of adult populations, in some cases with pheromone traps. There has even been success with biological control of at least two species.

As summer wanes, the coming autumn storm of harvest is never far from growers' minds. In preparation they'll continue to groom the orchard floor, weeding and sweeping, keeping the ground smooth in all directions, as far as the eye can see. A final run-through in early September with the flail grinds up nut blanks and twigs that have dropped, and readies the orchard for harvest.

SUMMER IN THE BREEDING PROGRAM

Summer life isn't quite so calm for the hazelnut research team. In the campus greenhouses, David Smith and his crew are watering, fertilizing, staking, tying, and pruning those seedlings from nuts they planted last winter, readying them for transport to the OSU research farm on the east side of the Willamette River. No longer babies, the young trees have gained four to five feet in height over the last five months, making them an unwieldy cargo on the trailer. It will take 14 trips to settle the entire collection in their new digs.

In the orchard, farm manager Randy Hopson oversees the big job of keeping 60+ acres of hazelnut trees of all ages in tip-top shape. "He does a terrific job overseeing all the irrigation, weed control, mowing and brush removal, and pitches in and lends a hand at planting time. He helps us look good," says Becky McCluskey.

And through it all, there are evaluations at every turn:

~ Evaluation of the harvested nuts from the previous year. There may be as much as half the harvest left in a cool storage room waiting to be scrutinized for all the characteristics on Mehlenbacher's very long wish list.

~ Evaluation of the maturing trees in the field, to determine which ones will be producing enough nuts to be a part of the team's harvest and which won't. "Shawn (Mehlenbacher) walks every row and looks at every tree in late summer, prior to harvest. He's literally doing the "hands on" work of selecting which seedlings will be harvested, and grabs one of us to record notes, in the true tradition of plant breeders," explains McCluskey. "Before we even start harvesting nuts, Mehlenbacher is evaluating for appropriate husk shape (which allows the nut to drop freely at maturity), shells that conform to industry standards, and nuts that are round instead of elongated."

Summer brings international visitors. So tours and talks merge into the ongoing tasks of research. McCluskey and Smith catch up on marking trees for discard, making sure tree labels are in place, and cutting out discard trees with the chainsaw.

AUTUMN

You can feel it in the air. The chill from the longer, colder nights that doesn't subside until mid-day. Then the heat is intense. This dramatic fluctuation in temperature preps the mature nuts for harvest. The outer husks swell with the heat and contract with the cold. Ultimately this helps to work the nuts loose and they drop to the ground. Not all at once. That would be too convenient! No, it's gradual at first. Then autumn winds rustle branches and move things along. At times, all you can do is stand off to the side and watch: it's raining nuts.

From Farm to Fork

A Year in the Life of the Oregon Hazelnut Industry
Growing and Improving the Best Hazelnuts in the World

AUTUMN IN THE ORCHARD

The equipment is readied. The tractor, sweeper and harvester all need a thorough going over. A breakdown in the middle of harvest is disastrous when you're racing against the weather. The refrigerator has been stocked with a week's worth of food that will be consumed quickly and simply, long after the sun has set and after a day's worth of dust and grime has been washed away.

Wooden totes, cubes measuring four feet on a side, have been trucked in and stand waiting. In family-run orchards, all members have their tasks. Even the young ones. A few days before harvest begins, the outer edges of the orchard are hand raked. "Raking the headers," is a good job for youngsters not ready to handle the big equipment.

A few days to go. Friends call and ask: "When's harvest?"

"Soon," they say.

And then finally...

It was harvest day at the Buchanan hazelnut orchards and I was in the middle of it. Literally. A 360 degree twirl brought tree after tree into view, with a thick green leafy canopy overhead. Shafts of light pierced through, transforming dust kicked up by the tractor operating several rows beyond my view into diagonal bars of gold.

By now, if you've been following this saga from the beginning of the cycle you know that unlike most other fruits and vegetables which are plucked from plants, vines and trees, hazelnuts are scooped from the ground. And so, once the nuts have fallen free of their frilly green husks, the race is on to capture as many of them as possible before the crop is consumed by mud from the coming rains.

Timing is everything, explained Dave Buchanan, who, along with his wife, Margy, planted their Corvallis-area orchard over 30 years ago on the century farm that his ancestors established. "You want all of the nuts to fall before you get out there to harvest, but if the weather turns so bad it's impossible to move the equipment through the orchard, then all will be lost."

So, once they feel the majority of the crop is down, Margy's task is to assemble the carpet of nuts into tidy, long rows with a nifty motorized blower/sweeper called a Flory Sweeper. Flory Industries makes some pretty fancy and finely equipped up-to-date models, but the Buchanans are fond of their quirky, fairly ancient vehicle. It has a steering wheel and gas pedal, but no brake, so to control speed Margy's constantly switching from neutral to forward to reverse. "Meanwhile," she laments, "you mangle yourself on a low-hanging branch."

It takes four runs down each row for Margy to get the nuts properly aligned. Then David comes along on his tractor, with the harvester in tow. This machine picks up everything in its path, spewing dirt and debris out the bottom while the nuts are carried up a metal conveyor belt to topple into the large wooden totes. It's a gritty job, and at the end of each day both people and machines are cloaked in dust.

The "first pick," as it's called, will be the bulk of the harvest. But as autumn winds rattle the rest of the crop from the trees, growers always hope to get back through the orchard for a "second pick" as well.

Like a lot of other hazelnut growers, the Buchanans grow things besides hazelnuts. In their case, the other major crop is wine grapes, which are turned into beautiful award-winning wines produced right on the farm under the Tyee Wine Cellars label. Their daughter Merilee Buchanan Benson is the winemaker, a big step up from raking the headers.

Wine grapes are an autumn crop too, and so once all of the nuts have been gathered (and sometimes before), it's time to bring in the grapes.

As their friend, I've grown to respect the strength and dedication the Buchanans have for their work. In 2008 the Oregon Wildlife Society, a statewide organization of wildlife biologists and ecologists, honored them for "their leadership as land stewards, conservationists, and sustainable agricultural producers in the Willamette Valley."

AUTUMN IN THE BREEDING PROGRAM

"September and October are just crazy," says David Smith. "You've got the unknowns of dealing with multiple varieties of hazelnuts, all ripening at varying times over about a five-week period. And you have to get them picked up before they mingle with each other or you've lost an entire year of evaluations. You're monitoring a crew that's not as familiar with the trees as you'd like them to be. You're keeping track of how the nuts are doing in the dryer at Hyslop farm before storage. And of course, there's the weather. "I remember some years of harvesting some late-maturing varieties at the end of October in a sleet storm," Smith recalled. "Let's just say we don't like to do that!

"The majority of the nuts that we harvest will not be good enough," says Smith. "They will not meet the criteria and the trees will have to be cut down. And then it's just an ongoing process of cutting and re-cutting discarded trees from each of the seedling plots."

By the second week of October, late-maturing varieties still need to be harvested, but Smith and his crew will break off to plant the 4000-6000 seedling trees they've been growing since spring before the ground gets too wet to use a mechanical planter.

"Helping operate a cleaning operation has been an adventure since I am not mechanically inclined in the least, but I persevered. There is a rhythm in the plant as the totes arrive and are weighed. Each lot is washed, debris removed and the clean nuts are shuttled into the dryers and when dry into waiting semis to be hauled to the processing plant. This is all done through a series of conveyors and bins with minimal human intervention. The noise is like a symphony of well-tuned instruments and the experienced ear can tell when something is not right."

Kathy Beutler, hazelnut farmer and processor

HARVEST

The Green Goose, a 1946 Chevy truck, spent the better part of a noble career on the Chambers family farm, just north of Albany, Oregon. Three generations of Chambers men, beginning with Edward , then his son, Elbert, and ending with grandsons Wayne and David, employed this sturdy workhorse in the hazelnut orchards, primarily as a water truck and for hauling totes of nuts to market. In the off season, she earned her keep hauling everything from prunes to beans to corn to table beets. Wayne keeps her in running condition, but she has a lifetime pass on harvest duties.

AFTER THE HARVEST—PROCESSING

At the end of a harvest, the totes are full and the farmers are exhausted. The whole year has come down to those rows of wooden totes, each filled to the brim with 1100 pounds of hazelnuts.

Some hazelnut farms are mechanized to the point where they can process and market their own nuts after harvest. But most growers take their totes to one of twenty major processors—they're actually called "handlers"—in the state, where their nuts are cleaned, weighed and sampled. Once a handler determines what a given grower will be paid, based on weight and quality, the nuts are co-mingled with those of other growers for the rest of the journey through the plant. First they're dried, which is an exacting and tedious process. At the Blue Diamond plant in Salem, for example, this is done in 4-story drying rooms maintained at 90 to 95 degrees F. Depending on the moisture within the nuts, it takes 12 to 36 hours before the nuts are down to the target moisture content of nine percent.

From the drying chambers, the nuts scoot along through the plant on conveyor belts where they are sorted for blanks and damaged nuts. At this point some of the nuts are almost at the end of their processing line because they will complete their journey to the consumer within their shells. The rest are shelled and graded by kernel size. Still more forks along the way send some of the shelled kernels straight into vacuum-sealed packages for shipping, while others will continue along to be chopped into pieces of various sizes.

It's an exacting, exhausting process. Another handler, Pat Ehli, president of P. J. Ehli Company, puts it this way: "It's funny how you can enjoy working a sixteen-hour day, seven days a week. Your growers are in and generally that's a good thing. And you get the camaraderie and everybody's all jacked up for harvest. So it's fun. Not many people can go to work in the morning and really have a passion or a love for what they do. And I've been extremely fortunate.

It's always nice when it's over, too. You can just about smell the finish line sometimes. When it's over, it's a very good feeling."

And where does all the product generating that good feeling go? For the industry as a whole, currently 60-65% of the crop is exported in-shell, along with 30% of the shelled nuts. The rest is consumed domestically in various forms.

AFTER THE HARVEST IN THE BREEDING PROGRAM

When harvest concludes, Shawn Mehlenbacher returns to his office (which he's pretty much ignored for two months) and tries to catch up with accumulated paper work, phone messages and emails. Then it's back to the lab at the farm. For six solid weeks the team cracks, roasts and in general evaluates all aspects of the year's research harvest. An immense amount of data must be compiled and put into comprehensible form.

"We've got Shawn, myself, Cristino, and one or two students part-time, coming in to crack out nuts," says David Smith. "Becky's (McCluskey) in the other lab working with her harvest. You see, we've got the process divided (between Becky's work and Shawn's work)…I'm working on the side with Shawn where we're evaluating new seedlings and our advanced selections. And then Becky is evaluating advanced selections also. We do the same ones so we can be tracking the parents. We've seen them from a breeder's eye view; she's looking at it more from a grower's eye view. She's busy doing her evaluations. We're doing ours. And we systematically go through the stacks, starting with the oldest seedlings and doing the advance selections that Shawn might want to use as parents. Again, we've got that December deadline looming and we've got roughly the last week of October plus November and the first week of December to get that information to him so he can make those decisions."

By mid-November, Mehlenbacher has only a few weeks left to complete the process and determine what combinations he wants to put together for the next round of crosses. He'll choose 25-50 trees, half of which will be enclosed in pollination cages, awaiting winter when their flowers emerge to be hand-pollinated.

Recently harvested seeds from the previous year's controlled crosses go into that aforementioned cold, dark, and damp storage facility. This technique nudges the seed's internal clock forward by months so it will come out of dormancy in research time rather than Mother Nature's, to start the yearly research cycle anew in March.

CHAPTER 2

How to Get the Best
Results from this Book

As carefully crafted as I've tried to make the recipes in this book, the one ingredient not included is your taste. I hope you will always take that into account and find ways to tune the recipes to your personal preferences.

In fact, if we ever meet and you happen to have your (my!) cookbook along, I would be most gratified to see a rumpled edition with sauce-stained pages and scribbles in the margins. My own blessed fortune once was to have a private visit with Julia Child. Not only did I have the good sense to bring along my copy of "Mastering The Art of French Cooking" in preparation for our meet, I also had the presence of mind to retrieve it from my briefcase for her to sign before we parted ways.

It was a book I had received as a teenager at least twenty years earlier. I handed it over and suddenly was struck by its dog-eared and tattered state. I was mortified and sure that Julia was going to be offended. But as she opened its cover and gingerly turned the pages, a smile spread across her face.

"Ah yes," she said, nodding her approval. "A well-used book."

So please, use this book with as much enthusiasm as you dare. There are sample menus in the last chapter. As designed, they will provide you with some interesting meals. But I'm hoping that they'll also stimulate your imagination.

Also, keep in mind that many of these recipes are multi-dimensional. As a very basic example of this concept, for instance, most of the salads in the chapter on side dishes can become main dishes with just a few more hearty ingredients tossed into them.

SAVORY RECIPES THAT MAKE GREAT GIFTS

RECIPES THAT ARE GOOD PICNIC FARE

RECIPES FOR HIKING, BACKPACKING, CROSS-COUNTRY SKIING, RIVER-RAFTING... JUST ABOUT ANYWHERE IN THE WILDS, REALLY!

Except where noted, all of these recipes will survive more than 24 hours without refrigeration.

GOOD POT-LUCK DISHES

PASTA PARTNERS (RECIPES TO TOSS WITH PASTA)

The balance of this chapter concerns certain techniques, common to many of my recipes, that are detailed here once to avoid needless congestion in the chapters.

MEASURES

Just to be clear, in this book all hazelnut measurements include specification of the form the nuts are to be in when measured. This is because a given volume of whole kernels can yield a different volume when chopped. The amount of difference, which is usually trivial, depends on the size and shape of the whole kernels, and the fineness of the chop. However, the best bet is just to measure nuts in the form specified.

Here are some equivalencies you will find handy when planning how many nuts to buy. Again, they are only close approximations, due to variations in nut characteristics.

1 pound in-shell hazelnuts

  = 1-1/2 cups hazelnut kernels

1 pound hazelnut kernels

  = 3-1/4 cups

SELECTING HAZELNUTS

Strict industry standards exist that are maintained when Oregon hazelnuts are processed at the regional handlers' plants. While still in their shells, they are cleaned, sanitized, graded and dried under carefully controlled conditions. Mandated quality control testing is systematically tracked by USDA. This is backed up by periodic unannounced plant inspections. Unshelled hazelnuts resulting from this process are beautiful to behold! There's that gorgeous hazel-brown color, for one thing, and a lovely sheen. They should look clean, with intact, unblemished shells. I do love eating raw hazelnuts out of hand. Most people do. Just put out a bowl of unshelled hazelnuts and a nutcracker at your next gathering and watch what happens.

For cooking, I prefer to buy shelled, whole, raw hazelnut kernels in the bulk food sections of grocery stores where I can evaluate their quality up close. Good ones will be generous in size, with a smooth surface. They'll have a rich, sweet and nutty aroma. So when you begin to scoop the nuts from the bin, pay attention. If they don't seem fresh to you, let someone in the store know about it so they can replenish the bin. Nobody in the hazelnut industry wants you cooking with less than perfect Oregon hazelnuts. You just don't have to when there are so many high quality ones available.

In most cases, store personnel won't be able to tell you what variety of hazelnuts they are selling, and they are usually mixed, anyway. In one sense, the question is moot, because the industry doesn't release inferior varieties for commercial planting in the first place, and the differences between marketed varieties are more subtle than, say, differences between apples. They tend to matter most to large-scale commercial users for various esthetic and mechanical reasons.

HAZELNUT STORAGE

Unshelled hazelnuts have the longest shelf life. They also look darned pretty in a bowl on the kitchen table. On the other hand, shelled nuts are far more convenient to work with and take up less room. I like to keep both raw and roasted kernels, prepped in various ways, in closed containers in the pantry so that when I crave a nut hit, they're ready to go. They're stable for at least a couple of months this way. And here's the good part. Once they get a little stale, you can easily restore them to their former glory with a gentle roast, or re-roast.

If you intend to squirrel away large quantities of hazelnuts keep in mind that exposure to air, light, warmth and moisture will hasten rancidity. That makes freezing the best course. Properly packed, frozen raw hazelnuts

Hazelnut Varieties

MY FAVORITE APPLE VARIETY IS FUJI, comice pears make me swoon, and Pinot Noir, of course, is my preferred beverage alongside a grilled Chinook. But hazelnut varieties? Do we have a choice?

Well, not usually. Perhaps the day will come when we're as finicky about the variety of hazelnuts we buy as we are about our apples, pears, and wine. But for now, most of us are pretty much at the mercy of the suppliers. And frankly, most of us simply don't know enough to ask what type of hazelnut we're buying. But at Hazelnut Hill, on highway 99 W between Corvallis and Monroe, Rob and Sally Hilles are educating their customers.

Within the hazelnut industry, their business is referred to as vertically integrated. They do everything themselves. They manage a hazelnut nursery, grow the trees, and process the nuts all the way to value-added end products. These products, which they sell through mail order and in their on-site store, range from raw and dry-roasted hazelnuts, through flavored nuts, to a variety of confections that incorporate chocolate, toffee and ice cream.

In their store, they have arranged a display where visitors can sample different hazelnut varieties side by side, observing subtle differences in size, taste and color.

Currently they're growing varieties named Lewis, Clark, Yamhill and Tonda di Giffoni. Each one has a distinct characteristic that makes it slightly more appropriate for a given end product. It's been a learning process, said Sally. "We began making hazelnut products from traditional in-shell varieties which we found were not particularly well suited for what we wanted to do. We need kernels to match the end result, whether that's chocolate covered, dry roasted, or buttered."

So what do they look for in kernel quality? "Depending on the end use," she said, "we look at oil content, blanchability (that's industry speak for a nut's ability to shed its skin readily), shape/size, and breakage."

Oil content creates the flavor, she explained. The Lewis, for example, "has such excellent flavor and high oil content that it is the one we prefer for a simple dry roasting." The Clark's outer skin has high blanchability, so it's their choice to pair with chocolatey confections, where skinned nuts are preferred.

As for future varieties, states Rob, "We still have orchards to plant and will do so with the eye towards end use."

They're intrigued with the varieties that Oregon State plant breeder Shawn Mehlenbacher has released—the Lewis, Clark, Yamhill, Sacajawea, and Jefferson. When they began working the Lewis and the Clark into their product line, "our customers were able to distinguish the difference and that encourages us to continue our search for superior kernel varieties," says Rob.

can have a shelf life of up to 24 months. Any treatment applied prior to freezing will reduce longevity. Roasted, whole hazelnuts tend to stay fresh in the freezer for at least 18 months; roasted and chopped, around 12 months. Nuts with various coatings? Unpredictable.

When packing nuts for the freezer, place them in as air-tight and moisture-free of an environment as you can create. If you have a vacuum-sealing system, great. Otherwise, at least tumble them into freezer-quality plastic re-sealable bags. Then you can remove a desired amount later, re-close the bag and pop them back into the freezer. Just remember that every time you do this, introduced oxygen shortens the shelf life of the residual nuts. It's an incentive to pack in smaller bags to begin with. Be sure to mark each package with the beginning storage date. I also like to write "new crop" on the package if I know for sure that they were from the previous Autumn's harvest. I wouldn't expect nuts from an earlier harvest to last as long in storage.

ROASTING HAZELNUTS

Three things happen when you roast a hazelnut: It gets more flavorful, it blushes from the inside, and it takes on a pleasing crunch. So you definitely want to roast them in most cases. Another way to look at it is that roasting almost always improves how hazelnuts perform in a given recipe. One exception is for chopped nuts used to coat something about to be grilled or oven-baked. In that situation, you can end up with chopped charcoal if you start with roasted nuts. Start with raw nuts, and they'll come out roasted just right in the end.

This is simple stuff, roasting hazelnuts. There is no absolute right way to do it. The pendulum swings from "low-and-slow" all the way over to "high-and-fast." I tend to go for the middle range, 350 degrees F. At that temperature you have quite a bit of control over the outcome. A medium roast only takes about 15 to 20 minutes. At higher temperatures, things move a bit quicker, and it's easy to overshoot your desired endpoint.

When you begin to smell the delicious toasty aroma, it's time to start checking the roasting progress. The longer you roast hazelnuts, the richer their flavor. You have to decide how deep of a roast you want based on how you're planning on using them. For instance, I prefer a dark roast when combining hazelnuts with all things chocolate. It just seems to produce a more elegant flavor experience. And apparently I'm not the only one who feels this way, since the industry standard for most candy and ice cream manufacturers is a dark roast.

Because of its dark skin, an unpeeled hazelnut doesn't make a dramatic color transformation during roasting. You have to pay attention to the more subtle visual cues and monitor kernel centers along the way.

LIGHT ROAST: The skins will have cracked on the majority of the nuts and the surface of the nut will still be a creamy-ivory color. Break into one of the nuts (careful, they're hot!). Its center will be a slightly darker color, a sort of beige.

MEDIUM ROAST: The skins will have cracked on the majority of the nuts and surfaces will still be a creamy-ivory color (just about the same color as the light roast). Centers will be notably darker than the surface color.

DARK ROAST: The skins will have darkened more and cracked on the majority of the nuts; surfaces will have darkened to a pale tan. Centers will be very dark (and getting darker faster at this point, so get those nuts out of the oven, they're done!).

SKINNING HAZELNUTS: THE LILY METHOD

The fact that most people prefer their hazelnuts skinned translates into a lot of frustrated cooks, since those pesky kernels do seem to love their pellicles and don't give them up easily. The time-honored approach to skinning involves lightly roasting the kernels, and then rubbing them around inside a towel. But you can count on only 40-60% success this way, depending on the variety of nut, and a big mess of skins

escaping your towel. I've tried lining the towel with every variation of plastic or rubber screen material I could think of to create more abrasion, without better luck. I've tried hand-rolling the nuts across a wire drying rack, with worse results and a bigger mess. Some have recommended replacing the roast with boiling in a solution of water and baking soda, so I tried that. What a horrible fate for an Oregon hazelnut! It does release the skins, but at the cost of ruining flavor and texture. Another no go.

The problem with any "rubbing" approach is that the kernels, being round, inevitably roll right over whatever abrasive they encounter, rather than sliding across it so it can get a grip on the skins. Any part of the skin not loosened by the roast just stays put. So the name of the game is to arrange for something to grip and pull the skin in one direction, while the kernel is, at least briefly, either stationary or moving in the opposite direction. It turns out that a particularly fine agent for this purpose is ... another hazelnut kernel! That's right. On the advice of my 6-year-old granddaughter, Lily, I just shake roasted kernels in a plastic box to get a big improvement over the towel method, with much less mess.

HERE IS WHAT YOU WILL NEED:

1) A RIMMED BAKING SHEET

2) A BOX A sturdy translucent rectangular half-gallon or so plastic container with a secure lid. An oblong shape is best. I use an inexpensive 58-oz bin widely marketed by Snapware, which has secure latches on all four sides of its lid. Size is not important so long as you leave plenty of room for the kernels to fly around in the container.

3) A PAN Optionally, a steel vegetable-grilling pan, approximately 12 x 12 x 3 inches deep, perforated with approx. 5/16-inch holes. These can be found wherever barbeque supplies are sold. Weber makes one, for example.

Begin by roasting your hazelnut kernels in a single layer on the baking sheet at 350 degrees F to the point of doneness called for by your end use. A minimal roast for skinning, just to the point that the aroma is becoming toasty and the skins are well-split, takes about 15 minutes. Allow the kernels to cool on the baking sheet until their skins stop crackling, at which point they will be quite cool. The assumption is that crackling equals releasing, so you might as well take full advantage.

Pour up to 3 cups of kernels into a half-gallon plastic bin (less in a smaller bin), and secure the lid. Now further secure the lid with a finger or two and vigorously shake the kernels for about 60 seconds. Try to get the nuts moving in as many directions as possible, and changing directions as often as possible, while bumping into the interior surfaces of the container as often as possible. That may sound complicated, but you will find that it's actually very easy to do. The goal is to generate as many impacts as possible between the kernels, particularly when they are briefly pinned against the container walls. The 60 seconds is only a guideline. You may need to shake for more or less time, depending on the variety of nut. Just keep an eye on progress through the sidewalls.

Once the shaking is complete, use the vegetable grilling pan like a colander to sift the skin fragments back onto the empty baking sheet. Voila! You now have a pan of mostly skinned kernels. It's easy to remove the few with retained skins to a separate container for uses not requiring skinning. You can dispose of the skins simply by stepping outside and blowing the them away from the baking sheet.

So that's it. For a small investment you've acquired some good multi-purpose equipment, updated your image with an unorthodox kitchen technique, and succeeded where so many have failed. Congratulations!

CHOPPING HAZELNUTS

Let's face facts. Hazelnuts are round and firm. Not perfectly round, of course. And more off-tender than rock-hard. But round enough and firm enough to scoot all over the place when you try to tackle more than a dozen of them at a time with a chef's knife. So unless you're willing to maintain a focused, unhurried technique when wielding a blade, the issue of chopping large amounts of hazelnuts needs to be addressed.

Let's start with containment. I have most success with a food chopper equipped with a blade array affixed to a spring-loaded plunger that you bang on from the top, forcing the blades down through nuts confined in a plastic cylinder. With each whack of your hand, the blades rotate slightly, attacking the pile from a different direction The cylinder actually has a removable bottom, so I can just place the chopper directly over a pile of nuts on the chopping surface and whack away.

If you only need a cup or so of coarsely chopped hazelnuts, another approach is to simply throw them into a sturdy plastic bag and lay it out on a cutting board, making sure that you arrange the nuts in a single layer. Whack them forcefully with a straight, heavy surface, such as the handle of a chef's knife or a rolling pin, until they are reduced to the desired size. I actually have a term for them: crushed.

If you're slicing with a knife, spread only about 1/2 cup of nuts at a time over a large chopping area and go slow to keep things under control. Using a chef's knife, grasp the handle with your dominant hand and hold the tip down with your other hand as you rock the blade up and down, pivoting and sweeping over the nuts. Laying the cutting board in a shallow pan helps to contain "flyers."

A food processor will also tackle hazelnuts for you. It works particularly well when you want a very fine chop, or if you aren't finicky about the range of size you need, since some of the nuts will succumb to the blade immediately while others just bounce around in the work bowl. The chop can be evened out somewhat if you begin by working the "pulse" button until the nuts have been coarsely chopped. Then let the motor run for longer intervals until you are satisfied with the outcome.

Since most of us like objective cues, I'm going to get very specific here, even though within most recipes there's so much wiggle room that I hope you would never feel compelled to hunt down a measuring tape. This is just to sort of calibrate my thinking for you, with respect to recipes in this book.

COARSELY CHOPPED: Chopped into an irregular range of sizes from about 1/4-inch up to about a third the size of a whole nut. You might even leave some of them in halves; that's perfectly okay in this category. I usually use my chef's knife, because it's fast, not messy, and I can control the overall ratio of sizes as I'm chopping.

CRUSHED/CRUMBLED: When I call for "crushed" or "crumbled" hazelnuts, that's your cue to not stress at all

over size. What I'm shooting for is a range from coarsely chopped to very finely chopped. I mostly use crushed or crumbled hazelnuts as a garnish, since the irregularity is visually appealing. To do so, simply tumble the nuts into a plastic bag and bang them with the handle of your chefs knife (careful!), or a rolling pin, until they break apart. You could use a hammer, but the maneuver requires quite a bit of control or you'll end up with very tiny crumbles.

CHOPPED: Chopped smaller than 1/4-inch, but not much smaller than 1/8 of an inch. I'll usually use either a chef's knife or my manual chopper with the spring-loaded plunger.

FINELY CHOPPED: Very small pieces, ranging from 1/16 of an inch down to "almost ground." I usually use my food processor when I want finely chopped hazelnuts.

GROUND: No visible pieces; the texture will be dry and powdery. I use my food processor to do this, starting with whole nuts and the "pulse" button in the beginning until the nuts have been coarsely chopped. Then let the motor run for slightly longer intervals until the nuts are very ground up and powdery. Don't let the blade run for too long at a time because it heats up the nuts and pretty soon if you don't pay attention, you'll have...

PASTE: Beyond ground, if you keep the motor of your food processor going, the blade action warms things up a bit and pretty soon the oils within the nut are released and the whole mixture turns into a soft-but-grainy purée. Paste is a wonderful thing in its own right, but you can observe a bit of magic if you keep turning that blade. In a brief moment, it becomes...

BUTTER: Beyond paste, the very end result in your food processor is when a batch of hazelnuts transforms from ground nuts to a granular paste, to, ultimately, a shimmery, creamy hazelnut butter. This is the stuff you keep hidden in the refrigerator at the verrry back on the bottom shelf, behind the box of baking soda. If you don't, you'll never have any on hand when you really need it!

MELTING CHOCOLATE

The most reliable way to do this is in a double boiler sort of arrangement, over barely simmering water. For the top portion, my preference is a wide round-bottomed copper bowl that nests into a lower pot with a slightly smaller circumference. The copper bowl is a great distributor of heat, so if you spread the chocolate out and up the sides of the gently sloping bowl in a fairly shallow layer, it will melt fairly evenly. There's less chance of over-heating the bottom layer of chocolate while the upper layer is just beginning to melt.

If you don't have that type of copper bowl, any metal or heat-proof glass bowl with a rounded bottom would be another option. Otherwise, use the traditional double-boiler arrangement.

The key is to not rush the process. Just place the pot on the burner, bring the water to a boil, then adjust the heat so that it settles back down to a gentle burbling simmer. Don't cover the upper container. When you've got the heat adjusted so the water is behaving itself, go do something else while the chocolate melts. Depending on the amount of chocolate that's melting, it can take anywhere from 5 minutes (for 1 to 6 ounces), up to about 15 to 20 minutes (for a 12-ounce bag of semi-sweet chocolate chips). Don't be fooled by the fact that chocolate chips retain their shape when melted, until they are stirred.

Remember, just leave the chocolate alone while it melts. Don't stir it or poke it with a spoon. Sometimes chocolate pokes back by doing strange things, like getting hard if you inadvertently inject a tiny bit of moisture from a damp spoon. Also be careful to avoid condensate dripping from the bottom of the pot when you transfer melted chocolate to another container.

SPECIAL INGREDIENTS AND EQUIPMENT

PONZU SAUCE: A citrus-flavored soy sauce used in Japanese cuisine. I use it widely in my cooking, particularly in place of soy sauce, because it brings a rich level of flavor. I started using it because my other favorite soy sauce substitution, tempura dipping sauce (made by Kikkoman), is not as widely distributed, which makes it difficult for my readers to acquire it in their local markets. You can make ponzu sauce from scratch, but it's one of those commercially made condiments that I'm content to purchase. I use the Kikkoman brand. You'll find it in the Asian food section of a well stocked supermarket.

TEMPURA DIPPING SAUCE: Used in Japanese cuisine, traditionally as a thin dipping liquid for freshly-made tempura, it has become a staple in my kitchen as a seasoning agent. I use it in place of soy sauce because it adds such a rich layer of flavor beyond traditional soy sauce. Like ponzu sauce, Kikkoman makes one which I recommend with confidence. You'll find it in the Asian food section of a well-stocked supermarket. It's a concentrated formula, which I use full strength in my recipes. If you were going to use it as an actual dipping sauce for tempura, then follow the directions on the label and dilute it in a 1 to 4 ratio (1 part tempura sauce, 4 parts water).

CHILI GARLIC SAUCE: This deep red-peppery purée is a heavenly seasoner, rich in chile and garlic, that can zoop up a stir-fry or vegetable sauté in a flash. I also use it to assemble tasty marinades and vinaigrettes. I use a commercially prepared version, of which there are many on the market. My favorite brand on the West Coast is Lee Kum Kee. You'll find various brands of it in the Asian food section of a well-stocked supermarket.

RIMMED BAKING SHEET: These are standard pieces of equipment, so chances are you have one in your kitchen. Any baking pan with about a 1-inch rim, and inner dimensions of at least 11-inches by 17-inches will work for my recipes.

SPRINGFORM PAN: This is a type of steel bakeware that features sides that can be removed from the base. In other words, the base and sides are separate pieces, held together when the base snuggles into a groove that circles the bottom of the side wall. The whole contraption is secured by a latch on the exterior of the side. Cheesecakes, tortes, tarts, and other types of desserts are prepared in springform pans. Any recipe in which there is a delicate bottom or where the finished dish can't be inverted for removal usually calls for a springform pan.

Okay, it's finally time to move away from the technical and on to the delectable. You're about to enter my world as I've come to love it: Hazelnuts at every turn, being used in sometimes surprising and most definitely delighting ways. Enjoy, have fun, and bon appetit!

CHAPTER 3

Just Nuts

A BIG RISK WITH TAKING ON A SINGLE-SUBJECT COOKBOOK is that one will get fed up with the subject. Day-in and day-out consumption of ANY food might do that to a person. Turn it into a tedious task. But through the course of this project, the one constant has been my appreciation of Oregon hazelnuts.

I really do love them.

I mean, really love them. Still! Even after months and months of daily intake, they're just as pleasing to me as they were when I wasn't writing an entire book about them. They're one of nature's most perfect foods—in all their forms.

Straight out of the shell, with their gentle, slightly sweet, slightly green—yet—nutty character? Love 'em.

Still hot from the oven? Heavenly. Roasting heightens the experience for me. Even just a light bronzing will add depth to a hazelnut's flavor profile. In fact,

lightly roasted hazelnuts garnished with just a dusting of popcorn salt are the perfect snack food. It's in this pure and simple state that I so often offer them to guests. Try it for yourself. Serve them to friends and notice just how well they compliment wines and craft beers. Unadorned as such a presentation is, it doesn't seem Spartan, because it rewards on so many levels, from the layers of flavor to the satisfying crunch of the texture.

Here are some recipes that celebrate the simple, savory side of Oregon hazelnuts. Further on, we'll certainly be exploring all the glorious ways that hazelnuts bring excitement to a meal. And when you reach the chapter on sweet celebrations, you'll encounter some dynamic candied variations that are amazingly simple also. But first, let's just focus on hazelnuts in their purest presentation. I use them to help me make drop-in guests feel special, kick off a party, garnish a side dish, or to nourish me along the trail when I'm hiking.

Makes about 6-1/2 cups

6-1/2 cups (about 2 pounds) raw hazelnuts

2 tablespoons butter, melted

2 tablespoons olive oil

1 tablespoon Worcestershire sauce

Salt to taste

"I was so excited I dragged it from room to room, showing my office mates!"

Dr. Sydney Piercy, Corvallis Clinic, on being given a 50 pound sack of in-shell hazelnuts by one of her patients.

The Aman Brothers Grilled Hazelnuts

I learned from second generation hazelnut growers Tim, Tom, Kevin, and Bob Aman that one of the easiest ways to wow a crowd is with a batch of fresh-off-the-grill roasted hazelnuts. "It's just something really great from the barbeque in the back yard - a really nice appetizer," says Tim, who has the opportunity to entertain lots of hazelnut folks since he's on the board of directors of one of the state's largest handlers, Hazelnut Growers of Oregon. "People are sitting around and having their favorite beverage, and these go along great. Really, once you get started on 'em you can hardly stop eating 'em."

First, give them a coating of butter, olive oil and Worcestershire sauce, he says. Then just roast them "slow and low" on your grill.

The Amans have been blessing friends and family with hazelnut treats for a long time. Parents Gertrude and Russell started the Mt. Angel-area orchard in 1968. The three brothers eventually took over orchard duties after graduation from college. They also have a thriving nursery business which produces hazelnut stock for growers. Of the fifty acres of hazelnut trees, they've dedicated 20 acres to one of OSU's new varieties, the Jefferson. "It's a beautiful tree," says Tim. "And a really a nice nut. The shell has such a sheen, and the kernel is nice and sweet, with a thin skin."

And even though that nice thin skin that peels easily, Tim points out that there are real strong health benefits to leaving it on, because "... that's where the antioxidants are. That's the benefit of leaving the skin on."

Tim says he and his brothers have great respect for the hazelnut industry: "The hazelnut-growing community is made up of really good people. It's a community that cares. That's why I've been involved in it as much as I can."

Place the hazelnuts in a bowl. Add the butter, olive oil and Worcestershire sauce. Stir well to evenly coat the hazelnuts with the butter mixture. Add the salt and stir again.

Place the seasoned hazelnuts in a perforated pan of some sort, something that will keep the nuts from falling down onto the coals. The ones designed to grill vegetables or fish work well. Grill the nuts over very low heat, stirring them occasionally, until they're golden brown. This will take about 30 minutes, says Aman, adding that at the point of doneness, they're "kind of crunchy. And then you take them off the grill, and you've got that buttery flavor on 'em, and they're nice and warm, and I'm actually getting hungry right now just talking about them!"

Serendipitous alternative: In one of my run-throughs of the Aman Brothers' recipe, I got called away from the kitchen just after I had tossed the hazelnuts with the melted butter, olive oil and Worcestershire sauce. I didn't get back to roasting them for TWO DAYS! In that interval those clever nuts had soaked up all of what had in effect become a flavorful marinade. At that point, I thought "What the heck, since I've already strayed from the original recipe, I might as well go all out." So I didn't even fire up the grill. Instead, I simply roasted them in a 350 degree F oven until they turned dark and fragrant, which only took about 20 minutes. Once removed and cooled, their flavor and crunch were delectable.

In search of the perfect hazelnut

For the 20-plus years I've known Dr. Harry Lagerstedt he's been "retired". Opportunities to act retired are numerous, considering that his closest neighbor is a Corvallis-area golf course. Yet Lagerstedt prefers spending his "leisure" hours in search of the perfect hazelnut (or peach, or nectarine) rather than the perfect swing. And so, if Carol Lagerstedt needs to negotiate a household chore out of her husband and he's not within earshot, or in the barn fiddling with some piece of farm equipment, then her search could involve their numerous acres of hazelnut, peach, and nectarine orchards.

I'm sure there are times when Carol really does wish Harry had taken up golf.

Harry was a professor in the Department of Horticulture at Oregon State University for 10 years before transferring to the U.S. Department of Agriculture in 1967 as a research horticulturist in the area of filberts and walnuts. For the next two decades his professional life would be dedicated to helping build the OSU hazelnut plant breeding program in its early days, under the direction of plant breeder Dr. Maxine Thompson.

In his first year with the USDA, said Harry "I made a call out to all the hazelnut growers. If there was something unusual in their orchards—a variety that was early, or larger, or seemed to have some disease resistance or more productivity—to bring it to our attention."

They ended up with about 20 varieties to consider. After evaluations, he and Thompson pared them down to 12 of the most promising ones.

"At that point," said Harry, "I called in the processors, with the idea that whatever we selected would have to be acceptable on the loading dock." Their wish list for the perfect hazelnut included a generous-sized kernel, high production, early maturation date, and resistance to disease and pests.

Based on that input, the varieties they continued to work with were Barcelona, Ennis, Butler, Ryan and Lansing. Of those five, said Harry, "Ennis and Butler floated to the top, and so we actually went ahead and introduced those varieties... I called them 'Grower Selections,' because they did not originate with the breeding program, or any one person or breeder, and my contribution to that was just to evaluate them and make sure that we weren't introducing an inferior variety."

Of course, if Harry hadn't "just" evaluated what was already at hand with an eye to immediate use, rather than merely in terms of long-term breeding program needs, the industry at large would have missed the early opportunity to benefit from Ennis and Butler. That's Harry, and it was just the beginning. Over a hundred research papers later, nothing much has changed about him, and the industry wouldn't be where it is today without his contributions, which continue to this day.

2 tablespoons butter (or half butter
and half olive oil)

1 tablespoon finely minced fresh garlic

2 tablespoons tempura sauce

1 tablespoon Dijon mustard

1/4 teaspoon Tabasco sauce

1/4 cup light corn syrup

3 cups lightly roasted and skinned
hazelnuts

Salt to taste

Teriyaki Garlic Hazelnuts

These nuts begin in a pot on top of the stove, but the real magic occurs in the oven as they bake to a golden, caramelized finish. Tempura sauce is sold alongside soy sauce in the grocery store. Kikkoman makes a good one. If you can't find it, opt for ponzu sauce, which is slightly more lemony.

Preheat oven to 350 degrees F. Place a rimmed baking sheet on the center rack in the oven to heat up.

In a medium-sized heavy-bottomed saucepan, melt the butter over medium heat. Add the garlic and let it simmer gently in the butter just until the garlic has softened. Don't let the garlic brown or it will burn in the oven during the roasting. Stir in the tempura sauce, Dijon mustard, Tabasco, and corn syrup. When this mixture has heated through, add the hazelnuts. Using a silicon spatula, scrape and stir for a minute or two so that the nuts become evenly coated with the butter sauce. Scrape the mixture out onto the baking sheet, spreading the nuts evenly into a single layer.

Roast for 15 to 20 minutes, just until the sauce turns golden. As the sauce begins to caramelize and thicken, you may need to scrape and stir the nuts once so they stay evenly coated during the final phase of roasting. But it's a thick enough sauce that this may not be necessary. I use a pastry scraper, which is a very efficient way to move a lot of nuts around at once.

While the nuts are roasting, spread a large sheet of waxed or parchment paper on a cutting board. When the nuts are done, remove them from the oven, salt them lightly, and scrape them out onto the paper, quickly spreading them out so they don't touch each other for the most part. Allow them to cool and then break them apart as desired into single nuts or clusters.

The pieces should be stored at room temperature in an airtight container, in which they can be kept for several weeks. Their crunchiness and flavor will continue to develop for the first 24 hours, so it's best to prepare them at least a day in advance of when they will be needed.

BEVERAGE THOUGHTS: For a wine, the spicy Asian qualities in the nut coating work well with a soft and floral Viognier, a dry Riesling, or a fruity Zinfandel. For beer, consider a classic wheat beer, such as Widmer Brother's Hefeweizen. A pale ale, like Rogue's Juniper Pale Ale, would be another good choice to cool the spice.

2 tablespoons butter

1 tablespoon finely minced fresh garlic

1 tablespoon ground chipotle chile powder

1 tablespoon spicy brown mustard
    (I use Gulden's)

1/2 teaspoon popcorn salt

1/4 teaspoon Tabasco sauce

1/4 teaspoon ground cayenne (optional)

1/4 cup light corn syrup

3 cups lightly roasted and skinned hazelnuts

Garlic-Chipotle Chile Hazelnuts

Smoky-spicy-garlicky, that's what you get with this simple treatment. A smoked paprika can be used in place of the chipotle chile powder.

Preheat oven to 350 degrees F. Place a rimmed baking sheet on the center rack in the oven to heat up.

In a medium-sized heavy-bottomed saucepan, melt the butter over medium heat. Add the garlic and let it simmer gently in the butter just until the garlic has softened. Don't let the garlic brown or it will burn in the oven during the roasting. Stir in the chipotle chile powder, mustard, salt, Tabasco and, if desired, the cayenne. Stir to combine, then add the corn syrup. When this mixture has heated through, add the hazelnuts. Using a silicon spatula, scrape and stir for a minute or two so that the nuts become evenly coated with the butter sauce. Scrape the mixture out onto the baking sheet, spreading the nuts evenly into a single layer.

Roast for 15 to 20 minutes, just until the sauce turns golden. As the sauce begins to caramelize and thicken, you may need to scrape and stir the nuts once so they stay evenly coated during the final phase of roasting. But it's a thick enough sauce that this may not be necessary. I use a pastry scraper, which is a very efficient way to move a lot of nuts around at once.

While the nuts are roasting, spread a large sheet of waxed or parchment paper on a cutting board. When the nuts are done, remove them from the oven, and scrape them out onto the paper, quickly spreading them out so they don't touch each other for the most part. Allow them to cool and then break them apart as desired into single nuts or clusters.

The pieces should be stored at room temperature in an airtight container, in which they can be kept for several weeks. Their crunchiness and flavor will continue to develop for the first 24 hours, so it's best to prepare them at least a day in advance of when they will be needed.

BEVERAGE THOUGHTS: This is a potent little nut that plays havoc with the taste buds, ruling out most wine choices. Riesling would balance the impact, but beer is an excellent choice here. The range could be anything from a light and thirst-quenching lager over to amber ales and brown ales.

Makes 3 cups

2 tablespoons butter

1/4 cup finely ground dry onion soup mix
 (see note)

2 tablespoons spicy brown mustard
 (I use Gulden's)

1/4 cup light corn syrup

3 cups lightly roasted and skinned hazelnuts

QuickTIP

When hazelnut growers Wayne and Joann Chambers pull a batch of roasted hazelnuts from the oven, the first thing they do is give them a light dusting of popcorn salt. The fine-grained seasoning coats the nuts more evenly than larger-grained salts, bringing out the flavor of the hazelnut in an elegant and understated way.

Onion Hazelnuts

These are simple, straightforward and satisfying.

Preheat oven to 350 degrees F. Place a rimmed baking sheet on the center rack in the oven to heat up.

In a medium-sized heavy-bottomed saucepan, melt the butter over medium heat. Add the onion soup mix, along with the mustard. Stir to combine, then add the corn syrup. When this mixture has heated through, add the hazelnuts. Using a silicon spatula, scrape and stir for a minute or two so that the nuts become evenly coated with the butter sauce. Scrape the mixture out onto the baking sheet, spreading the nuts evenly into a single layer.

Roast for 15 to 20 minutes, just until the sauce turns golden. As the sauce begins to caramelize and thicken, you may need to scrape and stir the nuts once so they stay evenly coated during the final phase of roasting. But it's a thick enough sauce that this may not be necessary. I use a pastry scraper, which is a very efficient way to move a lot of nuts around at once.

While the nuts are roasting, spread a large sheet of waxed or parchment paper on a cutting board. When the nuts are done, remove them from the oven, and scrape them out onto the paper, quickly spreading them out so they don't touch each other for the most part. Allow them to cool and then break them apart as desired into single nuts or clusters.

The pieces should be stored at room temperature in an airtight container, in which they can be kept for several weeks. Their crunchiness and flavor will continue to develop for the first 24 hours, so it's best to prepare them at least a day in advance of when they will be needed.

NOTE: To grind dry soup mix into a relatively fine powder, place a heaping 1/4 cup of it (shake or stir the mix before measuring to evenly distribute its dried onion flakes) into a small or medium-sized work bowl of a food processor and grind the contents to the desired consistency.

BEVERAGE THOUGHTS: A full-bodied Pinot Noir stands up to the onion and mustard and compliments the hazelnut character. Or try a spicy and lively Tempranillo, like the one produced in Southern Oregon at Abacela. My beer choice would be a nutty style, such as Rogue's Hazelnut Brown Nectar, or a soft and luscious wheat beer, such as Widmer Brother's Hefeweizen.

Makes 3 cups

2 tablespoons butter

3 large cloves fresh garlic, finely minced

1 tablespoon dry Italian herbs

1 tablespoon Dijon mustard

1/4 cup finely shredded Parmesan cheese

("the green box" is okay!)

1/2 teaspoon popcorn salt

1/4 cup light corn syrup

3 cups lightly roasted and skinned hazelnuts

"One of my favorite things to do when people come out to visit is to put 'em in the Gator and drive out into the middle of the orchard—especially in the good weather —and turn the engine off. You just sit there and feel the peace and quiet... it's so cool."

Darlene Chambers,
Albany area hazelnut grower

Parmesan-Herbed Hazelnuts

Amongst my taste-testers, this one seems to be one of the favorites within the "just nuts" category. If you do make a batch, consider making extras to garnish salads and vegetable sautés.

Preheat oven to 350 degrees F. Place a rimmed baking sheet on the center rack in the oven to heat up.

In a medium-sized heavy-bottomed saucepan, melt the butter over medium heat. Add the garlic and let it simmer gently in the butter just until the garlic has softened. Don't let the garlic brown or it will burn in the oven during the roasting. Add the dry Italian herbs and continue to gently sauté for about 30 seconds. Stir in the Dijon mustard, Parmesan, and salt. Stir to combine, then add the corn syrup and stir again. When this mixture has heated through, add the hazelnuts. Using a silicon spatula, scrape and stir for a minute or two so that the nuts become evenly coated with the butter sauce. Scrape the mixture out onto the baking sheet, spreading the nuts evenly into a single layer.

Roast for 15 to 20 minutes, just until the sauce turns golden. As the sauce begins to caramelize and thicken, you may need to scrape and stir the nuts once so they stay evenly coated during the final phase of roasting. But it's a thick enough sauce that this may not be necessary. I use a pastry scraper, which is a very efficient way to move a lot of nuts around at once.

While the nuts are roasting, spread a large sheet of waxed or parchment paper on a cutting board. When the nuts are done, remove them from the oven, salt them lightly, and scrape them out onto the paper, quickly spreading them out so they don't touch each other for the most part. Allow them to cool and then break them apart as desired into single nuts or clusters.

The pieces should be stored at room temperature in an airtight container, in which they can be kept for several weeks. Their crunchiness and flavor will continue to develop for the first 24 hours, so it's best to prepare them at least a day in advance of when they will be needed.

BEVERAGE THOUGHTS: A dry-style Gewürztraminer, such as Tyee Wine Cellar's plays off the herbs and cheese. Also a soft and playful Pinot Gris like the style at Spindrift has enough toast and complexity to work, as does a low-tannin Merlot or a fruity Sangiovese.

2 tablespoons butter

1 tablespoon onion powder

1 teaspoon dried dillweed

1/2 teaspoon popcorn salt

1/4 cup spicy brown mustard (I use Gulden's)

1/4 teaspoon Tabasco sauce

1/4 cup light corn syrup

3 cups lightly roasted and skinned hazelnuts

Mustard-Onion Hazelnuts

The spicy brown mustard comes across as a rich undertone.

Preheat oven to 350 degrees F. Place a rimmed baking sheet on the center rack in the oven to heat up.

In a medium-sized heavy-bottomed saucepan, melt the butter over medium heat. Add the onion powder, dried dillweed and salt and simmer gently to merge the dry ingredients with the butter. Stir in the mustard and Tabasco sauce. Stir to combine, then add the corn syrup, and stir again. When this mixture has heated through, add the hazelnuts. Using a silicon spatula, scrape and stir for a minute or two so that the nuts become evenly coated with the butter sauce. Scrape the mixture out onto the baking sheet, spreading the nuts evenly into a single layer.

Roast for 15 to 20 minutes, just until the sauce turns golden. As the sauce begins to caramelize and thicken, you may need to scrape and stir the nuts once so they stay evenly coated during the final phase of roasting. But it's a thick enough sauce that this may not be necessary. I use a pastry scraper, which is a very efficient way to move a lot of nuts around at once.

While the nuts are roasting, spread a large sheet of waxed or parchment paper on a cutting board. When the nuts are done, remove them from the oven, and scrape them out onto the paper, quickly spreading them out so they don't touch each other for the most part. Allow them to cool and then break them apart as desired into single nuts or clusters.

The pieces should be stored at room temperature in an airtight container, in which they can be kept for several weeks. Their crunchiness and flavor will continue to develop for the first 24 hours, so it's best to prepare them at least a day in advance of when they will be needed.

BEVERAGE THOUGHTS: A full-bodied Pinot Noir stands up to the onion and mustard and compliments the hazelnut character, just like I suggested in the onion-flavored version. And just so, another option would be a spicy and lively Tempranillo, like the one produced in Southern Oregon at Abacela. My beer choice would be a smooth, rounded beer along the lines of a brown ale, such as Rogue's Hazelnut Brown Ale, or a soft and luscious, slightly lighter wheat beer, such as Widmer Brother's Hefeweizen.

2 tablespoons butter

2 tablespoons light corn syrup

3 cups lightly roasted and skinned hazelnuts

1/2 cup (packed) light brown sugar

1/4 cup coarsely chopped fresh rosemary

2 teaspoons coarse kosher salt

1/8 teaspoon cayenne

Hot and Sugary Roasted Hazelnuts with Rosemary and Cayenne

These are an exquisite nibble! The rosemary compliments the toasty undertones with the caramelized sugar and hazelnuts. And the small bit of cayenne just keeps the experience alive a little longer! Place these out at happy hour and your guests will be very happy indeed.

Preheat oven to 350 degrees F. Place the butter and corn syrup in the center of a rimmed baking sheet and warm in the oven until the butter has melted. Meanwhile, in a medium-sized bowl, combine the hazelnuts, brown sugar, rosemary, salt, and cayenne. Transfer the mixture to the baking pan, stirring the mixture again with a flat-sided spatula to incorporate the butter and syrup. Bake until the sugar melts and caramelizes around the nuts, stirring every 5 minutes with a wide spatula or a pastry scraper, for about 20 minutes total baking time.

While the nuts are roasting, spread a large sheet of waxed or parchment paper on a cutting board. When the nuts and coating have darkened, remove the pan from the oven and immediately scrape them out onto the paper, quickly spreading the nuts out so they don't touch each other for the most part. Allow them to cool and then break them apart as desired into single nuts or clusters.

The pieces should be stored at room temperature in an airtight container, in which they can be kept for several weeks.

BEVERAGE THOUGHTS: The rosemary and toasty brown sugar are very complimentary to the herbal qualities of a big and fruity Zinfandel, such as Eola Hills' Lodi old vine Zinfandel. I would also consider a nice amber ale, such as Deschutes Brewery's Green Lakes Organic Ale. An edgier IPA, such as Ninkasi Brewing's Tricerahops Double IPA, is another refreshing alternative.

Makes 3 cups

2 tablespoons unsalted butter

3 cups roasted and skinned hazelnuts

1/4 teaspoon popcorn salt, more to taste

1 tablespoon fresh thyme leaves

Deep-fried Hazelnuts

Hazelnuts are exceptionally crunchy when French-fried. Heat oil to 365 degrees F. Submerge raw kernels for 30 seconds or until a light golden brown. Drain on paper towels and season lightly with salt.

Butter-Roasted Hazelnuts with Thyme

What a smashing way to serve one of Oregon's most special crops. Thyme adds an elegant lift to the smoky-toasty flavor within the nuts. You can serve them fresh out of the pan, or let them cool down and crisp up.

Melt the butter in a large skillet over medium-high heat. Continue to cook the butter briefly to lightly toast it. Add the hazelnuts and the salt and stir to evenly coat the hazelnuts with butter and salt. Stir in the thyme and continue cooking for a moment so its flavor has the opportunity to emerge. Scrape the nut mixture onto a large baking sheet to cool. Serve warm or at room temperature.

BEVERAGE THOUGHTS: Most certainly a medium-bodied Pinot Noir would play off the pure nuttiness and gentle herbed quality in this recipe. I'd go with a lighter style beer, something along the lines of a pale ale would not overpower the hazelnuts.

CHAPTER 4

Amuse-bouche

amuse-bouche \ a- myuź bush\ [Fr. Amuse the mouth]

    1. A small bite before the meal begins

    2. A gift of the chef de cuisine

If I had a chapter on hazelnut sauces, then some of these recipes would be there. The others, if push came to shove, could certainly reside in the appetizer section. But as you'll see, all of these recipes are so multidimensional that they deserved their own special little section. And so, in defining this collection, let's go with definition number two: They are my gift as self-declared chef de cuisine of this book, to you, the cook.

Oregon Hazelnut Dukkah

POUR A GLASS OF WINE. Chunk up some crusty artisan bread. Glug some really fruity olive oil into a saucer. Sprinkle some dukkah into a dish.

Sprinkle some what??? Dukkah. A savory melange of roasted and finely chopped hazelnuts, sesame seeds, and heavenly spices. When set out alongside that lovely olive oil and a platter of chunky, crusty bread, you've got about as instant an appetizer as you can hope for. I call it Party In a Dish. But it's also a great instant seasoner—of sautéed vegetables, roasted cauliflower, slices of heirloom tomatoes, and grilled steaks.

It's very ancient—as in, the Egyptians were making it long, long ago. And the fact that folks are still making it means that it's not only very ancient. It's also very good. In North Africa, street vendors will sell a flavorful sidewalk snack of dukkah, spooned into small paper cones, along with pita bread dipped in oil that you then use to dip into the dukkah. Of course, all vendors tout their own special blends, but a classic mixture includes sesame seeds, hazelnuts, dried chickpeas, coriander and cumin seed, black pepper and thyme.

I was introduced to dukkah by Oregon Dukkah founder Donna Dockins, a Portland area business woman and private chef who's fond of working with seasonal, regional, and flavorful dishes —particularly if they come with an ethnic twist.

She'd learned of dukkah through a friend who lives in New Zealand where dukkah has been around so long it's practically old hat. It immediately struck a chord with Dockins. After all, the main ingredient was hazelnuts. And here she was living in the middle of hazelnut country. The idea of building a business around such a healthy and sustainable product made perfect sense.

Dockins started packaging her Oregon Dukkah blends in 2005. Initially, she developed three blends: Zesty, Traditional, and Coconut & Sweet. Smoky Hot was added a couple years later.

Gearing up for such an endeavor was a challenge. No one else was producing dukkah in the United States, so she had to figure out all on her own how to do it on a commercial level. Hazelnuts, sesame seeds, and spices all needed to be roasted in bulk quantities. There were places where she could take her hazelnuts for roasting, but those places didn't want to deal with the smaller seeds and the spices.

So Donna ended up roasting her own mixtures with a barrel roaster, which is similar to a coffee roaster. As her company has grown, she's evolved her production practices, and now uses a completely different (read top secret) process. Donna's Dukkah blends are available in specialty food shops and on the internet (check the back of the book for contact information).

But since it's a straightforward process for the home cook—toast the hazelnuts, seeds and seasonings, chop them up, then combine and store—you should consider making it yourself. It's such a simple and delicious approach to entertaining. Here's a basic recipe, with plenty of adaptations. Perhaps you'll be inclined to bring it closer into line with your personal taste.

1/2 cup sliced almonds

1/2 cup sesame seeds

1/4 cup dehydrated chopped onion

1 tablespoon dehydrated minced garlic

1 teaspoon salt

1/2 teaspoon coarsely ground black
peppercorns

1 cup hazelnuts, roasted and skinned

A LIST OF FOODS TO ENJOY ONE WAY OR ANOTHER WITH DUKKAH WOULD BE LONG INDEED.

But if I had to make up a short list of particularly likely candidates, it would include:

~ potatoes, rice or refried beans

~ soups

~ steamed cauliflower

~ egg, chicken, or tossed green salads

~ sliced heirloom tomatoes and cheese
(blue, feta, or fresh mozzarella)

~ roasted vegetables, such as squash

~ grilled chicken, pork, fish, beef or lamb

Basic Roasted Hazelnut Dukkah

This is a classic mixture that is mild-flavored and lets the nut and sesame flavors shine through. As an appetizer, place some of it in a small saucer, alongside a saucer of good quality (read really fruity!) extra virgin olive oil. Round out the offering with a platter of crusty baguette slices. Show your guests how to enjoy by dipping a piece of the bread into the olive oil and then into the dukkah.

Dukkah is also a great addition to bread crumb coating mixtures, stirred into couscous or poultry stuffing, as a coating for cheese balls or cream cheese or fish (before grilling). Mix with fresh herbs and lemon juice and oil to form a coating for meat or fish prior to cooking.

Toast the almonds in a small non-stick skillet over medium-high heat until they begin to brown, tossing and stirring the nuts fairly frequently for even browning. Remove from heat and scrape the nuts onto a platter to cool thoroughly.

Return the skillet to the burner and add the sesame seeds, spreading them out into a single layer in the pan. Toast over medium-high heat until the seeds begin to brown and pop. Toss and stir the seeds occasionally for even browning. Remove from heat and scrape the seeds from the skillet onto the platter to cool thoroughly (keep them separate from the almonds because you will add them to the food processor before you add the almonds).

Return the skillet to the burner, add the chopped onion and cook briefly until most of the onion has lightly browned. This will only take about 30 seconds. Remove the skillet from the burner and scrape the onion onto the platter to cool thoroughly.

Place toasted sesame seeds, toasted onion, garlic, salt, and ground peppercorns in a food processor and process using the pulse button until the sesame seeds are partly ground up. Add the almonds and hazelnuts and continue to pulse until the mixture is ground to a consistency slightly coarser than cornmeal (with visible chunks of nut and seed). Do not allow the mixture to become a paste.

Store in an airtight jar or plastic container. Will keep at room temperature for about 2 months. If you plan to make large quantities of it (it's a great gift!), consider storing some of it in the freezer, where it will stay fresh much longer.

DUKKAH VARIATIONS:	JUST ADD:
BASIC DUKKAH BLEND	See recipe on previous page
MIDDLE EASTERN DUKKAH	2 teaspoons toasted cumin seeds 2 teaspoons ground coriander
ITALIAN DUKKAH	1 teaspoon dried rosemary 1 teaspoon dried basil 1 teaspoon dried thyme
SOUTHWEST DUKKAH	2 teaspoons ground cumin 1 teaspoon ground chili powder 1 teaspoon dried oregano
SMOKY-BARBEQUE DUKKAH	2 teaspoons ground chipotle chile pepper (or ground smoky paprika)

NORTHWEST WINES AND CRAFT BEERS
A Perfect Companion to Dukkah

WINE Old vine Zinfandels, Cabernet Sauvignon and Merlot, and full-bodied Pinot Noirs.

CRAFT BEER An American blonde ale such as Cascade Lakes' Blonde Bombshell Ale makes an interesting partner, because it leans in the direction of light-bodied, but is both refreshing and interesting on the palate.

WINE Old vine Zinfandels, Cabernet Sauvignon and Merlot, and full-bodied Pinot Noirs.

CRAFT BEER It's time to bring out a nice and hoppy English style bitter, such as Deschutes Brewery's Bachelor ESB, or a hearty India pale ale (IPA), such as Rogue Ale's Imperial Pale Ale. Also, Rogue Ale's Juniper Pale Ale would be refreshing on the palate while standing up to the spice and heat.

WINE Its rich nuttiness without a spicy back would compliment the gentler, more soft-spoken white wines, such as Pinot Gris, slightly oaked Chardonnays, a floral Vignionier, and gently spicy Gewürztraminer. Also, any light to medium-bodied Oregon Pinot Noir would be heavenly, as would a fruity Syrah.

CRAFT BEER I like to compliment this dukkah's toasty quality with an equally toasty nut brown ale, such as Rogue Ale's Hazelnut Brown Nectar. However, it would also be fun to go the amber ale route, particularly one that is as sweet, malty, spicy and floral as Full Sail's Amber Ale.

Romesco Sauce

THERE ARE SOME RECIPES THAT ARE SO SPECIAL YOU JUST WANT TO SHARE THEM WITH THE WORLD. Romesco sauce is such a creation. A dreamy blend of roasted tomatoes, peppers, and hazelnuts, thickened with fried bread, and spiked with red wine vinegar, fresh garlic and a smoky hint of Spanish paprika, this sauce comes packed with promise.

With the consistency of pesto and the reddish hue of a Tuscan sunset, this classic Catalan sauce does Spain proud. It enhances the delicate flavors of grilled prawns and vegetables, looks and tastes fabulous when tossed with creamy-white pasta, and adds a rich dimension to a simple appetizer of fresh ciabatta bread and extra-aged gouda. When stirred into a seafood stew or spooned over freshly-grilled halibut or scallops, it elevates the flavor profile in an elegant, understated way.

And it's been around for eons. Which is why I'm surprised that more people don't know about it. But there you have it. More often than not, when I share a bowl of romesco sauce at a party I get some curious looks. But once chunks of the afore-mentioned bread are dipped into it and tasted, the looks give way to contented sighs. It's that yummy.

Like anything that comes tagged with the term "classic," romesco sauce has a myriad of variations. Traditionally speaking, instead of plain old sweet red peppers, romesco is made with dried nora chiles, which are similar to the Mexican cascabel chile pepper, only sweeter and slightly milder. However, in most parts of the U.S., you're not going to find noras, or even cascabels for that matter, without journeying along the internet. So the most common variation on this sauce is to use fresh sweet red peppers that have been roasted and seeded, along with a hefty pinch of dried red pepper flakes for heat. This is the only way I've ever made my romesco sauce. But the results are magnificent, so I'm not worried.

I've also added a bit of ground chipotle chile, which is a close substitute for authentic and smoky Spanish paprika (another one of those hard-to-find items).

So give this amazing sauce a spin. Your family and friends will be impressed with your savvy. You'll feel lucky to have enriched your cuisine with such a versatile dish.

Makes about 3 cups

About 2 tablespoons of olive oil, divided

1 pound of Roma tomatoes
  (4 medium-sized)

1 red sweet bell pepper (see note)

2 (1-inch thick) slices of an Italian-style
  bread (measuring approximately
  6 x 3-inches in diameter),
    such as ciabatta or Pugliese

1 cup roasted and skinned hazelnuts

3 garlic cloves, crushed and peeled

1 to 2 teaspoons red pepper flakes

1 teaspoon Spanish paprika

1/2 teaspoon ground chipotle chile pepper
  (McCormick sells one in the spice aisle)

1/2 teaspoon salt

1/4 teaspoon freshly ground black pepper

1/4 cup red wine or sherry vinegar

1/2 cup extra virgin olive oil

Hot water, if needed

Romesco Sauce

This classic Spanish sauce is a melange of roasted tomatoes and peppers, olive oil, roasted hazelnuts and fried bread. It compliments many foods, including grilled shellfish and halibut, lamb, pasta, and even a simple offering of toasted bread (as a dipping sauce). It keeps for at least two weeks in the refrigerator.

Preheat oven to 400 degrees F.

Pool one tablespoon of olive oil on a baking sheet and place it in the oven while it is preheating. Halve the tomatoes lengthwise; cut out the core from each half. When the oven is hot, remove the baking sheet from the oven and place the tomato halves in the oil, cut-side up. Coat the surface of each tomato half with a bit more oil, which will help with browning. Roast for about 15 minutes, then turn the tomatoes over, cut-side down and continue roasting until the tomato skins begin to darken, crack, and pull away from the flesh. Remove from the oven and set aside until they're cool enough to handle.

Pierce the pepper in several places with a sharp knife to avoid bursting, then place it on the baking sheet. Place the pepper under a broiler and broil, turning several times, until it has blackened over most of its surface. Alternatively, you could blacken the pepper over a gas flame on your stove top, or in a grill.

Meanwhile, heat the remaining 1 tablespoon of olive oil in a heavy-bottomed skillet (you can use a non-stick skillet, but it won't impart quite as much toasty flavor to the bread). Fry the bread until golden brown and crisp on both sides. Remove from skillet and let cool.

Pluck the skins from the cooled tomatoes, reserving the juices. Place the flesh and juice in the food processor. Peel, core and seed the pepper, reserving the juice. Place the flesh and juice in the food processor. Add the bread, roasted hazelnuts, garlic, red pepper flakes, paprika, ground chipotle chile pepper, salt, and black pepper. Process until smooth (it will have a somewhat grainy appearance because of the nuts). With the machine running, add the vinegar. Let the motor run for a moment, then stop it and scrape down the sides of the bowl. Turn the motor back on and add the 1/2 cup of extra virgin olive oil in a slow, steady, very thin stream. The sauce will thicken slightly and hold together with a rich, rust orange/red color. If the sauce seems too thick (it should have a soft, pesto-like consistency), then with the machine running, drizzle in some hot water. Taste and make sure the sauce has plenty of piquancy and enough salt. If desired, with the machine running, add additional vinegar and salt. Romesco sauce can be prepared and refrigerated for at least a week (I've even used batches of it at the end of 2 weeks). Bring to room temperature before using.

NOTE ON ROASTED RED PEPPERS: If you want to trim a bit of labor from the project, you could use a store-bought roasted and peeled red pepper if you determine the quality is recipe-worthy. I've done just that and been satisfied with the results. Tassos makes delicious fire-roasted Florina Peppers. They come packed in a lovely oval-shaped jar and are in a light vinegar solution that contributes to the flavor of the sauce.

MORE USES FOR YOUR ROMESCO SAUCE: Serve over grilled lamb, fish and vegetables, or in a bowl alongside bread and roasted spring onions. Also delicious as a sandwich spread or a dipping sauce for asparagus. Stir it into seafood stews and vegetable soups.

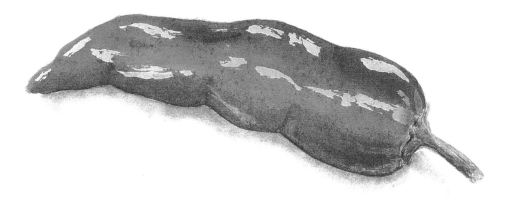

3 cups roasted and skinned hazelnuts
(about 1 pound)

1/2 teaspoon salt (optional)

1/4 cup granulated sugar (optional)

1/2 cup additional roasted, cooled,
and skinned hazelnuts (optional,
if you want a "chunky" hazelnut butter)

Nutella— what's in a name?

THE ORIGINAL RECIPE calling for the blending of ground hazelnuts, cocoa, sugar and oil, can be traced back to 1906 in Italy. For 40 years it remained below the radar for most of the world. Then in 1946, Italian pastry-maker Pietro Ferrero was looking for a way to stretch his limited supply of cocoa. Like so many other foods, it was in short supply in the post-World War II era. He turned to hazelnuts, which were in abundant supply in his Piedmontese town of Alba. He called his spread "Pasta Gianduja." Pasta means paste, and Gianduja was the name of a popular cartoon character of the region. The Pasta Gianduja was formed into loaves and wrapped in foil so that mothers could cut it into slices to use as a sandwich filling for their children. Of course, most children were prone to throwing away the bread and eating only the Pasta Gianduja. So, in 1949, Ferrero made his product creamier and sold it in jars as a spread. An instant hit, it was called "Supercrema Gianduja." Sales were solid. But when he renamed his recipe "Nutella" in 1964, sales went sky-high, reaching over 100 million pounds a year today.

Hazelnut Butter

For a richly-flavored butter, give the hazelnuts a longer roast than you might for some recipes. Let the nuts cool thoroughly before using. There's a honey option at the end of the recipe that's not to be missed by all you honey fans. How to use hazelnut butter? Well, any way you'd use peanut butter is a start. If you're going to pair it with jams, my choice is raspberry, which goes so well with hazelnuts. Hazelnut butter also is delicious smeared onto fresh chunks of apple.

Hazelnut butter can be stored for weeks at a time in your refrigerator, unless everyone else discovers your secret. Then all bets are off. So you'd better have a back-up jar hidden on another shelf!

Place the hazelnuts in the work bowl of a food processor. Using the pulse button, chop them until they resemble coarse meal. Then keep the machine running, stopping it every 10 or 15 seconds so the nuts don't get too warm. Keep processing until the nuts go from crumbly and grainy, to smooth and creamy. At any point along the way, add the salt and sugar if you are using it. It's not necessary; I just find the flavor deeper and more, well, flavorful! The creamy texture development is an amazing thing to watch, and occurs only after the nuts release their oils into the purée.

Once the mixture turns soft and creamy, you can throw in the additional 1/2 cup of roasted nuts and process briefly to make a "chunky" hazelnut butter.

HONEY-HAZELNUT BUTTER: Honey is an amazingly complimentary flavor to hazelnut butter. Instead of the 1/4 cup of granulated sugar, blend in 2 to 3 tablespoons of honey. Delicious!

HAZELNUT-COCOA BUTTER: Stir 1/4 cup of good-quality cocoa powder into the 2 cups of hazelnut butter. If you didn't add the 1/4 cup granulated sugar, then you will need to stir that in also.

STORAGE: Hazelnut butter will keep for several weeks at room temperature without developing off-flavors, but for longer periods, keep it refrigerated.

1/2 cup canola oil

1/2 cup roasted and skinned hazelnuts

1/3 cup cooked and drained garbanzo beans
   (canned is fine)

1/4 cup cooked and drained soybeans
   (canned is fine)

4 cloves garlic

1/2 cup water

1/2 cup fresh lemon juice (Meyer lemon juice
   is ideal but not essential)

1/3 cup nutritional yeast
   (see note below; this is not the same as
   "active dry yeast")

1 tablespoon Ponzu sauce (or soy sauce)

1/2 teaspoon salt

1/2 teaspoon dried basil

1/4 teaspoon ground cumin

1/8 teaspoon ascorbic acid
   (for "zing"—available in the health
   food section of most supermarkets)

Heavenly Sauce

My inspiration for this hazelnut-based sauce comes by way of Café Yumm!—a small, earth-friendly restaurant chain that got its start in Eugene, Oregon. Their Yumm! Sauce has enamored most who have ever tasted it. When you eat it, you go "Yummm!" This recipe is pretty close in flavor and texture. You could leave out the ascorbic acid, but it really does produce the extra kick that the original sauce has. I feel confident in calling it Heavenly Sauce, because it does taste heavenly, either on its own alongside a bowl of crudites, or as part of a main dish in a bowl of steaming jasmine rice with layers of fresh vegetables, cheese and beans. I've also enjoyed it as a simple sauce over gently steamed vegetables.

In a blender jar, combine the oil, hazelnuts, garbanzo beans, soybeans and garlic. Run the motor, stopping several times to scrape the sides of the jar and push the mixture into the blades. Once the mixture is a rough purée, add the water, lemon juice, nutritional yeast, Ponzu sauce (or soy sauce), salt, basil, cumin, and ascorbic acid. Continue blending until the mixture is relatively smooth (it will remain grainy because of the nuts). Scrape it into a container and store in the refrigerator for up to 2 weeks.

NOTE ON NUTRITIONAL YEAST: When Café Yumm! co-founder Mary Beauchamp created her Yumm! Sauce, she was attempting to make something nutritious for her young children. Hence, the nutritional yeast. It's loaded with vitamins, particularly B-complex and is a complete protein. Some brands are even fortified with vitamin B12, which is a difficult vitamin to get in your diet if you are a vegetarian. It also has a delicious, nutty, cheesy flavor, and it's color is a pale gold, sort of like powdered mustard. Don't confuse it with other yeasts, such as brewer's yeast. You'll find it in the nutritional section of any well-stocked bulk food aisle.

HOW TO USE YOUR HEAVENLY SAUCE: I have a specific recipe for constructing Heavenly Bowls on page 149. But in a nutshell, make a big pot of Heavenly Jasmine Rice (page 130). Then, place a serving of the rice (hot, warm, or cooled) in a bowl, add a spoonful of the Heavenly Sauce, and top it with a variety of vegetables and/or meats, and/or cheeses, sort of like building a burrito, tostada or taco. I like shredded cheese, diced avocado, chopped tomatoes, chopped green onions, roasted and chopped hazelnuts, sliced olives, and black beans. Then spoon on some more of the Heavenly Sauce. For an extra whang, spoon on a bit of your favorite salsa. Then, bon appetit!

MORE USES FOR YOUR HEAVENLY SAUCE: It's great as a dip for vegetables, and as a topping for baked potatoes and pasta dishes.

1-1/2 cups unsalted butter

3 large egg yolks, at room temperature

3 tablespoons fresh lemon juice,
    at room temperature

1/4 teaspoon salt

Pinch of cayenne pepper

3 tablespoons hazelnut oil

Hazelnut Hollandaise

First you make a simple beurre noisette, which in French, literally translates into "hazelnut butter," because it tastes like roasted hazelnuts. That gives you the first level of nuttiness, without even using a nut. Then, to form a classic butter emulsion—a hollandaise—you clarify that brown butter and drizzle it, while still hot, into a blender jar where it will join forces with egg yolks and lemon juice to form a splendid velvety smooth and barely thick sauce. Finish with a splash of hazelnut oil to deepen the nutty flavor and you've got a delightful sauce for poached or grilled salmon, Eggs Benedict, roast lamb, and fresh asparagus. You'll think of plenty more ways to enjoy it.

TO CLARIFY AND BROWN THE BUTTER (BEURRE NOISETTE): This can be done several days ahead and kept, covered, in the refrigerator. Cut the butter into chunks and melt it slowly in a small, heavy-bottomed pot over low heat. Continue cooking very gently; don't rush the process. After about 15 minutes, the milk solids will begin to separate as the liquid boils very gently. Eventually, the milk solids will turn a light brown and the surface of the butter will become fairly foamy. Keep cooking. At about the 30 minute mark, when the milk solids have turned a dark brown, remove the butter from the burner. Skim off the foam with the back of a metal spoon, then pour the butter into another container, leaving behind the browned milk solids.

TO PREPARE THE HAZELNUT HOLLANDAISE: Bring the butter to room temperature if necessary, then heat it in the microwave until it is very hot but not boiling. Place the egg yolks, lemon juice, salt, and cayenne in a blender jar and blend briefly. With the motor running, add the hot clarified butter, one drop at a time, until the eggs thicken. Once that occurs, you can start adding the hot butter in a slow, steady stream, as long as the sauce is remains thick. If the sauce breaks, go back to adding the butter drop-by-drop until it thickens again. Once the butter has been added, add the hazelnut oil in a slow steady stream. Stop the motor and scrape down the sides. Adjust seasoning if necessary.

The Hazelnut Hollandaise may be kept warm in the top part of a double boiler, but don't hold it for more than an hour, for safety. If you don't use it all at once, then share the left-overs with your neighbors (if they haven't had dinner yet) because you cannot re-heat hollandaise; it separates. But who says there will be any left over?

Hazelnut and Caramelized Onion Sauce

Makes about 2 cups sauce

1/2 cup plus 1 tablespoon extra virgin
   olive oil, divided
1 cup chopped yellow onion
1-1/2 cups roasted and skinned hazelnuts
About 1/4 cup dry white wine
   (such as an Oregon Pinot Gris)
Salt to taste
Freshly ground black pepper

Here's another hazelnut-based sauce. This one came into my world via hazelnut grower Margy Buchanan. She'd encountered it in a newspaper food section while traveling, took it home and gave it a whirl using hazelnuts in place of walnuts. She also used some of her house wine (Margy owns a winery, too!), the Tyee Pinot Gris, in place of water. Her reports were so encouraging I just had to give it a try. It's wonderful. So with a bit of fiddling, I present this delightful sauce. Margy served hers over pasta, but it was made famous (in its life as a walnut-based sauce) as an accompaniment to roasted asparagus at A16, a San Francisco restaurant. Consider using it on pizza dough (in place of the red sauce) before adding other toppings, with a ham and cheese grilled sandwich, on freshly sautéed vegetables, or as a dip for some seasonal crudites and toasted pita triangles.

Heat the 1 tablespoon of olive oil in a medium saucepan over medium heat. Add the onion and cook gently for at least 10 to 15 minutes, or longer if you have the patience, until the onion is soft and caramelized; remove from heat.

Scrape the onions into a food processor. Add the hazelnuts and the wine and process until the nuts are finely chopped. With the motor running, add the remaining 1/2 cup of olive oil in a slow, steady stream, processing until smooth and creamy. Adjust seasonings, adding salt and freshly ground black pepper to taste.

Makes about 1 cup

1/2 cup dark-roasted and skinned hazelnuts

8 to 10 medium-sized cloves fresh garlic,
    smashed and peeled

Scant 1/2 teaspoon salt

2 tablespoons warm water

1/4 teaspoon freshly ground black pepper

1/2 cup hazelnut oil
    (optional, use canola oil if unavailable)

Hazelnut Aillade

Aillade (pronounced "eye-yawd") is a French expression meaning "with garlic." In this case, it's hazelnuts with garlic. But it's so much more! It has the silky, creamy texture of a homemade mayonnaise, tinted a pale tan from the nuts, of course. The use of hazelnut oil gooses the nut flavor up a notch, but if you don't have any, just go with a good, fresh canola oil and you'll be fine.

If I have a jar of hazelnut aillade in the fridge, I reach for it throughout the week to use in so many ways: to flavor a vinaigrette; to layer onto chicken breasts, pork chops, or fish either before grilling, or right after they've come off the grill; as a topping for sliced tomatoes and grilled asparagus; to season a pasta salad, soups, and tomato-based sauces; and even as a sandwich spread. In the summer, when I'm making bruschetta (page 85), I sometimes give the fire-toasted slices of bread a thin layering of the hazelnut aillade before topping with my home-grown tomatoes and herbs.

Place the hazelnuts, garlic, salt, pepper and water in a blender. Blend, scraping down the sides of the jar as necessary, until the mixture is chopped (it will appear very rugged at this point). Add 1/4 cup of the oil and continue blending until the mixture is very smooth. With the motor running, add the remaining 1/4 cup of oil, drop by drop, until you have a thick and velvety sauce, which has the texture of a soft mayonnaise.

2 cups cooked and drained chickpeas
    (garbanzo beans), reserving the liquid

2 to 3 tablespoons liquid from the
    drained chickpeas

1/2 cup hazelnut butter (commercially made
    or homemade, page 59)

About 1/4 cup fresh lime juice

2 tablespoons olive oil

1-1/2 tablespoons chili oil

1 tablespoon mashed and finely chopped
    fresh garlic

1/2 teaspoon salt

Barb's Hazelnut Hummus

A traditional hummus recipe includes toasted sesame seed purée, which is called tahini. Barb Foulke of Freddy Guys Hazelnuts near Monmouth, Oregon had a brilliant thought: would her roasted hazelnut butter make a noble stand-in for the tahini? Well, beyond noble, it's just downright delicious. Rich and smoky, with a depth of flavor that I never seem to find in traditional hummus preparations. As Barb says, "Very simple!"

In a blender or food processor, combine the chickpeas, 2 tablespoons of the liquid from the drained chickpeas, hazelnut butter, lime juice, olive oil, chili oil, garlic and salt. Blend until puréed. Adjust seasonings, adding additional chili oil, lime juice, and salt to taste. If it is too thick, add additional liquid from the drained chickpeas.

The Essentials of Balsamic Essence

ONE CONSISTENT THEME IN THIS BOOK is the use of hazelnuts in two very distinct ways: as a bridge and as an accent. Their toasty-richness makes them the connect-the-dots sort of ingredient when other components are, perhaps, just a little bit far apart on the flavor continuum. Hazelnuts' strength as an accent is in their unique flavor and delightful texture.

Except for that texture thing, the same can be said for my use of balsamic reductions. A rich and mellow reduction of balsamic vinegar can bring all of the other ingredients into line. In the other direction, single drops or dollops of it on a plate, in the middle of a puddle of oil, or sprinkled over a freshly-grilled chop, is a dynamic accent.

In many cases, you'll find my recipes incorporating both ingredients—hazelnuts and balsamic reductions—because they play off each other so very well.

The wonder of a balsamic vinegar reduction landed on my radar back in the mid-90's. On a visit to Napa Valley, chef Michael Chiarello had invited me to his trendy wine-country restaurant, Tra Vigne, to sample his fare. The two most memorable offerings he shared both incorporated this syrupy-rich, tangy-yet-smooth ingredient; in each

case providing the kind of lick-your-plate perfection we all strive for in cooking.

The first dish was a simple appetizer playing off the subtle, flavorful layerings of a well-made fresh mozzarella and slices of backyard-ripened tomatoes and fire-roasted red peppers, resting on puddles of emerald-green basil-infused olive oil. Droplets of his balsamic vinegar reduction floated in the oil—liquid obsidian-toned capsules of intense flavor that I dipped into with young mozzarella cheese and fruity peppers and tomatoes.

Chiarello explained that garnishing with a good-quality (read very old and very expensive!) balsamic vinegar had been popular for eons, but the act of simmering the vinegar down to a syrupy-sweet concentrated version was still in its infancy, relatively speaking. He called it balsamic essence. And it truly was just that: the rich and savory-sweet essence of balsamic vinegar without a hint of whang.

Then came the polenta. Tender, golden triangles of roasted polenta, sitting in a buttery, beefy sauce that had such depth of flavor I just sighed. In response, Chiarello explained that, again, the sauce was invigorated with the use of a balsamic vinegar reduction.

Ever since, I've made sure that I always have a bit of this lovely essence tucked into the side pocket of my fridge. I keep it in a tiny squeeze bottle with a narrow spout so that it can be applied in a slender stream for controlled garnishing. I reach for it when my spaghetti sauce needs zooping up; when a chicken-vegetable sauté lacks oomph; when I want to wow our guests with a fancy, squiggly garnish alongside a platter of bruschetta or simple grilled meats. It's unique and special enough to not be considered passé. Ever.

One of the best parts of this concept is that you don't need to use the most expensive and aged balsamic vinegar to produce a delicious balsamic essence. In fact, with so many affordable balsamic vinegars on the market, I like to make up large batches both to have on hand for my own cooking and to give away to friends.

A Primer for Balsamic Vinegar Reductions

WHEN BOILING BALSAMIC VINEGAR DOWN into a syrupy essence, you're throwing a lot of steam and aroma into the atmosphere. So if you have an outdoor kitchen of some sort—a single burner on your gas grill, for example, that's where I recommend you do it.

A neat trick to help you track the reduction process is to visualize where the level of a balsamic reduction will end up in relation to the sides of the pot. The recipe will tell you how much vinegar you're starting out with and how much you'll have when it's reduced. The finished reduction is typically one third to one quarter of the original volume. So in the latter case if you're starting with 2 cups of balsamic vinegar, you'll end up with 1/2 cup. Pour 1/2 cup of water into the pot you're using. Now take a chop stick and stick it in the pot. Note the level of water on the chop stick. Then, when you're reducing the vinegar, you'll have a visual aid to show you how much more you have to reduce by sticking the chop stick in the simmering liquid and noting how high up on the stick it is.

Start with the real deal. To make a reduction of balsamic vinegar, it's a must that you start with genuine balsamic vinegar. On the other hand, do not use the REALLY good stuff that you so lovingly brought back from your adventure in Northern Italy last summer. I use the relatively inexpensive commercial balsamics that are becoming so available here in the U.S. In Italian, they are called industriale and a couple of good choices are Fini (this is on the high end of expense, however) and Cavalli. At the low end, I've found respectable brands through warehouse-style supermarkets. The basic flavor is less complex than the spendier artisan-made balsamics, but well-made commercial balsamic will at least have sweetness, accentuated by tartness and a lingering richness. There are plenty of imitation balsamics among the inexpensive brands, so be sure to read the label. The ingredients should include grape must and red wine vinegar (NOT cider vinegar). And because they're designed to behave like the well-aged balsamics, you'll also find corn syrup and caramel coloring.

Freddy Guys Hazelnuts

"It's been hard to be without the market, but thanks to the kindness of owner Barb Foulke, we've been able to keep Freddy Guys hazelnuts on hand all winter long. Barb drives in from Monmouth every two weeks or so, delivering boxes of freshly roasted hazelnuts to her Portland accounts during the off season. We're hooked on Freddy Guys hazelnuts. Taste them, and you'll see why they've induced a near-religious fervor in our kitchen. Barb and her husband Fritz farm 160 acres of hazelnuts, and unlike most growers, process their own harvest. They've been to Italy twice now to pick out the best possible roaster for their hazelnuts. It makes an unbelieveable difference in the finished product here at the bakery."

Elizabeth Beekley,
Two Tarts Bakery
March 13, 2009 blog

**2 cups balsamic vinegar (remember, you
     don't need to use the real good stuff!)**
1/2 cup coarsely chopped yellow onion
2 teaspoons granulated sugar
10 to 12 peppercorns

Basic Balsamic Vinegar Essence

This is simply balsamic vinegar that is reduced to a full-flavored, syrupy sauce, with a little seasoning. The recipe can easily be doubled or tripled or more, depending on how big of a pot you have and how much balsamic vinegar you want to start with.

In a medium-sized heavy-bottomed saucepan, combine the balsamic vinegar with the onion, sugar and peppercorns. Bring the mixture to a boil and simmer, uncovered, until the mixture has reduced down to about 1/2 to 1/3 cup and is thickened and somewhat syrupy. Let the mixture cool (it will thicken a bit more when chilled) and then strain through a fine sieve (be sure to press the onions with the back of a wooden spoon to squeeze out all of the juicy balsamic syrup).

Store the reduction in a tightly closed jar or squeeze bottle with a slender spout. It will keep for months and months. Use it to drizzle over tomatoes and fresh mozzarella, polenta, grilled chicken, vegetable sauté or roasted vegetables.

BUTTERY-RICH VERSION: While the vinegar mixture is boiling, cut 4 tablespoons of butter into small chunks. After the liquid has reduced, add the chunks of butter one-by-one, stirring thoroughly after each addition. Do not add another chunk of butter until the previous chunk has thoroughly melted. Makes about 3/4 cup sauce.

STORING YOUR BALSAMIC ESSENCE: Refrigeration isn't necessary from a food safety standpoint, but for long-term storage (more than a week or so), refrigerating the reduction will maintain quality. I keep a large batch of the sauce in a jar with a non-reactive lid. Then I transfer small amounts into little plastic squeeze bottles (they're about 2-ounce capacity) to make my artistic squiggle presentations. Look for squeeze bottles at restaurant supply stores, or in a well-stocked craft store (just make sure that the packaging states that they are "food grade.")

Makes about 1-1/2 cups

2 cups balsamic vinegar

1/2 cup chopped yellow onion

10 to 12 whole peppercorns

3 cups chicken broth (canned is okay)

3 cups beef stock (canned is okay)

1/2 cup butter

QuickTIP

For a simple appetizer using your Balsamic Essence, pour a small puddle of extremely good-quality extra virgin olive oil into the center of a lovely white plate, then scatter in a few droplets of the balsamic vinegar reduction. Now sprinkle some finely chopped roasted hazelnuts around the edges.

Provide slices of a crusty Italian bread for dipping...first into the oil and balsamic essence, then into the nuts.

Best Ever Balsamic Sauce

This sauce is a rich variation of my "Basic Balsamic Vinegar Essence." It incorporates two kinds of broth—chicken and beef. If you want to keep the sauce meat-free, then you could use a well-flavored vegetarian broth.

This sauce is fabulous served with the Roasted Polenta (page 126), alongside some grilled vegetables, or with grilled fish or chicken breasts. Don't forget to toss on a handful of richly roasted and coarsely chopped hazelnuts.

And if you want to go the extra mile for some special friends, use this sauce with the Pork Medallions and Grilled Pineapple recipe (page 154) instead of the Balsamic-Molasses reduction.

Add the vinegar, chopped onion, and peppercorns to a medium-sized, heavy-bottomed pot (about 8 quart capacity). Bring to a boil, reduce to a simmer and cook until reduced to a syrup consistency. You will now have about 1/2 cup of liquid remaining. Add the chicken broth and beef stock, bring to a boil again, then simmer until reduced to a sauce consistency. You will end up with about 1 cup. Strain the sauce through a wire sieve, pressing down on the onions with a wooden spoon or spatula to force the softened onions through the sieve for extra flavor.

The sauce may be refrigerated for several days or frozen for several months at this point. When ready to finish the sauce, bring it to a simmer, then whisk in the butter, 1 tablespoon at a time, until all of the butter has been incorporated. Keep hot until ready to serve.

CHAPTER **5**

Setting the Tone

If you want to instill a sense that something truly memorable is about to happen at the table, you need neither elegance nor extravagance.

THE KEY IS TO PROVIDE A REFRESHED CUISINE, something at least a little out of the ordinary, with well-matched flavors and textures working together to elevate the experience to a new level. And to do it from the start.

As I mentioned already, simply roasting a batch of hazelnuts straight over some coals—a la The Aman Brothers Barbequed Hazelnuts—is a delightfully unique way to get a party rolling. Just pass them around as they come off the grill, golden and glistening in a bit of melted butter and zesty Worcestershire sauce. Heavenly! I've also roasted them with fresh cloves of garlic, which takes their flavor in an entirely different direction. Plus, the resultant tender, juicy cloves are equally delicious served alongside the nuts.

Such basic treatment is just the beginning. Because the Oregon hazelnut has a special affinity for cheeses, artisan breads and grilled meats, it's easy to add depth and sophistication to the meal when you incorporate this versatile nut. Add hazelnuts to the savory pastry crust of your cheese tart. Sprinkle a handful of richly-roasted and chopped hazelnuts alongside a golden puddle of olive oil and balsamic vinegar for dipping into with slices of fresh ciabatta. Encourage guests to accent a freshly-grilled chicken satay by dipping it in a zesty hazelnut sauce, or giving it a double-dip of spicy mustard followed by chunks of roasted hazelnuts.

Certainly not to be overlooked is the hazelnut's relationship with two other Oregon specialties: wine and craft beer. It's a natural relationship, born of three noble gifts from the earth: The nut, the grape, and the hop.

The grape is in high regard here in Oregon, and deservedly so. In the Willamette Valley alone, which is Oregon's largest wine region, there are over 200 wineries. Each and every one has been built from a dream and a hope for sustaining future generations. Like the orchardists producing exquisite hazelnuts, Oregon wine producers are connected to their land, and interested in everything around them affecting their craft. In what has been described as a maritime climate, growers have the most success with cool-climate grape varieties, particularly Pinot Noir. In fact, the Pinot Noirs produced here are recognized as some of the finest in the world. But you'll also encounter luscious Pinot Gris, Pinot Blanc, Chardonnay, Gewürztraminer, Riesling, and Maréchal Foch. The list goes on and on, really. Which explains the healthy wine touring industry that has blossomed here over the last two decades.

And then there are the hops. To make good beer—and there's a lot of it in Oregon—you have to start with good quality hops. And boy do we grow great hops here in the Willamette Valley. Driving the back roads you'll encounter many hop farms that are inhabited by third and even fourth generation growers, with an average farm size of around 200 acres. Some of them grow hazelnuts as well.

Overall, the Oregon craft brew industry produces about 860,000 barrels of beer annually—equivalent to 1.72 million kegs or 285 million bottles of beer. That production ranks Oregon as the number two producer of craft beers in the U.S. These breweries are spread throughout the state, of course, but the highest concentration is surely in Portland. According to the Oregon Brewers Guild, beer lovers can take comfort in knowing that no matter where they are in that lovely city, they're less than 15 minutes away from a craft brewery. And it's all product that gets transported to every corner of the Pacific Northwest and beyond.

So pairing hazelnuts with beer and wine is a no-brainer. Time and again, I've found that my various hazelnut offerings can be brought even closer to perfection when served with the right wine or craft brew. So throughout the book, I'm providing tips on which wines or beers I've served with recipes. Take my observations in the spirit that they're given—strictly as loose guidelines for encouragement.

With that said, if you'd like to review a bit—let's call it "Food and Beverage Pairing 101"—then read on.

Thoughts on Connecting Wine with Food

THERE'S STILL A LOT OF DRAMA associated with bringing the right food into contact with the "correct" wine, which is too bad. Folks need to calm down about this. It's just choosing what flavors we like together, and aren't we all old hands at that? Part of the problem has been adherence to the old cant that red wine must be drunk with red meat and white wine with white meat, which is surely unreliable at producing good pairings. Nowadays, wine folk are more likely to consider cooking style, types of sauces used, and any other seasoning issues before deciding which bottle to pull from the rack.

But that still leaves plenty of room for insecurities if you don't have some understanding of where a given wine falls along the flavor continuum. One of the most basic questions to ask yourself (or that really helpful wine professional at the wine store) at the beginning of your pairing quest is: which wine is going to improve my dining experience? You might be saying, "Well, duh!" But think about it. Putting it this way, instead of in terms of "matching a food" leaves room for taking your personal tastes into account. Maybe you are only lukewarm about pinots in general, so narrow the field by ignoring them. This leads into first thinking in terms of styles of wines, rather than labels. Would it be a big, bold Pinot Noir with lots of fruit, earthiness, and oak?

A soft and delicate Pinot Gris? Or a spicy and aromatic Gewürztraminer or Riesling? For that "big" Pinot Noir, as an example, anything with an earthy-mushroomy-truffly-cheesy personality will be smashing. The shy Pinot Gris would be happy in the company of delicately prepared shrimp or crab or anything that's somewhat non-competitive on your palate. And the lovely spice and aromatic-exotic character of the Gewürztraminer or Riesling would be a delight in the presence of an exotic curry or Asian-themed offering, from dim sum to chicken satay. Plus, the slight sweetness in the Gewürz or Riesling (that's "off dry" in wine speak!) will balance the peppery-spicy quality in the food.

If you know the flavors and textures of the food you'll be serving, then you can get pretty darn close in your speculation—even when you can't take into consideration the variations any given grape exhibits from winery to winery, and year to year. All this means is that since there really are no hard-and-fast rules on the subject (so relax!), your pairing ability ultimately gets down to practice and observation. The more you experience, the easier it gets, and the more you can focus on specific labels and vintages to really dial a meal in.

Oh darn. So much wine and food. So little time.

Once I have a pairing set up, I make a point of analyzing a sip of the wine after I've had a bite of the food. I chew, swallow, sip. Then I ponder: Does the wine taste better or worse after that bite of food? It's really that simple. Either the food enhances the wine-drinking experience or it undermines it. And vice versa.

Of course, you can get into multiple levels of analysis. Does the food bring out subtle flavorings in the wine that you hadn't noticed when you were sipping it without food? Are the qualities in the wine that you expected to enjoy enhanced by the food? Was the slight bitter quality in the wine (that would be a red wine with lots of tannins, for example) reduced by the food? Then remember that for future reference, so when you're confronting a wine menu before a meal, you can hone in on the style of wine that just might get along perfectly with your food. Or, if you see a wine on that list that you simply HAVE to try, you'll be more likely to select an entrée that will heighten the experience.

Thoughts on Connecting Beer with Food

IN OREGON, LOVERS OF FOOD and beverage need look no further than the nearby supermarket for a vast selection of delightful regional beers and ales. Thus, there are plenty of times—with plenty of foods—when I'm just as likely to reach for a beautifully crafted regional ale as I am an earthy Pinot Noir. Indeed, as our beer savvy has blossomed, so have our opportunities for delightful pairings with food. For most beer lovers, whether they realize it or not, when the right beer is paired with the right food both components hum.

But for many, it's a totally mind-boggling experience, fraught with failure. With that said, I'm going to ask you to put those fears on hold and consider this: there are very few really right or really wrong approaches when the question relates to finding a good match between beer and food.

So again, relax. Discovering which foods taste best with which beers is a delightful journey to embark upon. And experimentation is part of the process. West Coast brew pubs are a great place to go for inspiration, since their chefs have taken the concept of food and beer pairings to a higher level. Far beyond buffalo wings and pizza, these days a brew pub menu is more likely to suggest a lively pilsner with caviar, an India pale ale with a bowl of chipotle chile hazelnuts, and a porter with a platter of mesquite-grilled ribs.

You don't have to be a chef to create successful pairings of beer and food. Just pick a starting point. You have two choices: the beer, or the food. Either way, think about how to create balance between the two. If you start with the beer, think about what you're tasting. What are the dominant flavors? Is the maltiness sweet or dry? Are the hops flowery or citric? What's going on with the yeast flavor? If you start with the food, is it richly flavored and highly seasoned or light and delicate? For example, a malty beer, such as a Scottish-style ale will fade next to a zippy, vinegary salad. Whereas a German-style pilsner might be the ticket, since its hoppiness will stand up to the oil and vinegar. And that Scottish-style ale will come to life in the presence of smoked sausage, beef bourguignonne, or roast pork and sauerkraut.

If you're looking for some general guidelines for a few of the most popular styles of beer, try this:

AMBER ALE: Probably your safest choice if you're really not sure which direction you want to go in your pairing. Most amber ales will compliment most dishes that aren't sweet. From soups and pizzas to Mexican or barbecue, this is a beer that will maintain a complimentary flavor profile and quench your thirst.

BITTER, PALE ALE, AND INDIA PALE ALES: Perfect choices for highly spiced cuisines, such as Thai and Indian. Fried and barbecued dishes also fare well with these beers because the hoppiness in the brew can cut through the greasiness. These beers are also great with beef, lamb, and game.

"The hop farm includes 44,598 square feet of processing sheds, two osprey nests, a riverside picnic area, and a chance to watch hops grow on the vine before they end up in your beer."

Rogue HQ, September 9, 2009, on the founding of The Rogue Hop Farm alongside the Willamette River, south of Independence, Oregon, where they are growing eight varieties of hops on 42 acres of land.

Start the Party with a Late Harvest Gewürztraminer, Huntsman Cheese, and Hazelnuts—an Exquisite Meeting of Flavors!

DURING THE HOLIDAY SEASON, I make sure my refrigerator is stocked with at least a pound of Huntsman cheese and a bottle of late harvest Gewürztraminer. The roasted hazelnuts, of course, are always close at hand in the pantry. It's a great combo for last-minute gatherings and very special drop-in guests. For the blue cheese and sharp Cheddar fans in your group, this is the ultimate experience, since it's a layering of English Stilton (a blue cheese) and Double Gloucester, which has the creamy-yet-powerful character of a sharp Cheddar.

Partnering such a complex and bold cheese with roasted hazelnuts and a late harvest Gewürztraminer is a brilliant maneuver. The hazelnuts act as that bridge you'll hear me speak to time and again throughout this book. In this case, they're bridging the rich-earthy cheese into a wine that is both sweet and complex. It has a classic Gewürztraminer nose of spice and floral accents, along with a flavor combination of apricot, pineapple, brown sugar and honey. But even with all those sweet notes, there's plenty of acidity for balance. So you can see where those hazelnuts come into play.

Then build the flavors to the next level by surrounding the cheese and nuts with thinly sliced rounds of sourdough baguette and some fresh grapes.

Wowie!

1/2 cup extra virgin olive oil

1/2 cup chopped red onion

1/2 cup chopped roasted and
    skinned hazelnuts

1/4 cup pitted and coarsely chopped
    Kalamata olives

1 large clove garlic, minced

3/4 cup crumbled blue cheese

Freshly ground black pepper to taste

1 French bread baguette,
    sliced into 1/4-inch thick rounds
    (Optional: for extra flavor and crunch,
    the slices can be lightly toasted)

1 bunch of sweet table grapes

Red Onion and Blue Cheese Spread

This is an elegant spread, featuring roasted bits of hazelnuts, gently warmed extra virgin olive oil and coarsely chopped Kalamata olives. Add a platter of grapes which compliment the blue cheese perfectly to push the flavor profile into the stratosphere.

In a small saucepan over medium heat, gently warm the olive oil with the onion, hazelnuts, olives, and garlic. Keep the mixture hot but not simmering, and cook until the onions are softened, about 10 minutes. Remove from heat. When ready to serve, place the blue cheese in the center of an attractive platter, then pour the warm oil mixture over the cheese. Add freshly ground black pepper to taste. Arrange the baguette rounds with grapes alongside on a separate platter and serve with the spread.

BEVERAGE THOUGHTS: I'd recommend you pull a lovely little bottle of Eola Hills Late Harvest Gewürztraminer from your refrigerator to share with your lucky guests.

A TRIO OF SPREADS

Whenever I know that there's going to be a heavy entertaining schedule to contend with, I fix up a tried-and-true trio of party spreads. All three hold really well for weeks in the refrigerator. Plus, they all compliment each other in color, texture, and flavor. I even find that similar wine styles can be paired with all three. My favorite wine preference is a medium to full-bodied Oregon Pinot Noir. A lightly-oaked Chardonnay is also lovely. Then, it's easy to round out the appetizer table with some tasty artisan breads, fresh crackers and vegetables, and some grapes. Two of these spreads incorporate my favorite regional nut. The third—my Muffuleta Relish—stands on its own without a nut back.

ONE: Mushroom Hazelnut Pâté

This is a wonderful pâté that I discovered through Margy and Dave Buchanan, Corvallis-area hazelnut growers and owners of Tyee Winery. The recipe has been adapted from one Margy found in a Sunset Magazine cookbook many (many!) years ago. They serve it in the wine tasting room during their annual Thanksgiving weekend open house.

Makes about 2 cups

1/4 cup butter

1 small onion, chopped

1 clove garlic, minced or pressed

3/4 pound mushrooms, sliced

3/4 teaspoon salt

1/2 teaspoon dried thyme

1/8 teaspoon ground white pepper

1 cup lightly roasted and skinned hazelnuts

2 tablespoons vegetable oil
   (preferably hazelnut oil)

Melt the butter in a pan over medium-high heat. Add the onion, garlic, mushrooms, salt, thyme and pepper. Cook, stirring occasionally, until the onion is soft and most of the pan juices created from the mushrooms have evaporated. Purée the hazelnuts in a food processor to form a grainy paste. With the motor running, add the oil and whirl until creamy. Add the mushroom mixture, and continue blending until smooth. Serve with crostini or fresh slices of a crusty baguette ("It's definitely best with thin slices of sourdough French bread," says Margy). It keeps in the refrigerator for two weeks or longer.

Makes about 2 cups

8 ounces (1 cup) softened cream cheese
  with chives
4 ounces (1/2 cup) crumbled Oregon
  blue cheese
12 ounces shredded (about 3 cups) sharp
  or extra-sharp Cheddar cheese
4 ounces (about 3/4 cup) shredded
  Parmesan cheese
1 tablespoon Worcestershire sauce
About 1/2 cup chopped darkly roasted
  and skinned hazelnuts

TWO: Oregon Three-Cheese Ball with Hazelnut Coating

Combine the cream cheese, blue cheese, Cheddar cheese, Parmesan cheese and Worcestershire in the workbowl of a food processor. Blend until the cheeses are thoroughly puréed. Scrape into a container and chill until firm. To form into a ball, scrape the mixture out onto a large piece of plastic wrap and gather up the edges of the plastic so that it's always between you and the cheese (less messy this way!). When it's formed to your liking, remove the plastic, spread the nuts out onto a work surface and roll the cheese ball around on top of them until it is thoroughly coated. Transfer to an attractive bowl and refrigerate until needed. Serve with crackers and toasted baguette slices.

DUKKAH VARIATION: Instead of just plain roasted and chopped hazelnuts, you could coat this cheese ball with one of the Dukkah mixtures (page 55).

Makes about 1-1/2 cups

1/2 cup coarsely chopped pimiento-
  stuffed olives
1/2 cup coarsely chopped pitted black olives
1/4 cup coarsely chopped red onion
1/4 cup coarsely chopped fresh Italian
  (flat-leaf) parsley
1/4 cup balsamic vinegar (more to taste)
1 tablespoon minced garlic
2 teaspoons drained and rinsed capers
1/4 teaspoon dried oregano, crumbled
1/4 teaspoon salt
1/4 teaspoon freshly ground black pepper
1/3 cup extra virgin olive oil

THREE: Muffuleta Garlic-Olive Relish

Muffuleta relish is a zesty spin on simple tapenade, having been kicked up a notch in garlic, olive oil and other goodies. It's really good stuff that can be used for plenty of seasoning maneuvers. In New Orleans, where the muffuleta sandwich was born, it's the hearty condiment on the region's famous submarine sandwich concoction of Italian-style meats and cheeses. Several years ago I began fiddling with the formula and created the following version, which makes the perfect party spread.

Place the olives, onion, parsley, vinegar, garlic, capers, oregano, salt and pepper in a food processor. Pulse the mixture until the ingredients are finely chopped. Add the olive oil and continue processing until the mixture is thoroughly chopped but not puréed. Adjust seasonings, adding additional vinegar if it needs a "zing," or additional olive oil if the mixture seems too "sharp." This marvel will keep in the refrigerator for at least one month. Since the olive oil solidifies at low temperatures, remove it from the refrigerator at least 30 minutes before serving.

Makes a generous 2 cups

1 cup oil-packed sun-dried tomatoes,
    drained well
1 cup grated Parmesan cheese
1 cup roasted and skinned hazelnuts
3/4 cup coarsely chopped green olives
3 tablespoons minced garlic
1/3 cup olive oil

Foley Station Green Olive and Hazelnut Pesto

Here's a wonderful recipe from Chef Merlyn Baker, owner of Foley Station in La Grande, Oregon. Chef Baker uses this mostly as a pasta sauce, but it's also a great appetizer, served alongside a thinly sliced baguette.

Combine the sun-dried tomatoes, Parmesan, hazelnuts, olives, and garlic in the workbowl of a food processor. Process until the mixture is finely chopped. With the motor running, slowly add the olive oil. If the mixture seems too thick after you have added the oil, add a small amount of water to reach a pesto-like consistency. Adjust seasonings, adding salt or additional Parmesan as desired.

BEVERAGE THOUGHTS: In the first go around, I tried this with a Belle Vallée 2005 Syrah, Rogue Valley. Wowie! It was amazingly delicious. It really brings out the toasty character of the hazelnuts. And the wine becomes soft and round and full-flavored. Another time, I enjoyed the Pheasant Court 2007 Syrah. Again, very delicious.

Makes 4 appetizer servings

16 (16-20 count) prawns, shelled
    and deveined
1 cup Romesco sauce, divided (page 57)

Grilled Prawns with Romesco Sauce

This is one of those simple, delicious uses for Romesco sauce, that hazelnut-infused Catalan specialty in Chapter 4.

Skewer the prawns lengthwise onto bamboo or metal skewers. Remove 1/2 cup of the Romesco sauce and set aside for dipping. Brush the prawns with the remaining 1/2 cup of sauce and grill over hot coals, or in a gas grill set on medium-high, until the prawns are opaque and lightly cooked, about 4 minutes. Remove to a platter and serve with the sauce alongside for dipping.

BEVERAGE THOUGHTS: Terra Vina's Sangiovese really loves the roasted tomato and red pepper in this sauce. A rich but not too pushy amber ale is nice also.

1 pound freshly cooked Dungeness
    crab meat
1/2 cup finely minced celery
1/2 cup finely minced sweet onion
1/2 cup coarsely chopped roasted
    and skinned hazelnuts
About 1/2 to 3/4 cup Lemon and
    Herb Sauce (recipe follows)
About 20 slices (cut 1/2-inch thick)
    of a good-quality French baguette
Handful of richly-roasted hazelnuts
    for garnish

Dungeness Crab Crostini in Lemon and Herb Sauce

The subtle, lemony character of the mayonnaise is the perfect foil for the delicate flavor of fresh Dungeness crab. Equally gentle sweet onions are the allium of choice. And the nut? A lightly roasted hazelnut, of course.

In a large bowl, combine the crab, celery, onion, and hazelnuts. Gently fold in some of the Lemon and Herb Sauce, adding more as needed to reach the desired consistency.

Place the baguette slices on a baking sheet and broil until golden; remove from oven. Spread the toasted side of each slice with a portion of the crab mixture, then return to oven and broil just until tops are golden.

Arrange the crab crostini on a platter and serve while they're still hot. Sprinkle the whole hazelnuts around on the platter.

BEVERAGE THOUGHTS: So as not to overpower the delicate sweetness in the crab, yet to stand up to the slight lemony character of the sauce, I chose a King Estate Signature Pinot Gris, which has a soft-yet-lively flavor of honey and citrus. For a craft beer, a complimentary choice is Widmer Brother's Hefeweizen, a full-flavored unbitter wheat beer that blossoms next to the lemon sauce.

1-1/4 cups good quality mayonnaise
2 teaspoons Dijon-style mustard
1-1/2 teaspoons grated fresh lemon zest
1 teaspoon fresh lemon juice
1 teaspoon granulated sugar
1/2 teaspoon minced fresh thyme
1/4 teaspoon paprika

Lemon and Herb Sauce

In a small bowl, whisk together the mayonnaise, mustard, lemon zest, lemon juice, sugar, thyme and paprika. Store in the refrigerator.

Makes 6 to 8 appetizer servings

1-1/2 cups balsamic vinegar

1/2 cup honey

1/3 cup finely chopped yellow onion

1/4 cup olive oil

2 tablespoons Dijon mustard

1/2 cup chopped raw hazelnuts

1/2 cup grated Parmesan cheese

2 pounds of chicken tenders
(these are the slender, very tender
portions that are attached to chicken
breasts, which are now being sold
separately; if unavailable, simply trim
several chicken breasts into
1- by 3-inch pieces)

Chicken Skewers with Savory Hazelnut Crust

Pay attention to the neat trick in this recipe of coating the chicken with a bit of mustard prior to coating with chopped hazelnuts. Two things happen: the nuts stay put during cooking and the mustard adds an extra bit of flavor and kick to the dish.

Preheat the oven to 350 degrees F.

In a small saucepan, whisk together the balsamic vinegar with the honey and yellow onion. Bring the mixture to a boil over medium heat. Simmer until it has thickened enough to coat a spoon and is reduced by 1/2. This will take about 10 to 15 minutes; set aside to cool.

In a saucer, whisk together the olive oil, mustard, and 1 tablespoon of the balsamic vinegar reduction (the remaining vinegar/honey reduction will be served as a dipping sauce).

Pat the chicken pieces dry with paper towels, then toss them with the mustard mixture, coating each piece well. In a separate, wide, shallow dish, combine the hazelnuts with the Parmesan cheese. Roll each of the tenders in the nut mixture, then thread each tender onto a bamboo skewer. Place the skewers on a baking sheet and bake until the chicken is thoroughly cooked (it will feel firm) and the crust is a light golden brown, about 25 minutes. Serve with the vinegar-honey dipping sauce.

BEVERAGE THOUGHTS: The hazelnuts, the mustard, the balsamic vinegar...all of these factors came ahead of the chicken, and so I went with a fruity, medium-bodied Oregon Pinot Noir, Belle Vallée's Reserve Pinot Noir, Willamette Valley. Another time, I brought out a Pheasant Court Maréchal Foch, Willamette Valley, which, again, addressed the nutty-yet-mustardy components in the chicken and still had plenty of fruit left over. For a craft beer, choose something that's medium bodied with a bit of bitterness but plenty of nuttiness to stand up to those hazelnut, mustard and balsamic components. For me, that meant Rogue Ale's Hazelnut Brown Nectar. I'd also recommend Widmer Brothers' Drop Top Amber Ale.

Its thirty minutes to air-time on KATU TV's 'AM Northwest' Set in Portland...

I'm prepping for a segment on bruschetta—Italy's simple toasted bread-and-tomato appetizer—
and the burning question of the morning seems to be:

> *"So Jan, do you say bru-SHETA or bru-SKETA?"*

> *"Bru-SKETA, Leslie. Bru-SKETA."*

> *"Good!"* said the executive producer.

No faux-pas on live television THIS morning.

Then one of the show's hosts, Dave Anderson breezes into the studio:

> *"Okay, Jan...I've heard it both ways. SO, is it..."*

> *"It's bru-SKETA, Dave. Bru-SKETA."*

> *"But it looks like it should be with an S-H. You know, SHETA.*
> *And I've heard it both ways."*

> *"I know. But in Italian, the "sch" is a hard sound. It's "SKETA."*

Then Steve the director drops by for his last-minute rundown. With several trips to Italy under his belt, I knew he'd weigh in. But he's more interested in reliving bruschetta experiences than pronunciation. His most amazing was a Tuscan adventure, where the bread was dense and richly toasted, and the simple topping was "a cloud of grilled sweet onions drizzled with an incredibly fruity olive oil. Heavenly! Simply heavenly!"

> *"Wait 'til you try my tomato-bacon-arugula-hazelnut-Gorgonzola topping,"* I say. He groans.

I tell him that only recently, good friends Jan and Rob Thurston had brought a platter of classic bruschetta (with tomatoes, basil, garlic and olive oil) to a party and it was such a refreshingly simple and delicious offering that we all stood around and Hoovered them up like starved teenagers. It wasn't pretty. Which is what gave me the idea for this morning's segment.

One minute to air and Dave's co-host, Helen Raptis roars onto the set.

> *"Looking forward to bru-SKETA, Jan!"* I just grin.

Forty minutes into the show, back from commercial, and Helen, Dave, and I are standing ready in the kitchen.
Dave looks into the camera and reads the intro for the segment off the prompter. Then, being Dave, he turns to us.

> *"So, is it bru-SHETA or bru-SKETA?"*

> Helen & Jan: *"Bru-SKETA!!!"*

That settles that.

Bruschetta

IF YOU'RE STILL STRUGGLING FOR A DEFINITION, bruschetta is, quite simply, a slice of fire-toasted bread topped with any number of ingredients, such as olive oil and salt, chopped tomato and basil, flaked tuna and capers, or a smear of seasoned white bean purée. The Bruschetta is served on a platter and presented as a little appetizer.

Bruschetta is so incredibly pure and simple that its toasty underpinning must be filled with flavor and texture, and the components on top equally flavorful and perfect.

THE BREAD

Go with dense-textured, crusty exterior, Italian-style. Make generous slices, cut a half inch thick or slightly more. And depending on how hefty a serving you want to offer, cut the slices in thirds, halves or keep them whole.

THE TOASTING

"Bruscare" is an Italian term referring to cooking over an open fire. So if you want to maintain an authentic presentation (and the most tasty), then the bread definitely should be toasted on both sides over coals before uniting with the topping. The second-best toasting modality would be a gas grill. But the extra layer of flavor created from time over coals is worth the effort. If you must, a toaster oven or broiler will do in a pinch. When I was prepping the bread for my morning cooking segment on *AM Northwest* I grilled them the night before and then gently reheated the slices in a 350 degree oven on the set. They came out great.

THE OLIVE OIL

Because olive oil is a major player in bruschetta, use the good stuff. It should be extra virgin, and full-flavored—either buttery/fruity or peppery, or a combination of both.

THE TOPPINGS

Well, after toasting the slices of bread, the most classic approach—during tomato season—is to first scrape the surface of each bread slice with a garlic clove for a whisper of garlic, and then have diners rub over this with the cut face of a tomato half. The tomato juices and flesh smoosh together with the toasted crustiness of the bread to form a remarkable morsel that is gobbled down on the spot before it has a chance to become soggy. Another classic topping during tomato season is to combine diced tomato with chopped basil, a sprinkling of salt, and a drizzling of olive oil. I also like to drizzle on a bit of a balsamic vinegar reduction.

8 (1/2-inch thick) slices good-quality crusty
    Italian-style bread

1 garlic clove, peeled and halved

3 ripe medium-sized tomatoes, chopped
    and drained

6 tablespoons extra virgin olive oil

3 slices bacon, fried, drained, and minced

1/4 cup fresh arugula, finely chopped

1/3 cup crushed roasted and
    skinned hazelnuts

Salt and freshly ground black pepper

About 1/2 cup crumbled Rogue Creamery
    Oregon Blue cheese

2 teaspoons balsamic vinegar (or balsamic
    vinegar reduction, page 66)

"Rogue River Blue reaches pungent
perfection within a year of its fall release.
Wrapped in grape leaves macerated in
local pear brandy, a deep, mellow flavor
underlies the cheese's bite. The Smoky
Blue is set over smoldering hazelnut shells
before aging. For a savory autumn meal,
serve both with Rogue River grapes like
Syrah or White Viognier and a handful of
hazelnuts."

'Brilliant Moves' from Rogue Creamery
Artisinal Cheeses catalogue.

Bruschetta with Tomato, Bacon, Arugula, Hazelnut and Oregon Blue Topping

Grill or toast the bread until nicely browned on both sides. Rub with the cut garlic.

About 10 minutes before serving, combine the tomatoes, olive oil, bacon, arugula, and hazelnuts in a small bowl. Toss gently and season with salt and freshly ground pepper to taste.

To serve, spoon the tomato mixture onto the grilled bread. Top each serving with a portion of the Oregon Blue, and then drizzle on a bit of the balsamic vinegar. Place the slices onto a hot grill (or into a hot oven) and cook just until the blue cheese begins to melt. Serve immediately.

FOR A SIMPLE-BUT-FABULOUS BRUSCHETTA COMBINATION: Prepare some toasts as described above, spread each one with a layer of Hazelnut Aillade (a garlicky, creamy sauce on page 63), then top with finely chopped tomatoes, and dollops of pesto and balsamic vinegar reduction (page 66).

BEVERAGE THOUGHTS: Sure, there are a lot of flavors going on in this one little preparation, but they're all pointing down the same road in my estimation, which is to a big and fruity Southern Oregon Syrah. I've enjoyed numerous ones, including a luscious offering from Del Rio Vineyards, as well as Pheasant Court's Rogue Valley Syrah and Belle Vallée's Rogue Valley Syrah. In the beer world, you can't go wrong with an amber ale that's won 14 gold medals since its introduction in 1989. And that's Full Sail's Original Amber Ale, which brings a sweet, malty, medium-bodied experience to the table, along with a slightly spicy-florally-hoppy finish. All of that stands up nicely to the blue cheese, tomato, bacon, hazelnut and arugula in this dish.

Three-Cheese Tart with Parmesan-Hazelnut Crust and Baby Greens Dressed in Pear Vinaigrette

The foundation for this savory tart is blue cheese. It's truly an amazing balance of flavors. Make sure that you've got a couple of ripened pears on hand for the vinaigrette.

Makes one 8-inch tart (enough for 16 slender slices)

1 pound good quality Oregon blue cheese, at room temperature

1 pound cream cheese, at room temperature

4 eggs

1 clove garlic, minced

1-1/2 teaspoons minced fresh rosemary

1/4 teaspoon salt

1/4 teaspoon freshly ground black pepper

Parmesan-Hazelnut crust (page 87)

Baby greens

Pear Vinaigrette (page 88)

Roasted hazelnuts

In a mixing bowl combine the blue cheese and cream cheese and mix until smooth. Add the eggs 1 at a time, beating well after each addition. Add the garlic, rosemary, salt and pepper and combine well. Scrape the mixture into the prepared Parmesan-Hazelnut Crust. Bake for 45 minutes to 1 hour, until the filling is golden brown and not loose in the center. Remove from heat to cool, then refrigerate up to 24 hours.

To serve, toss the baby greens with enough Pear Vinaigrette to generously coat the leaves. Arrange a serving of the greens on individual salad plates. Arrange a very slender slice of the tart on top, then garnish with roasted hazelnuts and drizzle a few drops of the vinaigrette around the plate edge of each salad.

BEVERAGE THOUGHTS: I've enjoyed this with a big, luscious barrel-fermented Chardonnay, which is in tune with the pears, rich cheese and toasty hazelnut flavors. In turn, all these flavors echo the nutty and creamy character in the wine. Consider Pheasant Valley's McDuffee Chardonnay from Hood River, with its aromas of pear and vanilla and touch of herbs. I've also enjoyed it with a fruity-spicy Gewürztraminer. But for an interesting alternative, consider a late harvest Gewürztraminer, such as Eola Hills' Vin d' Epics, or a late harvest Viognier like Pheasant Court's VICE wine.

Makes 1 unbaked tart shell if using an 8- or 10-inch springform pan, or 2 if using 8-inch pie pans

2 cups all-purpose flour

1/2 cup finely chopped roasted and
    skinned hazelnuts

1-1/4 teaspoon salt

3/4 cup finely grated Parmesan cheese

1/3 cup chilled shortening

1/3 cup chilled unsalted butter
    (cut into 16 pieces)

About 8 to10 tablespoons chilled water

Parmesan-Hazelnut Crust

Combine the flour, hazelnuts, salt, and Parmesan cheese in the workbowl of a food processor. Pulse briefly to mix. Add the chilled shortening and chilled butter, then pulse several more times until the shortening and butter are cut into the dough and the dough resembles coarse cornmeal. Drizzle in 8 tablespoons of the chilled water, pulsing constantly so that the water gets evenly mixed through the dough to form a firm mass (there may be a few dry spots, which you can gather up when you remove the dough from the workbowl). Add additional water if needed to form a dough that isn't too moist.

Remove the dough to a floured surface and gather/roll it into a ball; wrap tightly in plastic wrap and chill for at least 30 minutes (the dough can be prepared in advance and refrigerated for up to 4 days, or frozen for up to 6 months).

Let the dough come to room temperature (so that it's easy to roll out). On a well-floured surface, roll the dough out into a circle wide enough to cover the bottom of the pan and reach about half or two-thirds of the way up the sides of the pan. This is a very forgiving dough, so you can repair any thin or broken spots with pieces of the dough as necessary. Refrigerate the crust or proceed with tart recipe.

Makes 2 generous cups

2 (at least 4 ounces each) firm-ripe pears,
    peeled and coarsely cut into
    1/4-inch thick slices (for tips on ripening
    pears, page 102)
2/3 cup white wine vinegar
1/4 cup minced shallots
3 tablespoons granulated sugar
1 teaspoon finely minced fresh rosemary
1/2 teaspoon freshly ground black pepper
1 tablespoon Dijon mustard
2 teaspoons soy sauce
3/4 teaspoon salt
1 tablespoon chopped green onion
    (white portion)
1 cup vegetable oil
    (a mixture such as 1/2 cup each of
    extra virgin olive oil and canola)

Pear Vinaigrette

Combine the pears, vinegar, shallots, sugar, rosemary and black pepper in a skillet and bring to a simmer. Reduce the heat to low, cover, and simmer until the pears are tender, about 6 minutes. Remove from heat and transfer to a blender or food processor. Add the mustard, soy sauce, salt and green onion and purée. Scrape the mixture into a container, then whisk in the oils. Vinaigrette may be prepared up to 1 week ahead and refrigerated.

QuickTIP

Among our friends, Debbie Lauer is the queen of deviled eggs. In the spirit of exploration, she detoured from convention one night and brought a platter of her special eggs garnished with roasted and chopped hazelnuts instead of the usual paprika. We liked them a lot!

Makes 8 servings

2 tablespoons butter

2 pounds white or cremini mushrooms,
   thinly sliced

3 stalks of celery, chopped

2 yellow onions, chopped

1 leek (white part only), washed and
   chopped to measure about 1 cup

1 teaspoon salt

1 teaspoon freshly ground black pepper

8 cups chicken broth

1-1/2 cups full-bodied brown ale
   (such as Deschutes Brewery's Buzz-Saw
   Ale or Rogue's Hazelnut Brown Ale)

3 medium-sized Yukon Gold or other
   yellow-fleshed potato, peeled and
   chopped to measure a scant 4 cups

1 tablespoon apple cider vinegar

1/2 cup finely chopped roasted and
   skinned hazelnuts

1/2 cup sour cream

1 to 2 tablespoons heavy cream

For garnish: about 1 tablespoon dried
   crumbled sage (or fresh sage leaves);
   1/3 cup coarsely chopped roasted
   skinned hazelnuts

Mushroom Bisque with Leeks and Hazelnuts

This soup can be made several days ahead and refrigerated.

In a heavy 4-quart pot, melt the butter over medium-low heat. Add the mushrooms and sauté until the moisture they release has cooked off and the mushrooms begin to brown. Add the celery, onions, leek, salt and pepper and sauté for 5 minutes.

Add the chicken broth, ale, potatoes and vinegar and cook until the potatoes are soft, about 20 minutes.

Add the hazelnuts. Purée the soup in batches in a blender or food processor (or directly in the pot with a hand-held blender). Adjust seasonings, adding additional salt, pepper, and vinegar to taste.

Thin the sour cream by whisking in some of the heavy cream.

To serve, ladle into soup bowls and garnish each one with a swirl of the sour cream, a pinch of sage (or a whole sage leaf), and a sprinkling of chopped roasted hazelnuts. To make a pretty design with the sour cream, place a dollop in the center of each serving, then draw a skewer through it at several points to create the desired pattern before adding the sage and hazelnut garnishes.

BEVERAGE THOUGHTS: The rich, mushroomy-potato character of this soup is a great match for a full-bodied Pinot Noir, such as one of Spindrift Cellars' award-winning Pinot Noirs, which has a full compliment of oak, along with berry and earthy notes. As for a beer choice, with a full-bodied brown ale in the soup, it would be a delightful choice to serve alongside. Consider Deschutes Brewery's Buzz-Saw Ale or my go-to hazelnut-loving brew, Rogue's Hazelnut Brown Nectar.

Potato Cheese Soup with Hazelnut Cheese Crisps

I guess you could say this is the most traditional soup in the Dominguez household. When relatives hit town, this is the soup we make and pack along for day hikes in the Cascades, cross-country skiing, and winery touring. It's delectable, hearty-rich and cheesy. The Hazelnut Cheese Crisps add a festive crunch that crank it up a notch.

Makes servings for 8

4 cups chicken broth (homemade is best, but canned is fine too)

2-1/2 pounds Yukon Gold potatoes, unpeeled, coarsely chopped

2 cups chopped green onions— whites and about half the green stalks

1 quart half & half

1/4 cup soy sauce

1 teaspoon ground white pepper

6 ounces shredded Swiss cheese (about 1-1/2 cups)

6 ounces shredded Cheddar cheese (about 1-1/2 cups)

1/2 cup amber or brown nut ale (such as Deschutes Breweries Inversion IPA, or Rogue Ale's Hazelnut Brown Nectar), or sherry or dry white wine, or extra chicken broth if you prefer to avoid the alcohol

Hazelnut Cheese Crisps (recipe follows)

In a heavy-bottomed soup pot bring the chicken broth to a boil. Add the potatoes and simmer for 30 minutes, or until the potatoes are very soft. Add the green onions and remove the pot from heat. Add the half & half to the pot.

Purée the potato-broth mixture in a blender or food processor (you will have to do this in batches; when blending, fill the container only half full and cover the lid with a dish towel for extra safety because the soup "spurts" quite violently as it's being blended). Return the purée to the pot. Stir in the soy sauce and pepper and slowly bring the soup back to a simmer.

NOTE: The soup can be prepared to this point up to 48 hours ahead and refrigerated, or prepared and frozen for 3 months.

When ready to serve or pack into a Thermos, proceed with the recipe by placing the pot back on the burner, over medium heat. When the soup begins to simmer, stir in the grated cheeses gradually, a handful at a time. Now gently whisk in the beer, sherry, or wine (or extra broth).

To serve, ladle servings into bowls and float 2 or 3 Hazelnut Cheese Crisps on top.

BEVERAGE THOUGHTS: I would definitely serve this with Deschutes Brewery's Inversion IPA, or Rogue Ale's Hazelnut Brown Nectar, which are the ones I recommend using in the soup. They're both quite toasty and caramely in nature and go beautifully with the cheesy nature of the soup. Any beer in the pale ale to nut brown ale range would serve you well.

For a wine, we've paired it successfully with a number of different ones, including Tyee Wine Cellars' Estate Barrel Select Pinot Noir. A medium-bodied Pinot Noir is what you're after. Also, a fruitier option, such as a Southern Oregon Syrah or an old vine Zinfandel would stand up to the rich cheese character.

Hazelnut Cheese Crisps

Makes about 16 crisps

3 cups shredded extra-sharp Cheddar cheese

1 cup chopped roasted and
   skinned hazelnuts

These are simple and delicious. They're a delightful little appetizer. But I also like to use them as a flavorful garnish over salads and soups. And because you can make them before your party begins, they're hassle-free.

Combine the cheese and the hazelnuts in a bowl. Heat a large non-stick skillet or griddle over medium-high heat. Drop rounded tablespoons of the cheese-hazelnut mixture onto the skillet, leaving at least an inch between each portion, because the mixture will spread out a little as the cheese melts. Turn the crisps with a spatula when they have browned on the bottom. Continue cooking until the second side has browned. Remove to a paper towel to drain.

CHEESE VARIATIONS: Instead of extra-sharp cheddar, use extra-aged gouda or a good quality Parmigiano Reggiano.

BEVERAGE THOUGHTS: A medium to heavy-bodied Oregon Pinot Noir never fails to compliment these simple little offerings. In the craft beer world, a wide range of styles, from pale ale (My favorite? Deschutes' Mirror Pond) over to a richer brown ale (think Rogue's Hazelnut Brown Nectar).

An Insatiable Appetite for Unusual Side Dishes

ONE OF THE FEW CONSTANTS IN MY LIFE —besides an almost-perfect husband and a kitchen floor that requires daily mopping—is my insatiable appetite for unusual side dishes. You know, offerings beyond herbed rice and fingerling potatoes.

Although unique and perfectly-matched side dish/entrée combos abound, too often cooks ignore the important role the supporting cast should play in the overall production. A scintillating sidekick makes the star shine even brighter.

Most of the time, sides should be called middles because of what they bring to a meal. In fact, one spring evening I served two sides and no official entrée and my husband said: "This is a really good supper."

It wasn't Escoffier, by any means, or even Bobby Flay for that matter. It was jasmine rice with chiles and tomatoes and sautéed onions in one bowl; a salad of crunchy romaine, Parmesan, broccoli, and roasted hazelnuts, tossed with a vinaigrette of Dijon mustard, rice vinegar and hazelnut oil in the other. All of the components hummed together, creating a symphony of flavor on the palate, while remaining light on the waistline.

Around the Northwest, savvy chefs take their side dishes seriously. And in most cases these days, they're taking advantage of all that the Willamette Valley has to offer, including, of course, the Oregon hazelnut. At Jory Restaurant in Newberg, for instance, a side they've partnered with their grilled Muscovy duck breast includes a unique grain called farro, combined with wilted arugula, bacon and hazelnuts.

Higgins, in downtown Portland boasts a salad of spring greens, roasted hazelnuts, blue cheese and an herbed vinaigrette. Further north on Broadway, one of the Heathman's salads combines pears, apples and wild arugula with a roasted hazelnut vinaigrette.

Urban Fondue's house salad is a melange of greens tossed in a citrus vinaigrette with dried cranberries, spiced hazelnuts, goat cheese and sunflower seeds. The Singing Pig Salad at Toro Bravo is composed of grilled asparagus, chopped egg and hazelnuts, while Bread and Ink's salad features a hazelnut-crusted goat cheese with arugula. The house salad at Carafe is farm greens, roasted chicken, spiced hazelnuts and blue cheese dressing. And those spiced hazelnuts have even become popular as a side order all on their own. Then YOU get to decide what to pair them with. Very clever.

Nel Centro, another popular Portland restaurant, has featured a roasted beet salad with warm ricotta, blood oranges and hazelnuts.

As for my own repertoire, you'll see in the coming pages just how easy it is to zoop up a side dish with hazelnuts. But if you just want to do a little free-wheeling, then consider some of the speedy maneuvers you can do with a cache of hazelnuts: Combine them with grated cheese before turning your potatoes into a cheesy gratin, sprinkle them over a platter of backyard heirloom tomato slices, or onto a bowl of rice just before it hits the table. Layer them onto a halved and buttered winter squash that you're baking. Add them to a quick vegetable stir-fry for a rich smoky layer of flavor. And roast them right along with a pan of onions, garlic, and peppers. Hazelnuts also merge beautifully with cheeses—especially blue cheese and feta. Not surprisingly, they also are lovely with another Pacific Northwest specialty, salmon. I also find that topping a balsamic vinai-grette-based green salad with chopped hazelnuts makes most diners whistle a happy tune. In other words, just keep some hazelnuts on hand and use your imagination.

There are some things to keep in mind, such as if you want to retain a hazelnut's crunch, then you don't want

The Salad Box

to combine it with liquids for too long. In a quick sauté, you're fine. But with anything that's going to be stewed for a while, don't add the hazelnuts until close to the end or they'll come out somewhat soggy. I'm mindful of that in my rice dishes. In most cases I don't fold them in until after the cooked rice has been fluffed.

Also, keep an open mind as you skim through these recipes. Don't be afraid to think beyond their specific destinations in this book. There are some interesting hazelnut-based sauces in other chapters that can be introduced to some of these sides and your cooking style will be the better for it. If you're assembling one of the vinaigrettes, for example, and you have a batch of the garlic-flavored Hazelnut Aillade from Chapter 4 on hand, you can whisk some into your oil and vinegar solution to punch up the flavor without having to break into a bulb of garlic. My Heavenly Sauce recipe in that same chapter works wonders on steamed or sautéed vegetables, and certainly will heighten the dining experience when drizzled over a platter of home-grown tomatoes.

When composing the simple salads from this chapter, reach for your batch of spiced hazelnuts from Chapter 3. Anything to kick up the flavor and excitement factor in your everyday cuisine (while barely lifting a finger). So armed—with decent recipes and a curiosity about how to leverage them into more—you just may pull off an Escoffier move, or at the very least, a Bobby Flay.

YEARS AGO I DISCOVERED that the shelf life of my salad greens was dramatically extended by removing them from the produce bin and placing them in their own box. A Salad Box.

First, purchase a food-grade clear plastic box (with lid) that is large enough to hold the equivalent of at least five nights worth of salad greens. Obviously, it needs to be small enough to fit on a shelf in your refrigerator. My own box is a Rubbermaid model measuring 11 by 16 inches, and is 6 inches tall.

Purchase your salad greens. NOT the torn pieces of lettuce labeled "Salad in a Bag" from the supermarket. Although the wonderful, fresh, designer baby greens obtained at farmers' markets are fine, for the most part I'm talking about whole heads of lettuce, with all of the leaves still attached to the stem. I buy six-pack bags of romaine lettuce hearts from my local box store, but other fresh lettuces work just as well.

Prep your greens for the box by removing each and every leaf and rinsing in cool water. Vigorously shake the leaves (but don't dry them) and arrange them in the box. Put the lid on and store the box in your refrigerator.

That's it. You will be shocked at how dramatically this simple box will alter your attitude about throwing together the evening salad. No wrestling with grimy romaine leaves at the last minute. No pawing through slimy butterleaf in a clinging plastic produce bag. The box keeps the collection of greens hydrated and crisp down to the last leaf. And the prep work has already been done.

Added benefit? Once the lettuce has been removed from the produce bin, it's amazing how much classier all the other fresh veggies behave. It's like they graduated and moved out of the frat house.

3 cups red wine vinegar

3 tablespoons chopped fresh garlic

1-3/4 teaspoons salt

1 teaspoon sugar

1/2 teaspoon freshly ground black pepper

Jan's Amazing Vinaigrette Base

You know the biggest problem with homemade vinaigrettes? You store them in the refrigerator to keep all the herbs and garlic fresh, but when you go to use them—if you haven't thought ahead—the olive oil is thick and lumpy until it gets up to room temperature. So... I've developed this amazing "salad helper." It's a vinaigrette base made from red wine vinegar with gobs of minced garlic (it's a great way to use up handfuls of the peeled fresh garlic cloves—"box store garlic"—that we buy in large quantities at very little expense), lots of fresh-ground peppercorns, salt, and a pinch of sugar. Store THIS mixture in the refrigerator and keep the olive oil in the pantry at room temperature.

Then...when you're ready to toss the evening salad, just glug some of the zesty vinaigrette base over the greens with an equal glug of your room-temp olive oil and you've got a well-dressed salad in no time.

This recipe makes enough vinaigrette base to create at least 6 cups of finished vinaigrette dressing, using a ratio of 1 part vinaigrette base to 1 part olive oil. Some people prefer an oilier vinaigrette, in which case, your base will go considerably farther. I like to make large quantities of this and give it away to my kids and other special people. I use colorful Jose Cuervo tequila bottles, which adds to the recipe's charm as a gift. Usually.

Whisk together all of the ingredients in a bowl (preferably one with a pouring spout). Select a 3- to 4-cup capacity bottle or jar with a screw-top lid (consider using empty liquor or water bottles). Pour the prepared vinegar mixture through a funnel into the bottle and store in the refrigerator.

To prepare vinaigrette as needed, combine desired amounts of the vinegar base with good quality olive oil. You can either do this right in the salad bowl and toss with the salad ingredients, or you can whisk up a small amount in a separate cup then drizzle it over your salad before tossing.

1/2 pound fresh young spinach leaves, thoroughly washed with tough stems removed

1/2 head romaine lettuce (or local salad mix), thoroughly washed and dried

1/2 cup dried cranberries or cherries

1/2 cup chopped roasted and skinned hazelnuts

8 ounces feta cheese, drained and crumbled (leave some 1/2-inch chunks so it isn't too finely crumbled)

1 ripe Haas avocado, peeled and sliced into bite-sized pieces

2 Clementines, peeled and segmented (this is a seedless and very sweet variety of tangerine, also called "Cuties")

1/2 sweet onion, sliced into rings or strips

Tangy-sweet Sesame Vinaigrette (recipe follows)

Spinach and Salad Greens with Sweet Onions, Sweet Clementines, and Feta in Sesame Vinaigrette

Winter greens with citrus makes this a perfect salad for colder months. It's a pretty classic combo, but you're kicking it up a notch with the hazelnuts, dried cranberries or cherries, and sweet onion (which never used to be available outside of spring and summer).

After drying the spinach leaves, break the larger ones into bite-sized pieces. Place all of the leaves into a salad bowl. Reserve the dark green outer leaves of the romaine lettuce for another salad. Break the inner, brighter green leaves into desired size pieces and add to the bowl of spinach leaves.

To assemble the salad, add to the bowl the dried cranberries, hazelnuts, feta cheese, avocado, Clementines, and sweet onion rings. Give the vinaigrette a thorough whisking to mix the oil in with the rest of the ingredients, then drizzle about half of it onto the salad. Toss to coat all of the ingredients thoroughly. Then whisk the remaining vinaigrette again and drizzle more over the salad to taste.

BEVERAGE THOUGHTS: A fruity, floral Gewürztraminer would compliment the Asian-citrus flavors in this salad. A light, slightly fruity pale ale would be a delightful beer.

1/3 cup rice vinegar

2 tablespoons granulated sugar

1 teaspoon salt

1/2 teaspoon toasted sesame oil

1/2 teaspoon freshly ground black pepper

1/2 cup vegetable oil (such as canola oil)

Tangy-Sweet Sesame Vinaigrette

In a small bowl, whisk together all ingredients except the oil. Then whisk in the oil and adjust seasonings to taste.

3 medium beets

3 portobello mushroom caps

2 tablespoons olive oil

Salt and pepper to taste

1/2 cup plus 2 tablespoons extra virgin olive oil, divided

3 tablespoons red wine vinegar

2 tablespoons balsamic vinegar

1 teaspoon Dijon mustard

5 ounces baby arugula

5 ounces baby spinach

1/2 cup coarsely chopped roasted and skinned hazelnuts

2 shallots, sliced into thin rounds

1/4 cup fresh parsley leaves

About 4 ounces goat cheese

Warm Roasted Beet and Portobello Salad

Preheat the oven to 400 degrees F. Scrub the beets and place on a large sheet of aluminum foil. Drizzle with 1 tablespoon of the olive oil and fold the sides up to make a sealed pouch. Wash and dry the mushroom caps, then place them on another large sheet of foil or in a baking pan. Drizzle the mushrooms with another tablespoon of olive oil and season with salt and pepper. Do not cover the mushrooms; you want them to become a little richly colored. Place the beets and mushrooms in the oven. Bake the mushrooms for approximately 20 minutes, or until cooked through and darkened in color. Bake the beets for approximately 45 minutes, or until they are tender when pierced with a knife.

Meanwhile, whisk together the vinegars, mustard, and remaining 1/2 cup of olive oil. Whisk in salt and freshly ground black pepper to taste, then set aside.

When the beets and mushrooms are fully cooked, remove them from the oven. Slice the mushrooms into strips and place them back onto the foil or roasting pan. Toss the warm mushrooms with some of the vinaigrette and then cover with foil to keep warm. With a knife, remove the tops from the beets, and slide the skins off by hand. While the beets are still warm, slice them and drizzle lightly with some of the vinaigrette, then cover in the foil to keep them warm until serving.

In a salad bowl, toss together the arugula, spinach, hazelnuts, shallots, parsley and enough of the dressing to thoroughly moisten the ingredients.

To serve, arrange a serving of the arugula mixture onto each plate and top each one with portions of beets and mushrooms. Add a portion of the goat cheese, then drizzle on a little more of the vinaigrette.

BEVERAGE THOUGHTS: Either a rich and buttery barrel-aged Chardonnay or a medium- to full-bodied Oregon Pinot Noir plays well against the earthiness in the salad ingredients. A beer with a little extra kick of hoppiness plays out nicely too, such as Ninkasi Brewing's Tricerahops Double IPA.

2 tablespoons extra virgin olive oil

1 tablespoon butter

1 pound cremini mushrooms,
cleaned and thinly sliced

1 teaspoon fresh thyme leaves

1/4 teaspoon ground white pepper;
additional to taste

6 cups of mixed baby greens
(including baby arugula)

1 sweet onion, sliced thin

Hazelnut Vinaigrette (recipe follows)

About 3/4 cup of coarsely chopped,
roasted and skinned hazelnuts

4 to 6 ounces extra-aged Gouda cheese
(shredded in wide, slender sheets
using a vegetable peeler or the wide
side of a box grater)

Salt to taste

Warm Mushroom and Baby Greens Salad with Hazelnuts and Extra-Aged Gouda

Mushrooms and hazelnuts again! Two flavors that go so well together. In this version, the mushrooms are cooked. Plus, I'm bringing in the earthy-spicy quality of arugula and other young greens, and topping it off with a smoky, caramely extra-aged Gouda. Heavenly!

Heat the oil and butter in a large sauté pan over medium-high heat. Add the mushrooms and sauté until they begin to release their juices. Add the thyme leaves and continue cooking until the mushrooms become soft and golden. Season the mushrooms to taste with salt and if desired, more white pepper, then remove the mushrooms to a platter.

To serve, arrange the greens on 6 salad plates. Then layer the onions on top, followed by the mushroom mixture. Deglaze the skillet with the vinaigrette, then drizzle it over the mushrooms and salad greens. Sprinkle each salad with a portion of the hazelnuts and then generous sprinklings of the cheese. Serve immediately.

BEVERAGE THOUGHTS: Here's another salad that, because of all its earthiness, from the mushrooms and hazelnuts to the arugula and extra-aged Gouda, really works with a lovely Oregon Pinot Noir that's been crafted into a medium to full-bodied beverage. If you want a white wine though, consider a toasty, barrel-aged Chardonnay that would play off the mushrooms and other earthy components in the salad. As far as craft beers go, I've enjoyed this with a nutty brown ale, but a soft and round amber ale would also be a natural choice.

1/4 cup unseasoned rice vinegar

1 teaspoon Dijon mustard

1 tablespoon finely minced shallot

1 clove garlic, finely minced

2 teaspoons granulated sugar

1/2 cup hazelnut oil

Hazelnut Vinaigrette

Whisk together the vinegar, mustard, shallot, garlic and sugar. Slowly whisk in the hazelnut oil.

1 pound tender young spinach,
    trimmed of coarse stems
10 slices bacon, snipped crosswise into
    julienne strips before cooking
1/3 cup red or white wine vinegar
1 firmly packed tablespoon golden
    brown sugar
1/2 teaspoon salt
1/4 teaspoon freshly ground black pepper
1/2 cup extra virgin olive oil
10 mushrooms, washed, dried
    and sliced thin
1/2 cup chopped roasted and
    skinned hazelnuts
2 hard-cooked eggs, peeled and diced
Freshly grated Parmesan cheese

Spinach Salad with Brown Sugar Vinaigrette and Roasted Hazelnuts

Don't let the title confuse you. This is not a sweet salad. It's got just enough whang to go along with a wide range of entrées, from grilled salmon to roast turkey.

Wash the spinach well in several changes of cold water, shake or spin dry, then bundle in paper towels and refrigerate. When ready to proceed, mound the spinach in a large salad bowl.

Brown the bacon in a large heavy skillet over moderate heat for 3 to 5 minutes, until golden brown and crispy; drain the bacon bits on paper towels and set aside.

Drain off all but 2 tablespoons of the bacon drippings. Stir in the vinegar, scraping up all the cooked-on bits of bacon. Whisk in the brown sugar, salt, and black pepper. Add the olive oil, then adjust the seasonings; set the dressing aside while you assemble the salad ingredients.

Tear the spinach into bite-sized pieces, discarding tough stems. For individual servings, divide the spinach between 6 to 8 salad bowls or plates. Over each serving, layer the mushrooms, hazelnuts, and some of the dressing. Sprinkle each serving with some of the egg, crumbled bacon, and Parmesan cheese. For one large bowl of salad, prepare as above, and toss the salad at the table, right before serving.

BEVERAGE THOUGHTS: Because of all the earthy qualities in this salad—the mushrooms, the hazelnuts, and the spinach—I enjoy this wonderful salad with a medium- to full-bodied Oregon Pinot Noir. For a craft beer selection, you can't go wrong with a smooth, rounded beer with a nutty flavor, such as Rogue's Hazelnut Brown Nectar, Deschutes Brewery's Green Lakes Organic Amber Ale, or Widmer Brothers' Drop Top Amber.

How to Ripen a Pear

IT WAS TWO HOURS 'TIL THE THANKSGIVING turkey would be pulled from the oven, and a welcome lull had settled upon my kitchen. Time to make the pear salad. It was going to be a simple affair: fresh salad greens, tossed with roasted hazelnuts, dried cranberries, slivers of sweet onion, new-crop navels, crumbled feta, and, of course, some succulent chunks of Northwest pears. Before serving this simple seasonal melange, I was going to toss it with a tangy-sweet vinaigrette made to taste from white wine vinegar, sugar, black pepper, salt and olive oil, with just a splash of hazelnut oil.

I grabbed a comice pear from the fruit bowl and cradling it gently in my hand made my first cut into its creamy interior. Juice literally poured out, so I knew that this was an exquisite candidate. But I just had to taste for myself to "be sure." Immersed in rich pear aroma and flavor, it hit me at that moment just how lucky we are to live in a place that produces such treasures.

Indeed, eating a pear that has been properly grown, stored, and ripened can be one of life's most fabulous culinary experiences. And except for the apple, I can't think of a single other fruit that is so complimentary to both sweet and savory sidekicks. Be it cheese, pork, chocolate, or crème Anglaise, the humble pear plays its role to perfection. And with a late-harvest Gewürztraminer or fine sweet Sauternes, well, the experience is truly grand.

But to achieve such culinary drama, you have to take some care at the front end. Unlike other tree fruits, pears achieve their best flavor and smoothest texture when ripened off the tree. Tree-ripened specimens tend to develop an unpleasant sort of graininess and mediocre taste.

This off-tree ripening process requires patience, and proceeds best at room temperature. And since it ripens from the inside outward, if you're not vigilant it's easy to miss a pear's peak performance. Most varieties have very little color change as they ripen, so the best test is to check it for firmness—or the lack thereof. When the stem end yields to gentle pressure from your thumb, the pear is ripe. At this stage, it will also give off a heavenly aroma.

If you feel compelled to hasten the ripening process, you can place the pear in a paper bag to trap its natural ripening agent, ethylene gas, as it's emitted from the fruit. To slow down the process, or to maintain a pear for a day or two once it's ripened to the desired state, place it in the refrigerator.

Certainly, local pears can be found in just about every state. But as you probably know, Oregon and Washington provide most (84 percent) of the nation's fresh crop. When they're available, I buy them by the bagful and store them in the fridge, staggering the ripening process as necessary.

Makes 6 to 8 servings.

8 to 10 cups mixed baby spinach,
  baby arugula, and other salad greens,
  tough stems removed

1 sweet onion, peeled, halved and
  thinly sliced

Raspberry-Poppy Seed Vinaigrette
  (recipe follows)

2 ripe pears (preferably comice), peeled,
  cored, and thinly sliced

About 1/2 cup crumbled blue cheese
  (or feta)

Candied Hazelnut Garnish (recipe follows)

1/2 cup dried cherries or dried cranberries

Spinach and Pears with Candied Hazelnuts and Raspberry-Poppy Seed Vinaigrette

This is the salad I was making that day when I was one with the comice pear. It was inspired by a Spinach and Candied Pecan creation by fellow Oregon food writer, Maryana Vollstedt, which appears in one of her cookbooks, "The Big Book of Potluck."

To assemble the salad, place the spinach and other salad greens in a large bowl, along with the sweet onion slices. Toss with enough of the vinaigrette to evenly coat the leaves.

To serve, place a serving of the tossed greens on each salad plate. Divide the sliced pears among the plates, arranging them attractively on one edge of the greens. Sprinkle each serving with a portion of the blue cheese, then the Candied Hazelnuts and dried cherries or cranberries. Drizzle an extra bit of the vinaigrette over everyone's serving of pears.

BEVERAGE THOUGHTS: Because there's a fair amount of sweetness in this salad, a fruity Riesling works really well. A soft and fruity-styled Pinot Gris would also be nice. Pick a craft beer with a fairly light character, such as a lager or pale ale.

Chopped Salads and Hazelnuts

Hazelnuts belong in chopped salads! They bring depth and crunch to the collection of ingredients.

MY SUMMER CHOPPED SALAD: Tomato, corn, sweet peppers, local cucumbers, sweet onions, basil, garlic, roasted hazelnuts, olives

MY WINTER CHOPPED SALAD: Broccoli, cauliflower, sweet peppers, red onions, hothouse cucumbers, celery, red cabbage, green cabbage, carrots, roasted hazelnuts

THE MOVES: Whisk together your favorite vinaigrette, then toss and serve.

THE OPTIONS: Consider meaty additions, like grilled and finely chopped chicken, beef or pork; zesty accents, like finely chopped salami, ham, crisp bacon or prosciutto; shredded cheeses, like extra-aged Gouda, Monterey jack, or a smoky provolone.

1/4 cup raspberry vinegar

1 tablespoon packed brown sugar

2 teaspoons poppy seeds

1 teaspoon Dijon mustard

1/2 teaspoon Worcestershire sauce

1 finely minced clove of garlic

1/2 teaspoon salt

scant 1/4 teaspoon freshly ground
   black pepper

1/2 cup extra virgin olive oil

Raspberry-Poppy Seed Vinaigrette

This vinaigrette was designed to go with the Spinach and Pears with Candied Hazelnuts Salad. Beyond that, consider other spinach or baby green salads incorporating many other fruits, including (when in season) strawberries, apples, orange segments, avocados, and Asian pears.

In a bowl or pint-sized jar with lid, whisk together the vinegar, brown sugar, poppy seeds, mustard, Worcestershire sauce, garlic, salt, and pepper. Whisk in the olive oil.

Whisk thoroughly again just before using. May be prepared ahead and refrigerated until needed (the olive oil will thicken when cool, so remove from refrigerator ahead of serving time to allow it to re-liquify).

1 tablespoon butter

1 tablespoon packed brown sugar

3/4 cup chopped roasted and
   skinned hazelnuts

Candied Hazelnut Garnish

In a medium to small-sized skillet (non-stick is okay), melt the butter and brown sugar together over medium heat. Add the hazelnuts and cook for about 3 minutes, stirring fairly constantly, until the sugar caramelizes around the nuts and they are a rich golden-brown. Remove to waxed paper or aluminum foil and separate the nuts so they won't stick together when they cool. May be prepared several days ahead and stored in a covered container.

His pears are blue-ribbon and in less modern times, his peaches could have been bartered for doctors' services and cows.

Beyond Nuts

I HAVE A FRIEND WITH A KNACK FOR GROWING THINGS. What he grows the most of is hazelnuts. In fact, he's one of the Willamette Valley's major growers. But it doesn't stop there.

Beyond nuts, whatever characteristics any given type of produce should possess, Wayne Chambers' version will always come out on top, be it plumper, juicier, sweeter, or just all around more flavorful. When Wayne says "If you want to drop by for some garlic..." you'd be a fool not to. His pears are blue-ribbon and in less modern times, his peaches could have been bartered for doctors' services and cows.

Within the industry, Wayne is respected for his willingness to work with Oregon State University hazelnut researchers. It's a mutually beneficial relationship, because above all else, Wayne's a curious man. So he's just as anxious to see how a certain numbered variety will behave when planted out in the real world as the researchers are. When Wayne received the "Grower of the Year" award in 1994, the head of OSU's hazelnut breeding program, Dr. Shawn Mehlenbacher summed it up:

"Our grower this year is truly outstanding. In my contacts with him it is very clear that he is the leader in adopting new varieties of hazelnuts, in testing new selections from the OSU breeding program and getting them out to the commercial orchard setting. This is a tremendous service to the industry. Currently, he has several new varieties and over 50 numbered selections (that figure is currently at about 150 different cultivars). He has become an expert in propagation, including grafting and layerage. He is a leader and source of information to other growers on cultivars and propagation."

So when Wayne handed me a bag of Braeburn apples one December afternoon, I had high hopes. They were home grown, of course, and you could tell that they had thrived in Wayne's care. Even their outward beauty, red-blushed with almost-flawless skin, was most likely maintained by a gentle harvesting within the scope of Wayne's watchful eyes if not his very own hands. As expected, their innards were equally perfect, being everything I love in an apple: crisp, juicy, and with a richness in flavor that makes apple lovers hoard their caches.

One of the first things I did with a few of Wayne's Braeburns was to use them in a simple sauté. It's almost too simple to share. But if you haven't discovered the sublime experience of sautéing apples in butter, you'll have to give it a try.

Next up was a salad approach. I cored and cut a few of the Braeburns into slender chunks, tossed them with a zesty-but-slightly sweet vinaigrette and piled them onto a bed of crisp young greens, along with some blue cheese crumbles and one of Wayne's other loves in life (besides his wife Joann), roasted Oregon hazelnuts. Oh, you could jazz it up beyond that with dried fruits and a crispy crouton of some sort. But for an honest hit of fresh fruit playing off a savory pallette of simple greens, toasty nuts, and an elegant dressing, I found my original arrangement to be perfectly satisfying (You'll find a recipe for it on page 111)

In fact, it was so enjoyable it got me thinking of all the other winter salad combos featuring the fruits of the season that could dazzle during the holidays. Such a line-up would include pears, of course, as well as juicy navel oranges and ruby red grapefruits, crisp Fuyu persimmons, and ruby-toned pomegranates. Two regional nuts to consider from our own Willamette Valley are hazelnuts and walnuts. If you cast your net a bit farther, some lightly roasted California almonds also work well in these sorts of offerings.

3/4 cup fresh orange juice

1 tablespoon grated orange zest

3 tablespoons white balsamic vinegar

1/3 cup canola oil

2 tablespoons hazelnut oil

1/2 teaspoon salt

1/4 teaspoon freshly ground black pepper

1/4 teaspoon vanilla extract

1/4 teaspoon ground cinnamon

Pinch of nutmeg

About 6 cups of mixed salad greens,
     torn into 2-inch pieces

About 10 ounces total of baby spinach
     and baby arugula

1 large bunch watercress, stemmed
     (about 6 cups)

3 Fuyu persimmons, peeled, halved,
     and thinly sliced

1 red onion, thinly sliced into rings

2 cups coarsely chopped roasted and
     skinned hazelnuts

Salad of Mixed Greens with Fuyu Persimmons and Roasted Hazelnuts for a Crowd

Boil the orange juice and orange zest in a small heavy saucepan over medium-high heat until reduced to 1/4 cup. Transfer the reduction to a medium bowl. Whisk in the balsamic vinegar, canola oil, hazelnut oil, salt, pepper, vanilla extract, cinnamon and nutmeg. Add more pepper to taste if desired. Dressing can be made a day ahead and stored covered in the refrigerator.

To serve, place all the greens and half of the persimmon slices in a large bowl. Add dressing and toss to coat, then divide the salad among the plates. Top each with the remaining persimmon slices, onion rings and hazelnuts.

BEVERAGE THOUGHTS: This is another salad with a fair amount of sweetness, and so a fruity Riesling works really well. A soft and fruity styled Pinot Gris would also be nice. On the other hand, because it's one that you may be serving to a crowd, what would be more festive than a bit of sparkling wine? Pick one that's a bit fruity and off-dry. A craft beer with a fairly light character, such as a lager or pale ale, is a good alternative.

3 firm-ripe pears

1-1/2 teaspoons granulated sugar

Salt and freshly ground black pepper
   to taste

1/2 cup white wine vinegar

1/4 cup apple juice

1-1/2 teaspoons honey

About 1/2 teaspoon vanilla extract to taste

1/2 cup extra virgin olive oil

1/4 cup hazelnut oil

Roasted Pear Vinaigrette

Here's another variation on pear vinaigrette to consider using with the Three-Cheese Tart with Parmesan-Hazelnut Crust (page 86). It also works with the Simple Green Salad (page 112).

Peel, quarter, and core the pears. Arrange them in a lightly oiled roasting pan; sprinkle with the sugar, and salt and pepper to taste. Roast in a 375 degree oven for about 20 minutes, or until tender. Remove the pears and let them cool slightly, then place them in a blender or food processor. Deglaze the roasting pan by pouring in the vinegar and apple juice and using the flat side of a spatula or wooden spoon to scrape and stir the drippings loose. Add the vinegar mixture to the pears in the blender, along with the honey and the vanilla extract. Let cool, then blend until the pears are smooth. With the blender running, add the olive oil and hazelnut oil. Adjust seasonings, adding additional salt, pepper and vanilla to taste. Finally, achieve a perfect balance with extra oil or vinegar as necessary.

QuickTIP

If you have a jar of Hazelnut Aillade (page 63) in your refrigerator, then you can throw together a snazzy and delicious vinaigrette. Just whisk together about 1/4 cup of red wine vinegar, 2 teaspoons of the Aillade, 1 teaspoon of Dijon mustard, salt to taste, and about 1/3 cup of extra virgin olive oil or hazelnut oil.

IT WAS THREE DAYS AFTER CHRISTMAS and the first day of decent weather in a week. The good news to that scenario was that the crab boats which had been tied up at the docks during the storms were finally leaving Newport Bay in search of our favorite winter crustacean. They'd return to harbor in 18 hours. But, of course, our crab feast was in eight hours. So we re-named it a 'No-Crab Feast' and went to Plan B—Appetizers and a big salad.

That's the way it often goes at the beginning of Oregon crab season. Heavy winter storms can keep all but the largest vessels in port. Just when we're all at our most anxious to jump into commercial crab season, which always begins on December 1 and continues through to mid-August. The peak harvest occurs during the first eight weeks of the season, with up to 75 percent of the annual catch landed during this period. So those weeks of December and January are prime Crab Feast time.

For size, Dungeness falls between its East Coast cousin, the blue crab, and the West Coast Alaskan king crab. On average, the Dungeness weighs in from 1-1/2 to 3-1/2 pounds, whereas its Alaskan rival can come in as large as 20 pounds, with a leg span of nearly six feet. The genteel blue crab rarely grows larger than a pound. Although in the middle size-wise, I believe Dungeness is the hands down winner for flavor and texture.

If you've never thrown your own crab feed, the "how-to's" of it can be found towards the back of this book. Just know this: it's simple! It can be as straightforward as a big ol' green salad with a zesty Louie Dressing (page 114), and a crusty loaf of artisan bread. However, providing your guests with a twist on the salad concept is also a nice touch. The next three salads, while certainly not specialized for any particular cuisine, happen to be especially good for taking a crab feast to a whole new level. Bon appetit!

8 slices thick-cut smoked pepper bacon, diced

3 cloves garlic, chopped

1-1/2 cups chopped onion

1/2 cup balsamic vinegar

3/4 cup Rogue Toasted Hazelnut Brown Nectar (or another amber or brown nut ale)

About one-half head green cabbage, shredded to measure 5 to 6 cups

2 tablespoons wine vinegar

1 tablespoon olive oil

2 teaspoons chopped fresh thyme

1 cup chopped darkly roasted and skinned hazelnuts

Salt

Black pepper

Roasted Hazelnut Slaw

A warm and savory melange of tender-crunchy cabbage, smoky bacon and roasted hazelnuts. I love this dish! It's a wonderful accompaniment to fresh Dungeness crab. Likewise, it's delightful alongside grilled albacore, pork tenderloins, and so much more. In truth, it's a dynamite dish all on its own.

Place the bacon in a medium sauté pan and cook over medium heat until crispy, about 3 minutes, then transfer to a paper towel to drain. Add the garlic and onion to the pan and sauté in the bacon grease over medium-high heat for about 2 minutes. Add the balsamic vinegar and deglaze the pan by stirring and scraping the bottom to release all the cooked-on bits of food. Add the ale and cook until reduced by half, 3 to 4 minutes. Add the cabbage and cook just until wilted, but still slightly crunchy, about 1 minute. Remove from heat. Add the wine vinegar, olive oil, thyme, and hazelnuts and season to taste with salt and pepper. Toss in the reserved bacon (crumble it first) and keep warm until ready to use.

BEVERAGE THOUGHTS: This is such a simple, yet delectable side dish that I've found myself using it as a main dish. With that in mind, consider a lovely southern Oregon Syrah, which brings a bit of spice, fruit, and soft tannins to the table. If a white wine is needed, I'd go with a barrel-aged Chardonnay to compliment the earthy qualities of the dish. Of course, you'll also want to save some of that Rogue Toasted Hazelnut Brown Nectar that's IN the dish to pour at the table.

2 to 3 flavorful apples (such as Braeburn,
      Fuji, or Honeycrisp), cored, then sliced
      as described below
Balsamic Vinaigrette with Sweet Honey
      Mustard (recipe follows)
5 to 6 cups of mixed greens, including
      hearts of romaine leaves
      (the light green, crisp inner portion
      of a head of romaine lettuce),
      and baby arugula
Scant 1 cup of crumbled blue cheese
1 cup coarsely chopped roasted and
      skinned hazelnuts

Salad of Fuji Apples, Baby Greens and Roasted Hazelnuts with Sweet Honey Mustard and Hazelnut Oil Vinaigrette

Here's the salad I made with Wayne's Braeburn apples. You'll notice that in this case I'm calling for Fuji's. That's because they are typically easier to find. Everything clicks in this mixture, as long as you select apples with exceptional flavor and crispness. And among the things it goes wonderfully with is Dungeness crab.

To prepare the cored apples, cut lengthwise into 1/4-inch thick slices, then cut each slice into thirds. Place the apples in a small bowl and toss with enough of the vinaigrette to coat the pieces. You can prepare the apple mixture up to an hour ahead. If you hold it any longer the apples will absorb enough vinaigrette to overwhelm their flavor.

To serve, arrange the mixed greens on individual salad plates. Divide the apple mixture among the salads. Top each serving with a portion of the cheese and then a portion of the hazelnuts. Drizzle an extra bit of the vinaigrette over the greens and around the edges of the salad.

ALTERNATIVELY: You could substitute feta or Cheddar cheese for the blue cheese. Another serving option would be to assemble the entire salad on a large platter instead of on individual salad plates.

1/2 cup red or white wine vinegar

2 teaspoons balsamic vinegar

1 teaspoon granulated sugar

1 teaspoon Sweet Honey Mustard
(I use the Inglehoffer brand made
by Beaverton Foods)

1/2 teaspoon salt

1/2 teaspoon vanilla extract

1/3 cup hazelnut oil

1/3 cup canola oil

Balsamic Vinaigrette with Sweet Honey Mustard

I designed this vinaigrette to go with my Salad of Fuji Apples, Baby Greens and Roasted Hazelnuts. It's also a wonderful dressing to have on hand for any number of your winter salads incorporating fresh greens, fruits, and nuts. The hint of vanilla gives it a lovely toasty quality that compliments the nuts and some cheeses, such as Cheddar, feta, blue cheese, and provolone. Even shavings of a good-quality Swiss or extra-aged Gouda would work.

In a container, whisk together the vinegars, sugar, mustard, salt, and vanilla, then whisk in the oils.

NOTE: If you have trouble finding the hazelnut oil, simply use all canola oil.

2 quarts of mixed spring greens,
torn into pieces

2 avocados, peeled and sliced

1/2 pound fresh Pacific shrimp, rinsed
and drained well, then patted dry

1/4 pound blue cheese, crumbled

Dijon Vinaigrette (recipe follows)

1 cup hazelnuts, roasted, skinned
and chopped

Simple Green Salad with Dijon Vinaigrette

Sometimes less is more! Particularly when you're working with stunningly fresh and flavorful ingredients. Lovely and pure with tender, mild-mannered Pacific shrimp.

In a large salad bowl, toss together the salad greens, avocados, shrimp and blue cheese. Toss with enough of the vinaigrette to evenly coat the ingredients, add the hazelnuts, toss again and serve.

1/3 cup red wine vinegar

2 tablespoons Dijon mustard

1 teaspoon Worcestershire sauce

2 cloves finely minced or pressed
   garlic

1/4 teaspoon salt

1/8 teaspoon freshly ground black pepper

2/3 cup extra virgin olive oil

Dijon Vinaigrette

Whisk together the red wine vinegar, Dijon mustard, Worcestershire sauce, garlic, salt, and pepper. Whisk in the extra-virgin olive oil. (Note: if you want to use Jan's Amazing Vinaigrette Base on page 96, then follow this recipe, but use 1/3 cup of the vinaigrette base in place of the unseasoned red wine vinegar, and omit the garlic, salt and pepper).

QuickTIP

Our book designer, Joanne McLennan, brought a lively salad to one of our hazelnut potlucks. The kicker was the dried fruit that she had soaked in Rogue Spirits' Spiced Hazelnut Rum. Then, she whisked some of that soaking liquid into the vinaigrette before tossing the salad greens with the fruit and the rum-laced vinaigrette. Amazingly good.

A final thought about crab feeds

When I'm opting for a simple tossed green salad to accompany our crab feeds, the following Louis Dressing is always a part of the party because it's such a delicious partner to fresh Dungeness crab. You can make it days ahead (although you have to hide it in the very back of the refrigerator until the feast begins or it will disappear).

Additionally, the Tomato-Pesto Mayonnaise and Buttery Cocktail Sauce are very special and delicious accents to consider.

Makes about 1-1/2 cups

1 cup mayonnaise

1/4 cup chili sauce (it's like ketchup, only spicier; Del Monte makes one)

2 tablespoons finely chopped green or red sweet bell pepper

2 tablespoons finely chopped yellow onion

2 tablespoons chopped parsley

1/8 teaspoon cayenne pepper

1 teaspoon Worcestershire sauce

1 teaspoon prepared horseradish

1 hard-cooked egg, finely chopped

Classic Louis Dressing

Here's our family favorite dressing for a crab feed. Set it out alongside a big ol' tossed green salad, where it will be handy for mingling with both the salad and the crab, along with melted butter and fresh lemon juice, of course.

In a small bowl, whisk together the mayonnaise and chili sauce. Add the peppers, onion, parsley, cayenne, Worcestershire, horseradish, and chopped egg. Stir this mixture thoroughly and then taste to determine whether it needs additional chili sauce, Worcestershire sauce, or horseradish. Use immediately or cover and refrigerate for up to 1 week. If the dressing seems a bit thick, you can stir in 1 to 2 tablespoons of milk.

Makes about 3 cups

2 tablespoons olive oil

3 tablespoons minced yellow onion

1-1/4 cups peeled, seeded, and chopped
    tomato (use Roma style tomatoes,
    if possible)

1/4 teaspoon salt

1/8 teaspoon coarsely ground black pepper

2 cups good quality mayonnaise

1 teaspoon commercially prepared
    or homemade pesto (more to taste)

1 tablespoon brandy (optional)

Tomato-Pesto Mayonnaise for Crab

This is a wonderful alternative to the classic red seafood cocktail sauce. But actually, I like to serve it alongside the red sauce so folks can sort of mingle the two together if desired.

Heat the olive oil over medium heat in a small skillet. Add the onion and gently sauté until the onion is lightly caramelized. This will take about 10 minutes. Avoid scorching the onions with too much heat. Add the tomatoes, salt, and pepper, and adjust the temperature up to about medium-high and continue simmering until the tomato mixture has softened, and all of the liquid released by the tomatoes has cooked away, creating a thick mixture. This will take 15 to 20 minutes. Scrape the mixture into a mixing bowl and set aside until cool.

Mix in the mayonnaise, pesto, and brandy, then adjust seasonings, adding additional pesto, salt and pepper as needed. Chill until ready to serve. May be made and refrigerated up to a week ahead.

Makes 1-1/4 cups sauce

1 cup seafood cocktail sauce

4 tablespoons butter

Buttery Cocktail Sauce

Margy and Dave Buchanan always have this simple and delicious twist on cocktail sauce at their annual Tyee Wine Cellars crab feed. It's become my favorite way to serve cocktail sauce.

In a microwavable bowl, combine the cocktail sauce with the butter. Loosely cover with plastic wrap to prevent splatters and microwave on high just until the butter is mostly melted. Whisk it into the hot cocktail sauce and serve. Alternatively, heat the cocktail sauce and the butter in a small pot over medium heat, whisking until the butter is incorporated into the sauce.

Makes 4 to 6 servings

6 tablespoons butter

4 cups chopped leeks (white and pale green portions only, about 4 large leeks)

2 tablespoons dry sherry

1/4 teaspoon salt

1/4 teaspoon white pepper

1/3 cup heavy cream

1/3 cup coarsely chopped, lightly roasted and skinned hazelnuts

1/4 cup coarsely grated Monterey Jack cheese

1/4 cup freshly grated Parmesan cheese

Leeks Braised in Butter and Sherry Au Gratin

This simple dish is a wonderful accompaniment to steak or roast chicken.

Melt the butter in a heavy, oven-proof skillet over medium-high heat. Add the leeks and sauté until softened, about 3 minutes. Add the sherry, salt, and white pepper and continue to cook until the leeks are tender, about 5 minutes. Stir in the cream and cook for a couple of minutes longer to reduce the liquid slightly; remove from heat. Combine the hazelnuts with the two cheeses and sprinkle over the leek mixture. Place the pan under the broiler and broil just until the cheese melts and begins to turn golden around the edges, about 3 minutes. Serve immediately.

QuickTIP

When a recipe calls for roasted and chopped hazelnuts, consider substituting one of the flavored Dukkahs (see recipe, page 55) for different taste and texture.

1 cup uncooked wild rice

4 tablespoons butter

1/4 to 1/2 pound thinly sliced pancetta,
    minced (see note)

2 leeks, washed and thinly sliced (white
    and pale green portions, about 2 cups)

1 bunch of red Swiss chard, chopped
    (if not available, use regular)

4 ribs celery, coarsely chopped

1 cup uncooked barley

1 bay leaf

1/2 cup dry sherry

7 cups homemade or canned chicken broth

Salt and freshly ground black pepper
    to taste

Minced fresh or dried thyme to taste

1 cup coarsely chopped roasted and
    skinned hazelnuts

Leeks with Barley and Wild Rice Pilaf

Rinse the wild rice in a strainer under cold running water several times. Heat the butter in a large sauce-pan and sauté the pancetta, leeks, chard, and celery over low heat for 15 to 20 minutes. Stir in the wild rice and barley and cook for several minutes, stirring, until the barley turns slightly golden. Add the bay leaf, sherry, broth, salt, pepper, and thyme. Bring to a boil, then cover, reduce the heat to low, and cook for about 40 minutes, or until the rice and barley are tender. If there is any unabsorbed liquid, simply uncover and boil until it is gone. Stir in the hazelnuts just before serving.

This dish can be prepared up to 2 days in advance (without adding the hazelnuts), covered, and refrigerated. Reheat in a microwave on high or in a preheated 350 degree F oven, covered, adding more liquid if necessary. Stir in the nuts just before serving.

NOTE ON PANCETTA: This is Italian-style bacon. If unavailable, consider using a good quality ham. You could also use regular bacon, which would add more of a smoky flavor.

"The early varieties start around the 20th of September. And then, hopefully, by the end of October we would do the final go-around with the late trees. That last one's after you're out of the mood to harvest."

"You mean tired," I ask.

"Grumpy."

Wayne Chambers,
Oregon hazelnut grower,
when asked how long the
harvest typically lasts.

Makes 6 servings

1 teaspoon finely minced garlic

1 tablespoon hazelnut oil

1 pound fresh sugar snap peas

Salt and freshly ground black pepper
   to taste

Sugar Snap Peas with Garlic and Hazelnut Oil

My friend Mary Miner knows her way around vegetables. I once watched her transform a bowl of sugar snap peas into a heavenly delight. I didn't think that was possible with a vegetable that I consider perfect straight out of the gate - no heat or seasonings need apply. But Mary really showed me something. First she gently sautéed a bit of garlic in some olive oil. This was done very slowly and deliberately so that the garlic cooked through without getting bitter. Then, just before we were ready to sit down to dinner, in went the peas. While the rest of us scurried around readying platters of beef and salad, Mary focused on those plump and crunchy peas, turning them in the pan in a purposeful way so that each one received a shiny coating of garlic-infused oil. Then, before they lost their snap, she spooned them into a serving dish.

They were divine.

With such a low-key, understated presentation, I knew that hazelnut oil would add a rich and toasty element. Perfect for your summer grills of smoked loin pork chops and chicken.

In a large, heavy-bottomed skillet over medium-low heat, gently sauté the garlic in the hazelnut oil until it is softened. Be careful not to let the garlic brown. Just before serving, add the peas and continue to gently sauté them over medium-low heat, turning each one so that all surfaces get a brief moment in the oil and the heat. This process will only take about 3 to 4 minutes, tops! Remove them to a serving dish before they lose their crunch.

1 pound cipolini onions (if unavailable,
   use fresh pearl onions)

2 tablespoons olive oil

1/4 pound of 1/4-inch thick pancetta slices,
   finely diced

1 tablespoon balsamic vinegar

1/2 cup chicken broth

1 teaspoon chopped fresh rosemary

Salt and freshly ground black pepper
   to taste

1/3 cup chopped roasted and
   skinned hazelnuts

Balsamic Glazed Cipolini Onions with Pancetta, Hazelnuts and Rosemary

These gently cooked and glazed little onions add magic to the plate. And for so little effort! They serve a cook well in so many dishes, such as ham, a very special piece of grilled tenderloin, or even a Thanksgiving turkey.

Place the cipolinis in a bowl and cover with boiling water. After 2 minutes, drain the onions and plunge them into cold water to stop the cooking and cool them enough to handle. Trim away the stem end from each onion and peel away the papery outer skin. Trim away most of the dark portion of the root end, but leave the root intact or the onion will fall apart during cooking. Set the onions aside.

Heat the oil in a large, heavy-bottomed skillet over medium-low heat. Add the pancetta and sauté slowly, until the meat has released its own oils and browns. This will take 10 to 15 minutes.

Remove the pancetta from the skillet with a slotted spoon and set aside; drain off all but 2 tablespoons of the fat. Increase the temperature to medium, add the onions and sauté briefly. Add the vinegar and half of the chicken broth, along with the rosemary and a little salt and pepper to taste (about 1/4 teaspoon of salt). Cover and cook until the cipolinis are tender when pierced with the point of a sharp knife, about 20 minutes.

Remove the lid and increase the temperature to medium-high. Return the pancetta to the skillet and cook, stirring the cipolinis frequently to avoid scorching, until the onions are turning a golden brown and most of the liquid has cooked off, forming a glaze on the bottom of the skillet. Add the rest of the chicken broth and continue stirring and scraping the bottom of the pan to dissolve the cooked-on bits of food and heat the broth. Add the hazelnuts just before serving, along with an additional splash of balsamic to balance the flavors if necessary.

QuickTIP

Hazelnut grower Margy Buchanan keeps a wide variety of prepared hazelnuts in the freezer, from raw whole nuts to roasted and chopped. Then, no matter what form a recipe calls for she's instantly prepared.

Serves 8

2 pounds of fresh, slender green beans, trimmed (if they're large, consider French-cutting)

3 tablespoons butter

2 tablespoons chopped fresh thyme, divided

2 teaspoons Dijon mustard

1/2 teaspoon salt

1/2 cup coarsely chopped darkly roasted and skinned hazelnuts

Green Beans with Hazelnuts and Thyme

This is a simple and elegant way to enjoy fresh, tender, green beans. And it's a wonderful way to incorporate hazelnuts into your summer barbeques because these beans are a healthy natural alongside all forms of grill fare, from chicken and pork to steak, albacore, and wild salmon.

Bring a large pot of salted water to a boil. Add the beans and cook just until the beans are becoming tender and still have their brilliant green color. Remove from heat and immediately plunge the beans into ice water to stop the cooking and set the color. Drain well and set aside for up to several hours in the refrigerator.

When ready to serve, melt the butter in a large skillet over medium high heat. Add 1 tablespoon of the thyme and gently sauté for 1 minute. Add the mustard and salt and stir to blend it into the butter. Add the beans to the skillet and sauté until the beans are just barely tender, which will take about 7 minutes. Toss with most of the hazelnuts and then transfer the beans to a serving bowl. Sprinkle with the remaining hazelnuts and the remaining 1 tablespoon of thyme.

QuickTIP

The earthy flavors within even the most common mushroom makes it another powerful match for the Oregon hazelnut. And when you get into the muskier wild varieties that show up in Oregon markets in Spring and Fall—the treasured chanterelle and, most especially, the exotic morel—the experience is nothing short of dynamic.

1 pound green beans, trimmed

1 Walla Walla Sweet onion, peeled
    and cut into 1/4-inch thick rings

1/2 cup sliced black olives

Ponzu Vinaigrette (recipe follows)

1/2 cup crumbled blue cheese

1/3 cup chopped roasted and
    skinned hazelnuts

1-1/2 cups of local cherry tomatoes, halved

Fresh basil leaves for garnish

Green Beans and Sweet Onions in Vinaigrette with Blue Cheese and Roasted Hazelnuts

This is a great make-ahead salad for summer barbeques that has evolved from one I found in fellow Oregonian Maryana Vollstedt's wonderful cookbook, "The Big Book of Potluck." Make sure the green beans are young and tender.

In a large pot of boiling salted water, cook the beans uncovered until tender-crisp, 6 to 7 minutes. Drain immediately and plunge into cold running water to stop the cooking process and set the color. Drain well, then place the beans in a medium bowl, along with the onion and the vinaigrette. Toss well to coat. Cover and refrigerate several hours or overnight. The beans will not retain their bright green color, but the flavor from the marinade certainly compensates!

To serve, drain the marinade from the bean mixture (you can save it in the refrigerator up to 2 weeks for re-use) and place the beans on a lovely serving platter. Sprinkle with the blue cheese and nuts, then arrange the tomatoes around the perimeter of the platter. Add a few basil leaves for garnish.

Makes about 3/4 cup

2 tablespoons fresh lemon juice

2 tablespoons red or white wine vinegar

Splash of balsamic vinegar

1 tablespoon finely chopped fresh basil

2 teaspoons Dijon mustard

1 teaspoon ponzu sauce

2 cloves finely chopped fresh garlic

1 teaspoon granulated sugar

1/2 teaspoon salt

About 1/4 teaspoon freshly ground
    black pepper

1/2 cup canola oil

PONZU Vinaigrette

In a bowl, whisk together the lemon juice, wine vinegar, balsamic, basil, mustard, ponzu sauce, garlic, sugar, salt and pepper. Whisk in oil.

5 cups broccoli spears

4 tablespoons butter, divided

2 tablespoons all-purpose flour

1/4 teaspoon salt

1/8 teaspoon white pepper

1-1/4 cups milk

4 ounces cream cheese, cut into chunks

2 tablespoons crumbled Oregon Blue cheese

1 cup coarse dry bread crumbs,
   preferably sourdough

Broccoli Casserole with Oregon Blue Cheese Sauce

Oregon blue cheese is produced by the Rogue River Creamery, located in the southern portion of the state. It's not quite as creamy as its American and European counterparts, but is a delightful cheese all unto itself.

Preheat oven to 350 degrees F.

In a medium saucepan over high heat, cook the broccoli in enough boiling salted water to cover for 3 minutes and drain thoroughly. Place broccoli in a single layer in an 8 x12-inch glass baking dish lightly coated with cooking spray or oil.

In a saucepan over medium heat, melt 2 tablespoons of the butter. Add the flour, salt, and pepper and stir until bubbly. Add the milk and stir constantly until thickened, about 2 minutes. Add the cream cheese and blue cheese and stir until the cheeses are melted and the sauce is well blended, then pour it over the broccoli.

In a small saucepan over medium heat, melt the remaining 2 tablespoons of butter. Stir in the bread crumbs and mix well. Sprinkle this mixture over the casserole. Bake, uncovered, until the casserole is bubbly and its top is golden, about 30 minutes.

QuickTIP

Hazelnuts merge beautifully with cheeses—especially blue cheese and feta.

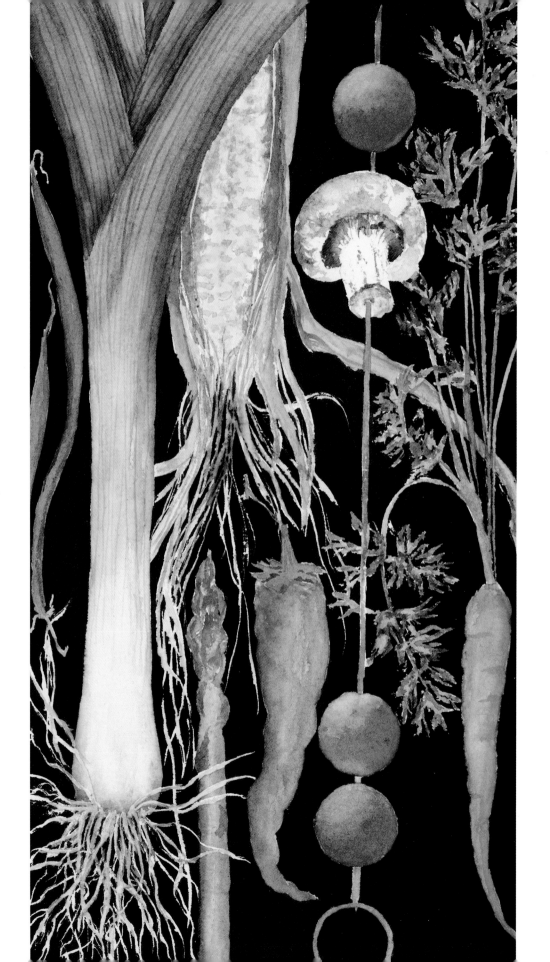

Makes 4 servings

1 cup roasted, peeled and coarsely
　　chopped hazelnuts (optional)

FOR THE MARINADE:

1/3 cup red or white wine vinegar

1/4 cup dry red wine (such as Zinfandel,
　　Cabernet, or Pinot Noir)

2 tablespoons soy sauce

1 teaspoon Worcestershire sauce

1/4 teaspoon salt

1/4 teaspoon freshly ground black pepper

3 cloves finely minced garlic

2/3 cup extra virgin olive oil

VEGETABLES FOR GRILLING:

1/4 pound mushrooms (halved or whole,
　　depending on size)

1 red bell pepper, seeded and cut in strips

1 yellow bell pepper, seeded and cut in strips

1 whole sweet onion, cut into thin strips
　　or rings

Other fresh vegetables of the season,
　　such as summer squash, corn, or
　　asparagus spears (remove tough
　　lower portion, then cut into
　　1-inch pieces)

Jan's Marinated and Grilled Veggies

This is my all-time favorite way to grill a pile of fresh vegetables. After marinating in my zesty marinade for an hour or two, I drain the vegetables and simply stir-fry them over charcoal or a gas grill. This requires a special grilling pan with medium (about 5/16-inch) holes so that small pieces of food or fish won't fall through during cooking. If you don't have one, this is the perfect excuse to make the purchase.

Combine the vinegar, wine, soy sauce, Worcestershire sauce, salt, pepper, garlic and olive oil. Place the vegetables in one large container or two re-sealable plastic bags. Pour the marinade over the vegetables and marinate for 1 to 2 hours.

When ready to cook, remove the vegetables from the marinade (the marinade will keep for a couple of weeks, so refrigerate in a sealed jar for another round of veggies within that time-frame). Place the grill pan on top of the grill grate over hot coals or gas flame and let it heat through. Add the vegetables and let them cook, turning and tossing the veggies sort of as you would for a stir-fry, only slower, until they're lightly bronzed and cooked through.

Remove from heat. If desired, toss in the hazelnuts before serving. Delicious with my Heavenly Rice (page 130), Roasted Polenta with Best Ever Balsamic Sauce (page 68), or even in a sandwich. If you want to introduce a bit of meat into the festivities, try them along side my Tenderloin of Beef on a Bed of Arugula, (page 159). Yum!

 BEVERAGE THOUGHTS: If this dish turns into an entrée, then consider any number of wine directions: certainly, a rich barrel-aged Chardonnay would be delicious. I've enjoyed it with a spicy Gewürztraminer, as well as a fruity, peppery Syrah.

Best Ever Balsamic Sauce (page 68)

3 cups chicken broth

    (I use either homemade or Campbell's

    double strength, undiluted)

3 cups heavy cream

1/4 teaspoon ground white pepper

1 cup polenta meal

1 cup semolina meal

1/2 cup grated Jarlsburg cheese

1-1/4 cups grated Parmesan, divided

BEVERAGE THOUGHTS: Over the years, I've served this with a number of different wines. But it always comes back to Pinot Noir. Especially if I'm serving this alongside a platter of grilled vegetables and salmon or pork tenderloin. For beer choices, consider a wide range, really, from pale ales to amber ales, with varying levels of hoppiness.

Roasted Polenta with Best Ever Balsamic Sauce

Before Chef Michael Chiarello gained celebrity status on the Food Network with his popular show, "Easy Entertaining with Michael Chiarello," he was wowing Napa Valley foodies at Tra Vigne. On one visit, I learned from him that a very tender and moist polenta can be created by using equal parts polenta meal and semolina (Bob's Red Mill, a Portland-based company, makes both). I keep a pre-mixed batch of it in my pantry. He also taught me that a reliable ratio of liquid and dry ingredients for a basic polenta is 3 to 1.

Prepare the Best Ever Balsamic Sauce ahead, but do not whisk in the butter until ready to serve the polenta.

In a heavy-bottomed pot, combine the chicken broth, cream, and pepper (if using homemade chicken broth, you might want to add up to 1 teaspoon of salt). Bring this liquid to a boil, then whisk in the polenta and semolina in a steady stream. Continue stirring and cooking over moderate heat. The mixture will begin to thicken after a few minutes. Continue stirring. The polenta is ready when it is very thick and begins to pull away from the sides of the pot (approximately 7 to 10 minutes).

Remove from heat and stir in the Jarlsburg and 3/4 cup of the Parmesan. Immediately pour the polenta out onto an oiled baking pan, spreading it out into a rectangle or square about 3/4-inch thick. Cool at room temperature, then cover with plastic wrap and refrigerate up to 48 hours in advance of roasting.

To roast, cut the cooled polenta into squares, triangles or diamonds. Using a spatula, transfer the pieces onto a lightly oiled baking pan, sprinkle generously with the remaining 1/2 cup of Parmesan, and place in a pre-heated 500 degree F oven. Roast until golden brown and slightly puffy, about 7 minutes.

While the polenta is roasting, bring the Best Ever Balsamic Sauce to a simmer and whisk in the 1/2 cup of butter in tablespoon-sized chunks. Keep hot until ready to serve.

To serve, pour a bit of the sauce onto each plate, then top with 1 or 2 portions of the roasted polenta. This is great alongside a selection of grilled vegetables (I like to use mushrooms, wedges of onions, sweet bell peppers, and zucchini chunks), and grilled fish or chicken.

CARAMELIZED ONION VARIATION: For another level of flavor that is exquisite, gently sauté 1 cup of chopped yellow onions in 2 teaspoons of extra virgin olive oil in a skillet over medium heat until they have softened and turned a pale gold; remove from heat and set aside. Stir them into the polenta when you are stirring in the cheeses. Wowie!

1 pound cauliflower

2 yellow onions

1/3 cup olive oil

Salt and freshly ground black pepper

4 to 6 tablespoons dukkah (page 55)

Roasted Cauliflower and Onions with Roasted Hazelnut Dukkah

This is a heavenly roasting of cauliflower florets, onion wedges and olive oil, along with a roasted-nutty sprinkling of flavored hazelnuts.

Preheat the oven to 450 degrees F.

Wash and dry the cauliflower and cut it into 1- to 2-inch florets. Trim the root and stem ends from the onions, then peel and cut each one horizontally into halves. Cut each half into thirds.

Place the vegetables into a roasting pan large enough to accommodate them in a single layer. Drizzle the vegetables with the olive oil and toss to evenly coat them. Add a light sprinkling of salt and pepper, then roast until the cauliflower begins to brown and is tender when pierced with a sharp knife. Remove from oven, sprinkle with some of the dukkah and toss to coat the veggies on all sides.

To serve, arrange the vegetables in a serving dish and sprinkle on more of the dukkah to taste.

1 (10-inch) flour tortilla

1 cup roasted and skinned hazelnuts

1 green onion (white only) coarsely chopped

1 cup shredded Gruyère cheese

1/2 teaspoon fresh basil

1/2 teaspoon fresh thyme

1/4 teaspoon fresh marjoram

1/4 teaspoon freshly ground black pepper

1 medium egg, lightly beaten
    (or 1 large egg with 1 teaspoon removed
    after lightly beating)

Vegetable oil for frying

Roasted Hazelnut Cakes

Created by Foley Station Owner/Chef Merlyn Baker in La Grande, Oregon. Chef Baker's creations are always, well, creative and flavorful. This is a great side dish for pork, chicken or seafood. It also makes a good appetizer, topped with a little crab meat or bay shrimp.

Cut the tortilla into 1-inch pieces and bake in a 350 degree oven until crisp; set aside.

In the work bowl of a food processor, combine the tortilla, hazelnuts, green onion, cheese, basil, thyme, marjoram and black pepper. Process using the pulse button until the mixture is a coarse meal. Scrape the mixture out into a bowl and stir in the egg until well blended.

Divide the dough into 4 cakes. Fry in a heavy-bottomed skillet with a small amount of the oil, until golden brown, about 3 minutes on each side.

16 fingerling potatoes, thoroughly scrubbed

2 teaspoons salt

Salt and pepper to taste

2 tablespoons extra virgin olive oil

2 teaspoons fresh thyme, chopped

1 teaspoon fresh rosemary, chopped

Fingerling Potatoes Pan Roasted with Herbs

Sometimes all a meal needs are a few lovely fingerling potatoes, gently cooked and seasoned. Leave the peelings on for extra flavor and color.

Place the potatoes in a large pot with enough water to cover. Add the salt, cover and bring to a boil. Cook just until the potatoes are fork tender, about 8 minutes. Remove from heat and drain, then cool the potatoes by adding cold water to the pot; set aside. This can be done several hours ahead.

About 15 minutes before serving, slice the potatoes in half lengthwise and season with salt and pepper.

Heat a large, heavy-bottomed skillet over medium-high heat with the olive oil. Add the potatoes, cut sides down, and cook until they have browned on the bottom. Turn the potatoes, add the thyme and rosemary, and continue cooking until the potatoes are brown and crisp on the second side.

1 large yellow onion

1/2 cup butter

3/4 cup half & half

2 pounds Yukon Gold potatoes, peeled
     (or not, or partially peeled)

2-1/2 teaspoons salt, divided

Mashed Yukon Golds with Caramelized Onions

This is the mashed potato that I serve with many (many!) of my entrées, from grilled hazelnut-crusted halibut to the Herbed and Grilled Beef with Vegetable and Hazelnut Sauté.

To prepare the onion, cut it in half lengthwise from stem to root end. Trim off stem and root ends and peel. Place the onion halves on a cutting board, cut-side down and slice into 1/4-inch thick slices. Cut each half ring into half again. Cut enough onion pieces to measure 2 cups.

Place the prepared onion and the butter in a medium-sized heavy-bottomed pot over medium heat. Cook until the onion softens and turns a pale gold, about 20 minutes. Reduce heat to low.

Meanwhile, cut the potatoes into 2- to 3-inch sized pieces and place them in a large pot with enough water to cover. Add 2 teaspoons of the salt. Cover and bring the water to a boil over high heat, then reduce heat and simmer until the potatoes are tender, about 15 minutes.

While the potatoes are cooking, add the half & half to the butter and onion mixture and bring it just to a boil. Turn off the heat and set the mixture aside.

When the potatoes are tender, drain well into a colander. Return the potatoes to the pot and mash with a potato masher. Add the remaining 1/2 teaspoon salt and continue mashing to mix in the salt. Stir in most of the hot cream, butter and onions and combine. The potatoes may seem too thin at this point, but you'll notice that they soon thicken. Add additional cream/butter mixture to reach desired consistency. Add additional salt, if desired.

MORE STUFF! Other things to stir into your potatoes include grilled corn kernels, roasted peppers, roasted garlic cloves, smoky bacon, blue cheese, extra-aged Gouda...

Heavenly Jasmine Rice

With so many varieties of rice in the world to choose from, it would seem ridiculous for me to pick a favorite. And yet, jasmine rice is it. Not its aromatic sister, basmati, or its chubby Italian cousin, arborio. California's medium-grain Calrose has a lovely name and used to be my house rice, but that was Before jasmine. Even those popular long grain Southern Belles from Arkansas, Mississippi, Louisiana and Texas - so widely appreciated throughout the world for their firm, non-sticky character - simply can't speak to my spirit in the way that this exotic Thai beauty does.

It brings so much to the kitchen. First, there's that aromatic character. Open the bag and inhale. Even before you add water and heat, jasmine rice has an exquisite, almost floral smell that tells you you're about to prepare something delicious; that these grains harbor a pureness in quality that makes your time in the kitchen worthwhile. Aroma-therapy for cooks.

Then there's its complex personality. Oh sure, jasmine rice is a long grain variety, just like the Southern Belles. But jasmine comes across fluffy-yet-chewy thanks to a higher amylose content. Not as sticky as the medium-grained Calrose or the very glutinous and sweet California Mochi rice. Just fluffy and resilient enough to be interesting all on its own.

If I keep a bowl of cooked jasmine rice in the fridge my spontaneous side has more to work with during the week. Unlike most long-grain rice, jasmine's outer surface remains tender and fluffy at cold temperatures instead of turning hard and brittle. So it's a great base for last-minute salads and sautés.

Now you know, there are many ways to prepare jasmine rice. For one thing, some prefer a liquid to rice ratio as low as 1 to 1. I just happen to like a ratio of 2 to 1 that yields very tender, moist, rice with just a hint of stickiness without being, well, sticky! Beyond that, I like to complement all of that heady jasmine rice aroma with butter and onion. Heavenly!

Makes 6 to 8 servings

1/2 cup chopped yellow onion

2 tablespoons butter

1-1/2 cups jasmine rice

3 cups water

3/4 teaspoon salt

In medium-sized heavy-bottomed pot over medium heat, sauté the onion in the butter until the onion is soft and translucent (about 5 minutes). Add the rice and sauté to evenly coat the grains. Add the water and salt, increase the temperature to medium-high and bring the water to a boil, stirring occasionally with a flat-bottomed utensil so the rice won't scorch. Once the water has boiled, reduce the temperature to low, cover, and cook the rice at a very slow simmer for 20 minutes without uncovering the pot.

After 20 minutes, check the rice. If all the water has been absorbed, the rice is done. Gently fluff it with a fork. If not serving immediately, place a paper towel over the top of the pot and put the lid back on to keep the rice hot (the paper towel absorbs condensation that would otherwise drip back down on the rice and make it soggy).

Makes about 2-1/2 cups

1/2 cup yellow onion, finely chopped

1 tablespoon extra virgin olive oil

2 cups whole, fresh cranberries

1 cup firmly packed light brown sugar

Juice and grated zest of 1 orange
     (about 1/2 cup juice)

1/2 cup brandy

1/3 cup apple cider vinegar

1/3 cup dried cherries

1/3 cup dried Mission figs,
     each one cut into 8 pieces

2 tablespoons freshly grated ginger root

3/4 teaspoon ground cinnamon

1/2 teaspoon ground nutmeg

3/4 cup chopped roasted and
     skinned hazelnuts

Gingered Cranberry, Hazelnut and Fig Conserve

A delicious side to serve with smoked turkey! I'd call it a chutney because of it's spicy nature, but once you've added hazelnuts, it officially becomes a conserve.

In a medium, heavy-bottomed pot, over medium to medium-high heat, sauté the onion in the olive oil just until the onion softens, about 2 minutes. Add the cranberries, brown sugar, orange juice and zest, brandy, vinegar, cherries, dried figs, ginger root, cinnamon, and nutmeg. Bring the mixture to a boil, then reduce the heat and simmer, stirring occasionally. The mixture will foam at first, but that will subside and then the liquid will thicken and turn glossy.

Remove from heat. Serve warm or chilled. May be prepared up to one month ahead and refrigerated.

4 firm, ripe pears, such as Bosc or comice

1 cup coarsely chopped raw hazelnuts

2 tablespoons balsamic vinegar

1 tablespoon olive oil

2 teaspoons minced fresh thyme

3/4 teaspoon salt

1/2 teaspoon freshly ground black pepper

1 tablespoon melted butter

4 ounces Oregon blue cheese, crumbled

Balsamic and Thyme Roasted Pears and Hazelnuts with Blue Cheese Crumbles

This is a delicious partner for your turkey or ham feast.

Preheat oven to 350 degrees F.

Peel and cut each pear in half, removing the core. Place the pears in a bowl, along with the hazelnuts. Toss the pears and nuts with the balsamic vinegar, oil, thyme, salt and pepper. Drizzle on the melted butter, which will begin to harden the minute it comes in contact with the pears. Transfer the contents of the bowl to a lightly oiled roasting pan large enough to hold the pears and nuts without crowding, with the pears resting cut side down. Roast until the pears and nuts are golden brown, about 25 to 30 minutes. Set aside until ready to serve.

To serve, arrange on a platter and sprinkle with the blue cheese.

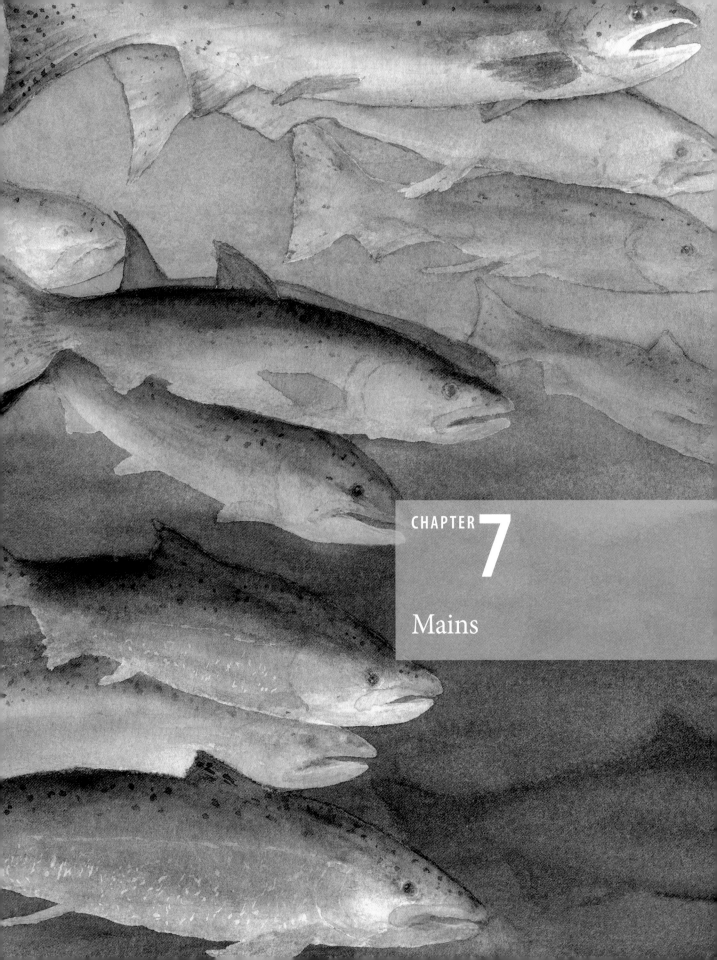

CHAPTER **7**

Mains

HEARTY MAIN DISH SALADS

Side salads become a main dish in so many simple ways. Adding meats, cheeses and eggs, of course, or beans and grains. Roasted vegetables, still warm and caramelized from the oven, draped over some spring greens and sprinkled with some Oregon Blue is a jazzy maneuver too.

In all these cases, that extra depth I keep speaking of that hazelnuts provide is the factor that elevates them beyond the ordinary. So don't take the concept lightly. It's simple, and it works. When I'm garnishing main dish salads with hazelnuts, I like them to be extravagantly varied in size, the way they become when crushed gently with the handle of a chef's knife.

THE MAIN DISH Well, this is where Oregon hazelnuts really shine. On so many levels! But let's talk about the simplest thing first: garnishing. At least, for lack of a better word, that's what we'll call it.

So far, I've made plenty of reference to this concept. Tossing a few hazelnuts around on a platter of appetizers. Sprinkling some onto a salad. But now that we're into the main dish, so to speak, let's really explore the issue. I can't stress enough to you how a simple handful of deeply roasted and chopped hazelnuts, sprinkled over a platter of freshly-grilled steaks adds such depth to the meal. In fact, just about anything I bring off the grill is complimented by the nature of hazelnuts. So I've learned to garnish the platter with a handful of roasted hazelnuts just before bringing it to the table. It's a smooth move that hasn't really been done much. But it works, because the earthy-toasty character within the nut forms a rich layer of flavor—a bridge, if you will—between the freshly grilled meat and accompanying side dishes. An integrative measure like this steps up the quality of the meal as a whole.

As part of a stuffing for chicken, trout, or a big, fat, pork chop, hazelnuts bring crunch and a sweet nutty goodness to the party. And when combined with two other flavorful-but-complimentary ingredients—arugula and feta cheese—you've got a dynamite mixture to nestle into a butterflied piece of pork tenderloin before grilling.

The earthy flavors within even the most common mushroom make it another ideal accomplice for the Oregon hazelnut. And when you get into the muskier wild varieties that show up in Oregon markets in Spring and Fall—the treasured chanterelle and, most especially, the exotic morel—the experience is nothing short of dynamic. Working off that synergy, consider a simple accent at your next salmon bake: sautéed mushrooms, Walla Walla Sweets and roasted hazelnuts.

Then there's the whole concept of coating your meal in nuts. Chef Cory Schrieber of Wildwood in Portland's historic Northwest district offers a delectable twist on that concept: roasted hazelnuts and sage-crusted halibut with roasted pears and Crater Lake Blue Cheese.

If you're wanting to go meatless, hazelnuts are a powerful way to punch up a rice or pasta dish. There's that natural toastiness and gentle crunch. Plus, a sophisticated flavor that's rich and complex, yet not overpowering.

Makes 4 servings as an entrée

2 poached or grilled chicken breast halves,
    finely diced

Salt and freshly ground black pepper

1 fresh lemon

Extra virgin olive oil

1/2 head firm iceberg lettuce, finely diced

1/2 head curly-leafed lettuce, finely diced

1 heart of romaine (the light green
    inner leaves), finely diced

1 medium bunch watercress,
    coarsely chopped to yield 1 cup of leaves
    and tender stems

1 avocado

About 1 cup of a good vinaigrette
    (see note on next page), divided

6 slices crispy cooked bacon, crumbled

3 hard-cooked eggs, peeled and diced

2 tablespoons minced fresh chives
    or green onions

4 ounces good-quality blue cheese

3/4 cup chopped darkly-roasted
    and skinned hazelnuts

2 medium-sized ripe, firm tomatoes,
    finely diced

The Almost-Traditional Cobb Salad

In 1936, Robert Cobb, president of a restaurant group that owned the Hollywood Brown Derby Restaurant, wandered into the Derby's kitchen and put together a salad for his pal, Sid Grauman (of Grauman's Chinese Theater). According to legend, the pickin's were slim that night, and yet Cobb was able to assemble an interesting creation with the leftovers lurking in the restaurant's refrigerator: good quality blue cheese, perfectly seasoned and poached chicken, avocado, bacon, hard-cooked eggs, tomatoes and a variety of salad greens and fresh herbs. He gave everything a fine dice, and then for presentation arranged those ingredients in tight but separate formation, with the greens on the bottom. At the table, after his guest got to appreciate the colorful array, Cobb tossed it all together with a fine vinaigrette.

The combination of flavors and textures was perfect, and a classic was born. Over 70 years later, variations abound. But in my mind, the successful alterations are strictly architectural—nobody has fiddled with the ingredients and come up with an improvement. My favorite spin-off was created in a San Francisco restaurant, MacArthur Park, back in the early 1970's. Individual salads were built up layer by delectable layer in porcelain soufflé bowls and crowned with a topping of Roquefort dressing. The result was a delightful stratification of colors and flavors, but not much real difference after all was said and, ah, crunched.

Enter the hazelnut. I've already maintained that its crunchy-toasty-sweet-yet-smoky character partners beautifully with such things as bacon, blue cheese, chicken, avocado, and tomato. Wait a minute, that's sounding an awful lot like a Cobb Salad. Well, what do you know? The addition is a winner. Give it a try!

Toss the chicken in a small bowl with a sprinkling of salt and pepper and a drizzling of fresh lemon juice and olive oil. Cover and refrigerate until ready to serve.

Choose a fine, big salad bowl with a wide shape. Place the iceberg lettuce, curly-leafed lettuce, romaine and watercress in the bowl, tossing to combine them.

Halve the avocado, then peel and dice it into 1/4-inch pieces. Turn it into a small bowl and sprinkle with a few drops of the fresh lemon juice and extra virgin olive oil.

To serve, toss the greens with about 1/3 cup of the vinaigrette. Arrange the other ingredients in strips across the top of the greens. From left to right, lay on the avocado, bacon pieces, hard-cooked eggs, chives or green onion, blue cheese, hazelnuts and tomatoes. Bring the salad to the table, then toss with additional vinaigrette.

NOTE ON VINAIGRETTE: consider using the Balsamic Vinaigrette with Sweet Honey Mustard (page 112), the Hazelnut Vinaigrette (page 100) or the Dijon Vinaigrette (page 113). Alternatively, if you have a batch of Jan's Amazing Vinaigrette Base on hand (page 96), then combine a scant 1/2 cup of it with 2/3 cup of extra virgin olive oil.

NOTE: If you wish to arrange the salad in advance, do not toss the greens with any of the vinaigrette before bringing it to the table or the greens will become limp; simply cover with plastic wrap and refrigerate, then toss with the vinaigrette at the table.

VARIATIONS: you could take your cue from the San Francisco restaurant MacArthur Park and layer the salad in individual souffle dishes. Each guest can then toss his or her own—or not—as desired.

BEVERAGE THOUGHTS: With all of the salad components, there's a complex flavor profile to consider that has always sent me in the direction of a crisp, clean, straightforward wine, such as a lovely Pinot Gris or Pinot Blanc. A nice craft beer choice would be something that is equally simple and clean-tasting, such as pilsner, which would be light-bodied with a bit of malt and floral character to it.

Quick TIP

For a speedy Beef Salad: Season and cook skirt steak to desired doneness. Whisk together 1/4 cup red wine vinegar, 2 teaspoons Dijon mustard, 1/4 teaspoon salt and freshly ground black pepper, a pinch of sugar and 1/3 cup extra virgin olive oil. Toss this vinaigrette with salad greens, sliced steak, a healthy crumbling of blue cheese and a handful of roasted and coarsely chopped hazelnuts.

3 to 4 grilled and cooled boneless,
    skinless chicken breasts, cut into
    1/2-inch chunks to measure 4 cups

1 cup halved or coarsely chopped lightly
    roasted and skinned hazelnuts

1 cup shredded Farmstead Brindisi cheese
    (see note)

1 cup chopped celery

1/2 cup chopped sweet onion

3/4 cup mayonnaise

1/4 cup Oregon blue cheese

2 tablespoons white wine vinegar
    (or rice vinegar)

1 tablespoon Dijon mustard

2 teaspoons Worcestershire sauce

1 fresh pineapple (preferably, a
    super-sweet "Golden" variety)

Grilled Chicken Salad with Oregon Blue, Brindisi, and Grilled Pineapple

This recipe came to be after hazelnut grower Wayne Chambers came for lunch one day and handed over a bag of a beautiful-but-not-ready-for-prime-time hazelnuts. In other words, they were one of OSU researcher Shawn Mehlenbacher's test cultivars that Wayne was growing in his orchard.

"Wow!" said I. "These are so sweet and flavorful."

"What's the variety?" asked my husband, Steve.

"These don't have a name yet. They're just a number," said Wayne. "I doubt they'll make it out of trial, because the darn things split during processing."

Well, even though they may not be up to Oregon hazelnut industry standards in all ways, I wasn't about to let them go to waste. So the following week I threw together this salad. My goal was to play off the rich and smoky characteristics of these lovely no-name nuts. In my first go-'round, I used some poached chicken that was lurking in the refrigerator. But on reflection, it didn't really stand up to the rich, blue-cheesiness of the sauce. It could have been any meat. Grilled chicken, however, was going to be the perfect balance for the sauce. Plus, it would be a bridge for the smoky-toastiness of the hazelnuts, bringing all of the ingredients into harmony. Steve said it more succinctly: "Yeah, grilled chicken is the better back."

In a medium bowl, combine the chicken breast, hazelnuts, Brindisi cheese, celery, and onion. Mix well.

In a blender or food processor, combine the mayonnaise, blue cheese, vinegar, mustard and Worcestershire sauce. Blend until smooth, then scrape out onto the chicken mixture. With a spatula or wooden spoon gently stir until the creamed mixture is evenly distributed. Chill for at least 30 minutes while flavor develops. Can be prepared up to 24 hours ahead.

While the salad is chilling (or several hours ahead), prepare the grilled pineapple as directed in the recipe for Pork Medallions with Grilled Pineapple, Feta, and Tangy Balsamic-Molasses Reduction (page 154); set aside.

To serve, spoon the salad onto plates and arrange the pineapple slices alongside.

VARIATION: Instead of grilled pineapple slices, I've had great success with fresh pears. Just make sure they have been lovingly ripened and are very sweet and juicy. Core and wedge 3 of them and distribute them between the servings of salad.

NOTE: Farmstead Brindisi cheese is made by Willamette Valley Cheese Company. It's an aged Jersey cow's milk cheese. But if you can't locate it, an extra-aged Gouda (I like the Rembrandt brand) or extra-aged sharp Cheddar from Tillamook or another regional artisan cheese similar to one mentioned above would be dandy substitutes.

BEVERAGE THOUGHTS: A spicy, fruity, berry-tinged old vine Zinfandel would compliment some of the main components in this dish, including the grilled pineapple slices. However, a well-oaked Chardonnay would also be a nice choice, even with the blue cheese. For beer, I'd go with a nice hoppy-floral India pale ale, such as Ninkasi Brewing's Tricerahops Double IPA, which would balance the richness of this salad, yet provide a refreshing, thirst-quenching character.

QuickTIP

As long as your grill is already loaded and lit for a meal, take advantage of the situation by roasting some hazelnuts on the side with a bit of olive oil or butter on a piece of aluminum foil shaped into a shallow pan. I even throw in some fresh garlic cloves. Serve alongside the evening meal.

Grilled Chicken Salad with Jalapeño Dressing

If you like Waldorf salad, you probably won't like this. Just kidding! Sort of. This is Waldorf salad on vacation in Albuquerque. The hazelnuts compliment the feta, apple, and cherries. This is one of those great "Ladies Luncheon" sorts of offerings. It would even be a lovely addition to a brunch buffet. Steve says he'd put in an extra pepper and take it to a tailgater. What a man!

Makes 4 servings as an entrée

3/4 to 1 cup Chile Mayonnaise
    (recipe follows)
4 boneless, skinless chicken breast halves
    (6 to 8 ounces each), grilled, chilled,
    and cut into bite-sized chunks
1/2 cup chopped celery
1/4 cup dried cherries
1/2 cup chopped apple
1/2 cup chopped roasted and
    skinned hazelnuts
Salt and freshly ground black pepper
    to taste
2 cups chopped mixed salad greens
2 Roma tomatoes, cored and sliced
1/2 cup crumbled feta cheese

To serve, combine the mayonnaise with the chicken, celery, cherries, apples, hazelnuts, salt, and pepper. Mix well. Serve on top of mixed greens with sliced tomatoes on the side and a crumbling of feta on top.

BEVERAGE THOUGHTS: The chiles, dried fruit and fresh apples make this a great match for a luscious Gewürztraminer. For beer drinkers, a lightly hopped ale with a bit of fruit would be nice. In that regard, consider Stumptown Tart Ale from Bridgeport, which would play off the fruits in the dish.

Chile Mayonnaise

Makes about 1-1/8 cups mayonnaise

1 fresh serrano pepper
1/2 fresh jalapeño pepper
3 cloves peeled garlic
2 tablespoons fresh lemon juice
1 cup mayonnaise

Remove stems, seeds and membranes from the peppers and coarsely chop. Purée the peppers, garlic and lemon juice in a blender or food processor. Scrape the mixture into a small bowl, then whisk in the mayonnaise.

Makes 4 servings as an entrée

4 skinned and boned chicken breast halves,
    grilled, cooled and cut into
    1/4-inch cubes

1/2 cup Sesame and Poppy Seed Vinaigrette
    (recipe follows)

6 cups of salad greens
    (I prefer to use half romaine and half
    baby arugula leaves)

2 Roma (Italian plum) tomatoes, diced

2 ripe Haas avocados, peeled, seeded,
    and diced

1 cup Sugar-Glazed Hazelnuts
    (recipe follows)

1/4 cup minced sweet onion

Salt and pepper to taste

Additional salad greens for plating

2 ripe pears, cored and sliced for garnish

Additional tomato wedges for garnish

2 hard-cooked eggs, sliced for garnish

Grilled Chicken Salad with Sugar-Glazed Hazelnuts and Sesame and Poppy Seed Vinaigrette

Thanks to the toasted sesame seeds in the vinaigrette, there's a hint of bacon flavor in the salad. And what goes well with bacon? Uh-huh, hazelnuts. In this case, they're sugar-glazed.

Combine the chicken with the vinaigrette, salad greens, tomatoes, avocado, sugar-glazed hazelnuts and onion. Add more vinaigrette as necessary to reach desired consistency. Salt and pepper to taste.

To serve, arrange additional salad greens on four plates, then divide the salad mixture between them. Garnish with the pear slices, additional tomato wedges, and the sliced egg.

BEVERAGE THOUGHTS: This salad has a nutty-bacon profile that goes beautifully with a medium to full-bodied Pinot Noir. A pale ale is another approach that works very well.

Makes 1 cup

1 cup coarsely chopped lightly roasted and
    skinned hazelnuts

2 tablespoons granulated sugar

Sugar-Glazed Hazelnuts

Place a sheet of waxed paper on the counter. Warm the chopped hazelnuts in a non-stick skillet over medium-high heat. Sprinkle on about 2 tablespoons of sugar, stirring constantly with either a silicon spatula or a flat-sided wooden spoon, and cook until the sugar melts around the hazelnuts. Sprinkle on more sugar as necessary to glaze all of the hazelnut pieces. Remove from heat and quickly scrape the hazelnuts onto the sheet of waxed paper in a single layer to cool.

1/4 cup red or white wine vinegar

1 tablespoon granulated sugar

2 tablespoons lightly toasted sesame seeds
    (see note)

1 tablespoon poppy seeds

1 tablespoon coarsely chopped onion

1/2 teaspoon Worcestershire sauce

1/4 teaspoon paprika

1/2 teaspoon salt

1/3 cup vegetable oil, such as canola

Sesame and Poppy Seed Vinaigrette

Because of it's hint of bacon flavor (thanks to the toasted sesame seeds), this vinaigrette is delicious with a wide range of salad components, including shredded cabbage, sliced Fuyu persimmons and young salad greens. It works as well on a plethora of baby spinach salad combinations incorporating any number of fruits, including pears, oranges, and apples.

Place the vinegar, sugar, sesame seeds, poppy seeds, onion, Worcestershire sauce, paprika, and salt in a blender or food processor. Blend until most of the sesame seeds are ground, stopping the motor several times along the way to scrape down the sides of the container. Scrape the contents into a small bowl, then whisk in the vegetable oil in a slow, steady stream.

NOTE ON TOASTING SESAME SEEDS: Place in a small non-stick skillet over medium-high heat. Gently shake the pan while stirring the seeds with a flat-edged spatula until the seeds begin to brown. They will crackle and pop and try to jump out of the pan. That's when you know they're done! Scrape them out onto a dish to cool.

A top-notch Oregon food experience

CORVALLIS-BASED WHITE WATER RIVER GUIDES JOY AND BOB HENKLE handed me a most delightful assignment. It began with a note: "We have a Rogue River rafting business that is based out of Corvallis and we are big foodies here. We grow a lot of the food we serve our guests in our Willamette Valley gardens. Also, we serve Oregon hazelnuts to our rafting guests each summer (we buy them direct from a local farmer), and get rave reviews.

"We're very interested in giving our guests the highest quality local foods, especially since many of them come from the California area and really appreciate our efforts to supply them with a top-notch Oregon food experience. We're always looking for the 'perfect' river lunch salad. I make one with homemade pesto, but do you have any other ideas for great river salads?"

This started me on a nostalgic jog down memory lane to my own ultimate river salad experience: The year was 1978. It was the first day into a 3-day white water rafting trip on the North Fork of The American River in Northern California. We'd beached the rafts for a break.

"What's for lunch," we paddlers wondered. The guide and his crew had set out cutting boards on a big fat log and were pulling fresh carrots, celery, green onions, cucumbers, bell peppers, and hard-cooked eggs from their dry bags.

"Tuna salad sandwiches," said our guide as he tumbled his pile of chopped veggies and egg into a huge pot. Out came the cans of tuna, some fresh mayonnaise, and sliced olives. All of these ingredients combined into the most amazing tuna salad sandwich I have ever experienced.

Now, I'm sure that ambiance had a bit to do with it, as well as a hearty appetite from a morning of paddling through class 3 rapids. But still, it was a dynamic combination of ingredients I have savored ever since.

5 large Anaheim chiles, roasted and
    peeled (see note)

1 large Walla Walla Sweet onion
    (if unavailable, another fine variety
    will do)

2/3 cup pitted and halved Kalamata
    olives, drained

5 ripe local tomatoes, cored and diced
    to measure about 3 cups

1 cucumber, peeled and diced

The kernels from 3 freshly cooked ears
    of corn

5 grilled boneless skinless chicken breast
    halves, cooled and chopped

3/4 cup coarsely chopped darkly roasted
    and skinned hazelnuts

2 tablespoons finely chopped fresh basil

2/3 cup red or white wine vinegar

2 tablespoons Dijon mustard

4 cloves garlic, minced

1 teaspoon salt

1/2 teaspoon freshly ground black pepper

1 cup extra virgin olive oil

About 2-1/2 cups crumbled Rogue Creamery
    Oregon Blue (or other good quality
    blue cheese)

Crusty artisan bread, sliced

Rogue River Salad

I patterned this salad after a salsa I created under similar circumstances: outdoors, on a camping trip in the Oregon coast range, with a bag full of sun-ripened tomatoes and a couple of luscious Walla Walla Sweet onions. My fellow campers were the official taste testers and Walla Walla Salsa Salsa was given thumbs up all around at Happy Hour.

To meet Joy's criteria for a river-worthy lunch salad, I added chicken, basil, hazelnuts and an Oregon blue cheese from (where else?) Rogue Creamery. Also, because the Henkles are running the Rogue in the summer, I decided that fresh corn would be an outstanding ingredient to include as well. When you carve it off the cobs, be sure to leave it in the chunky "rafts" instead of breaking it up into individual kernels. It adds so much interest to the dish. I'm hoping that this is one salad that I'll enjoy someday alongside its namesake, after a day on the water. Bon Appetit, Joy. Thanks for the challenge!

Remove the stems, seeds, and inner membranes from the roasted chiles, then chop.

When ready to serve the salad, combine the chopped chiles with the onion, olives, tomatoes, cucumber, corn kernels, chicken, hazelnuts, and basil in a large bowl. In a small bowl, whisk together the vinegar, mustard, garlic, salt and pepper. Whisk in the olive oil.

Toss the salad mixture with enough of the vinaigrette to moisten it thoroughly (you'll probably have enough left over to marinate a few chunks of chicken for another meal). Serve in individual bowls. Top each serving with some of the blue cheese, along with crusty slices of a good artisan bread.

NOTE: To roast the Anaheim chiles, poke each chile once with a sharp knife to avoid explosions in the oven. Place the chiles on a baking sheet and broil until the skin has blistered and is fairly blackened on all sides. This takes 6 to 8 minutes total. Alternatively, you could roast them on the grate over a gas burner or on a grill. Just make sure that the skin gets blistery and blackened in most spots all the way around. Remove from the heat and let cool. The skin will peel away very easily.

BEVERAGE THOUGHTS: The boldest components in the salad—the anaheims and blue cheese—would be very comfortable around a lovely, spicy, fruity southern Oregon Syrah. Of course, if you're packing along some beer and you actually are by a river, let's hope it's a refreshing pale ale.

RICE DISHES

I love combinations of nuts and rice. The nuttiness in both components is a great starting point for whatever else you're adding to the dish. If you want to maintain the crunch in your hazelnuts, hold them out until the end of cooking. But sometimes they're lovely when they've had a chance to absorb the flavored broth right along with the grains of rice.

Makes 4 servings as an entrée

2 fresh jalapeños, seeded and sliced

4 cloves garlic, peeled and chopped

About 1 tablespoon freshly grated
      ginger root

3 tablespoons firmly packed brown sugar

3 tablespoons tempura sauce or ponzu sauce
      (if unavailable, use soy sauce)

Juice and lime zest from half a fresh lime

1/4 cup unsweetened coconut milk
      (commercially canned; available in the
      Asian food section of supermarkets)

About 1/3 cup coarsely chopped fresh
      basil leaves

2 tablespoons vegetable oil

1/2 teaspoon salt

1/4 teaspoon coarsely ground black pepper

1 pound peeled and deveined raw shrimp

Jasmine Rice with Coconut, Lime and
      Roasted Hazelnuts (recipe follows)

Mango Salsa (recipe follows)

Coconut Ginger Shrimp and Jasmine Rice with Lime and Roasted Hazelnuts

Here's a delicious preparation for jasmine rice. I've also included a recipe for a simple Mango Salsa that is a great addition. If you have a batch of Heavenly Sauce on hand (page 60), then a dollop of that will elevate the experience even higher.

In a medium-sized mixing bowl, combine the jalapeños, garlic, ginger root, brown sugar, tempura sauce, lime juice and zest, coconut milk, fresh basil, vegetable oil, salt, and pepper. Add the shrimp and stir to coat them evenly. Marinate the shrimp in the refrigerator for at least 30 minutes (or up to 4 hours).

Meanwhile, prepare the jasmine rice and the Mango Salsa. When ready to proceed, heat a large nonstick skillet or wok over high heat. Remove the shrimp from the marinade (reserve the marinade) and place them in a single layer in the pan. Stir-fry the shrimp until they are nicely browned, taking care not to over-cook them. This will only take about 3 minutes. Remove the pan from the burner and spoon the shrimp onto a warm serving platter. Pour the reserved marinade into the pan and bring to a boil over medium-high heat, then simmer gently for about 5 minutes for safety (the shrimp were raw) and to leave it slightly thickened.

To serve, arrange a portion of rice on each of 4 dinner plates. Arrange a serving of shrimp on top of the rice, then pour some of the hot marinade over each portion. Add a bit of the Mango Salsa on the side, reserving the remainder to pass at the table.

BEVERAGE THOUGHTS: the exotic, aromatic qualities within this dish, from the ginger and chiles to the mangos and lime all push me in the direction of a Gewürztraminer. It's a lovely pairing. A floral, well made Viognier would also work here, as would a wheat beer or a slightly fruity pale ale.

Jasmine Rice with Coconut, Lime and Roasted Hazelnuts

Makes 4 to 6 servings

1 cup jasmine rice

1 cup unsweetened canned coconut milk

1/2 cup water

1/2 teaspoon salt

Zest from 1/2 lime

1/2 cup coarsely chopped darkly roasted
    and skinned hazelnuts

Beyond coconut shrimp, this is a wonderful rice to have in your repertoire for all sorts of meals. It's great as a base for sautéed vegetables, quick chicken or shrimp sautés, and main dish salads. It also makes a slightly more exotic and flavorful base for my Heavenly Bowls (page 149).

In a medium-sized heavy-bottomed saucepan, combine the rice, coconut milk, water, and salt. Bring to a boil, cover, reduce the heat, and gently simmer without opening the lid for 15 minutes. Then check the pot and if all of the liquid has been absorbed the rice is done. If not, cover and continue cooking another 3 minutes or so. Remove from heat, fluff with a fork and stir in the lime zest and hazelnuts.

Mango Salsa

Makes about 1 cup

1 fresh mango, peeled and chopped

3 green onions, finely chopped
    (white and pale green portions)

2 tablespoons chopped fresh basil

About 3 tablespoons fresh lime juice

About 1/4 teaspoon salt

About 1/4 teaspoon pepper

Combine the mango, onions, basil, and lime juice in a small bowl. Add salt and pepper to taste.

Makes 4 servings

1 recipe of Heavenly Jasmine Rice (page 130)

1-1/2 cups of Heavenly Sauce (page 60)

2 to 3 cups shredded sharp Cheddar cheese

2 ripe Haas avocados, peeled, seeded, diced

2 to 3 medium tomatoes, cored and chopped

1 cup sliced black olives

About 3/4 cup chopped green onion

1 cup black beans, canned or fresh-cooked

1-1/2 cups salsa (use a high quality
　　fresh one from the refrigerated case)

Heavenly Bowl

My inspiration for the Heavenly Bowl concept comes by way of Café Yumm!, a small, earth-friendly restaurant chain that got its start in Eugene, Oregon. I've provided my own variation on their popular sauce on page 60.

Café Yumm! founders Mark and Mary Ann Beauchamp built an entire menu around their amazing sauce. The most popular item, of course, is the Yumm! Bowl. It begins with rice (their favorites are jasmine and brown) and ends with Yumm! Sauce. In between, the layers can include such complimentary delights as black beans, avocado, shredded cheese, fresh salsa, sliced olives, and sour cream. Here's how I do it...

To serve, place the rice, heavenly sauce, cheese, avocado, tomatoes, olives, onions, black beans and salsa in individual bowls. Set the bowls out on the counter or at the table. Let each diner assemble their own Heavenly Bowl.

General directions for assembling individual Heavenly Bowls: Place a serving of the rice (hot, warm or cooled) in a bowl, then top with a bit of the Heavenly Sauce, followed by the other ingredients listed and ending with the salsa. Add another dollop of the Heavenly Sauce, and bon appetit!

BEVERAGE THOUGHTS: A medium to heavy-bodied Pinot Noir is a nice compliment to the toasty components in the sauce and doesn't fight the various ingredients that are assembled in the bowls. A toasty brown ale would be a lovely beer choice.

For each quesadilla, you will need:

**About 1/3 cup of shredded sharp Cheddar
(or Monterey jack, or medium-sharp
Cheddar)**

**1/4 cup finely chopped raw or lightly
roasted hazelnuts**

1 flour tortilla (8- or 10-inch)

**Desired fillings, such as: sliced and sautéed
mushrooms (I sauté them until they're
golden brown in a bit of butter,
Worcestershire, chili garlic paste,
and a splash of sherry or brandy),
diced tomato, salsa, guacamole,
sautéed or grilled meat, sour cream,
taco sauce**

Golden Quesadillas

Here's a quick and tasty meal that comes with a great boost of flavor from an "accident" run amok. You know how when you sprinkle cheese onto a flour tortilla as it's warming in a skillet, some of the shreds "accidentally" fall down onto the surface of the pan and immediately turn into a golden, delectable crunch? Those tidbits have always been my favorite part. So one night I decided to make an entire pan of them. Well, one thing led to another and this recipe is the result of that experiment. It was a huge success—fast, simple, and absolutely DELICIOUS, especially once it occurred to me to work in a handful of hazelnuts.

Heat a non-stick skillet over medium-high heat until it becomes very warm to the touch. Meanwhile, combine the cheese with the hazelnuts. Sprinkle the cheese mixture directly onto the surface of the pan, spreading it out to cover the approximate diameter of the tortilla. As soon as the cheese begins to melt (which is pretty much right away), overlay the tortilla and press it gently into the melting cheese (the pressure from your hand helps the cheese adhere to the tortilla). Let the tortilla sit undisturbed in the pan for about 30 seconds, then gently test it around the edges by sliding your spatula under the tortilla and lifting slightly to see whether the cheese has turned golden and is adhering to the tortilla. Once this has happened, then go ahead and slide your spatula completely underneath the tortilla and flip it over to brown its other side slightly, which will take another 20 to 30 seconds, Then slide the tortilla onto a plate, cheese side up.

Arrange the desired fillings down the center of the tortilla, then fold both sides inward over the filling and enjoy!

NOTE: For feeding several folks, it's a good idea to have two pans going at the same time, or use a non-stick griddle.

BEVERAGE THOUGHTS: A nice frosty lager, such as a Dos Equis or your favorite Oregon pale ale, such as Deschutes Brewery's Mirror Pond, or Rogue's Juniper Pale Ale, will hit the spot.

MEAT DISHES

Makes 4 servings

1 tablespoon all-purpose flour

1 teaspoon poultry seasoning

1 teaspoon garlic powder

1 egg

1 cup chopped raw hazelnuts

4 boneless, skinless chicken breast halves

1/4 teaspoon salt

1/4 teaspoon white pepper

2 tablespoons extra virgin olive oil

1 cup half & half

1/2 cup Oregon Blue cheese
   (or other good quality blue cheese)

2 teaspoons Dijon mustard

Mashed Yukons with Caramelized Onions
   (page 129)

Lightly steamed broccoli florets

BEVERAGE THOUGHTS: A fruity Zinfandel or Southern Oregon Syrah can hold its own with the blue cheese and really compliments the nutty flavor profile. Beer could be as light and simple as a pale ale, or as rich and toasty as a Scottish style ale, such as Pelican Brewery's MacPelican's Scottish Style Ale, which would introduce a rich malty sweetness and kiss of smoke to the meal.

Hazelnut-Crusted Chicken with Oregon Blue

You will be shocked at just how easy it is to prepare the blue cheese sauce used in this dish.

Preheat the oven to 350 degrees F.

Combine the flour, poultry seasoning and garlic powder on a pie plate. Place the egg on a second pie plate and whisk thoroughly.

Place the chopped hazelnuts on a piece of waxed paper or plastic wrap on a cutting board or kitchen counter.

Season each piece of chicken with some of the salt and pepper, then turn each piece in the flour mixture. Next, turn each floured breast first in the egg and then in the nuts, thoroughly coating each side. Place them on a baking sheet or plate until ready to cook. They can be held up to several hours in the refrigerator prior to cooking.

When ready to cook, heat a nonstick skillet with an oven-safe handle over medium-high heat. When the skillet is heated through, add the olive oil. Once the oil is hot, place each piece of chicken in the skillet and brown both sides, which will take about 1-1/2 to 2 minutes per side. Remove the pan from the heat and transfer it to the preheated oven. Finish cooking the chicken, which will take about 8 more minutes.

While the chicken is baking, warm the half & half in a small heavy-bottomed pot over medium heat. Add the cheese and stir gently until it melts. Stir in the mustard, then turn down the heat and keep the sauce warm until ready to use.

To serve, place a breast on a dinner plate and drizzle on some of the Oregon Blue Sauce. The Mashed Yukons with Caramelized Onions make a delicious accompaniment. And the lightly steamed broccoli adds both color and balance of flavor.

Makes 4 servings as an entrée

1 cup balsamic vinegar

1/2 cup finely chopped yellow onion

1/4 cup honey

3 tablespoons Dijon mustard, divided

4 boneless, skinless chicken breast halves

3 tablespoons olive oil

1 cup finely chopped lightly roasted
   and skinned hazelnuts

1/3 cup freshly grated Parmigiano-
   Reggiano cheese

BEVERAGE THOUGHT: I like this with either a soft and fruity Pinot Blanc, or a medium-bodied Pinot Noir. Both wines are nice with the roasted nuts, chicken, and kiss of the grill. A simple pale ale or IPA would keep everything in balance as well, but you might thrill some of your beer lovers if you bring out one of those slightly richer and maltier ales, like Pelican Brewery's MacPelican's Scottish Style Ale.

Dijon Chicken with Parmesan-Hazelnut Crust and Balsamic-Honey Reduction

Here's where you get to learn one of the tricks of the trade: how to get nuts to stick to meat during cooking. In this case, it's a layer of mustard that holds the nuts in place while adding its own flavor. The same technique can be applied to any fish or meat, so feel free to improvise down the road. You can alter the flavor by choosing different mustards, from very zesty and grainy, like a German brown style, over to a hot and spicy Chinese mustard.

To prepare the Balsamic-Honey Reduction, combine the balsamic vinegar, onion and honey in a small, heavy-bottomed saucepan. Bring to a boil over medium-high heat, stirring occasionally. Reduce heat to a vigorous simmer and continue cooking, stirring occasionally to prevent scorching, until the mixture has reduced by half and has thickened slightly. Remove from heat and whisk in 1 tablespoon of the Dijon mustard; set aside. This can be prepared several days ahead and refrigerated. Re-heat when ready to use.

Preheat the grill or oven to 375 degrees F. If grilling, arrange the grill for indirect cooking, so the breasts can be offset to the side of the heat source, rather than directly over it.

Pat the chicken breasts dry with paper towels. If they are especially plump at one end, consider pounding the thickest portion with a kitchen mallet or rolling pin to achieve even cooking (to avoid a mess, I put the breasts in a plastic bag before doing this).

Whisk together the olive oil with the remaining 2 tablespoons of mustard in a wide, shallow dish. Combine the hazelnuts and cheese in a second wide, shallow dish. Dip both sides of each breast in the mustard, then dip one side only in the nut/cheese mixture.

If grilling, place each breast on the hot grill with the nut-side up (remember, offset the breasts from direct flame or hot coals). Grill the breasts without turning them over until they are golden brown on the bottom and firm to the touch, about 25 minutes.

If baking in the oven, place the breasts nut-side up on a baking sheet, leaving several inches around each one for even cooking. Bake until nicely browned on top and firm to the touch, about 25 minutes.

Serve immediately, with the Balsamic-Honey Reduction on the side for dipping.

If you've been taking this book seriously at all...

then by now you have acquired a bottle of ponzu sauce or tempura sauce, some chili garlic sauce, and some Madeira. With that in mind, a really quick and handy (because you have those condiments in your pantry) stir-fry would go something like this:

Whisk together about 3 tablespoons of either ponzu or tempura sauce, 3 tablespoons of Madeira, 2 tablespoons of chili garlic sauce, and a teaspoon of sesame oil. Now cut up your favorite stir-fry veggies. Mine, in the order that I place them in the hot wok, are sliced mushrooms, sliced yellow onions, whole baby carrots, florets of cauliflower and broccoli, sweet bell pepper strips, slender wedges of red cabbage, strips of green onions, and whole sugar snap peas. Allow a little cooking time between additions, so everything reaches doneness at the same time. When the vegetables are just about done, drizzle on the sauce and continue stir-frying to get everything glazed and flavorful. Then add the hazelnuts and toss just to heat through. Serve. Consider soba noodles or medium-grain rice to round out the offering.

The last time I did this I served it with a bottle of Lumos 2008 Oregon Gewürztraminer (Temperance Hill Vineyard) and it was amazing. The spicy Gewürz, with just a hint of fruit, really balanced the heat and spice of the stir-fry.

For a more substantial stir-fry, I've included chunks of tofu that I've fried separately in a tiny bit of oil in a non-stick skillet, then added to the wok at the end. Of course, you could also add any type of beef, pork, chicken, shrimp or other seafood.

QuickTIP

For a quick, light supper or elegant side dish, simmer a 12-ounce box of frozen potato pierogi and 3 cups of broccoli florets in water until tender; drain. Sauté 1/2 cup chopped onion in olive oil until soft; add 1/2 cup chopped roasted hazelnuts, a pinch of red pepper flakes and the pierogi mixture. Heat through and season with salt and a splash more olive oil.

1 whole, fresh ripe pineapple (preferably a
     super-sweet "golden" variety)

1-1/2 cups balsamic vinegar

2 tablespoons molasses

2 or 3 sprigs fresh sweet basil leaves

1/4 cup coarsely chopped yellow onion

2 natural (not brine-injected) pork
     tenderloins (approximately 1-1/4
     pounds each)

About 1/2 teaspoon salt

About 1/2 teaspoon freshly ground
     black pepper

1 tablespoon extra virgin olive oil

2 teaspoons butter

8 ounces feta cheese, crumbled

1 cup coarsely chopped lightly roasted
     and skinned hazelnuts

BEVERAGE THOUGHTS: The rich, sweet flavor of grilled pineapple, as well as the sweet-yet-tangy balsamic reduction sauce are a great match for an Oregon Gewürztraminer. If you want to go red, consider a medium-bodied fruity Syrah. A light, slightly fruity pale ale, such as Deschutes' Mirror Pond, would be an excellent beer choice.

Pork Medallions with Grilled Pineapple, Feta, and Tangy Balsamic-Molasses Reduction

This is a wonderful meal to prepare. The grilled pineapple is a perfect counterpoint to the meat, feta, and sauce.

Grasping the pineapple by its tuft of leaves (be careful, the leaves are sharp!), keep the pineapple upright as you trim away the tough outer skin with wide, downward strokes, using a large, sharp knife. Remove the remaining "eyes."

Now turn the pineapple on its side and slice it into 1/2-inch thick rings. At this point, you could trim out the core from each slice, but I prefer to leave it in. It has a delicious flavor and slightly chewy texture that makes for an interesting contrast. Set the slices aside for grilling later.

To prepare the Balsamic-Molasses Reduction, combine the balsamic vinegar, molasses, basil, and onion in a saucepan. Bring the mixture to a boil, then cut it back to a lively simmer and cook until the sauce has been reduced to about 2/3 cup and is thick and syrupy. Strain, then return it to the pot and keep warm (or re-warm it when ready to serve). This can be prepared up to a week ahead and refrigerated.

Twenty minutes in advance of serving, grill the pineapple slices over medium-hot coals (or a gas burner), cooking on both sides until the edges are golden brown and the slices are still juicy. Keep hot until ready to use.

Meanwhile, preheat the oven to 400 degrees F. Cut a total of 12 half-inch thick slices from the thickest parts of the tenderloins (you may have some pork remaining; refrigerate for another use). Salt and pepper both sides of each medallion. Heat a large, heavy pan over medium-high heat. Add the olive oil and butter and continue heating until the butter has melted, then sear the medallions on both sides and a bit on the edges. Remove to a baking pan, making four groups of three medallions each (the 3 medallions in each group should touch each other and form the shape of a 3-leaf clover). Place a generous crumbling of the feta on top of each group, then sprinkle a portion of the hazelnuts on top of the cheese and bake for 5 to 6 minutes.

To serve, place a grilled pineapple slice on each plate and top with a group of three medallions. Drizzle the balsamic-molasses reduction over the medallions. Serve with a simple rice or pasta dish.

ALTERNATIVELY: If you're willing to make a little greater effort, then substitute the Best Ever Balsamic Sauce (page 68) for the Balsamic-Molasses reduction.

3 tablespoons minced shallots

1 medium onion, chopped

4 cloves garlic, minced

2 tablespoons extra virgin olive oil

3 cups crusty French bread chunks (pulled
   apart into rough 1/2-inch pieces)

8 ounces pork sausage

3 ribs celery, chopped

1 tablespoon crushed fennel seed

1 cup fresh parsley, chopped

2 tablespoons minced fresh rosemary

2 tablespoons minced fresh thyme

2 thick-cut slices bacon, chopped

Salt and hot pepper sauce to taste

1 pork loin roast (about 3-1/2 pounds),
   boned, rolled, and tied

2 cups dry white wine (an inexpensive Pinot
   Blanc or Pinot Gris, for example)

1/2 cup chopped, roasted and
   skinned hazelnuts

Balsamic Reduction Sauce (recipe follows)

Stuffed Pork Roast with Balsamic Reduction Sauce

In a medium-sized heavy-bottomed skillet over medium-high heat, sauté the shallots, onion and garlic in the olive oil, stirring frequently, for 5 minutes, or until the onions are softened. Add the bread pieces, sausage, celery, fennel, parsley, rosemary, thyme and bacon. Cook uncovered, stirring occasionally, until the sausage and bacon have browned, about 10 to 15 minutes. Season with salt and hot pepper sauce.

Untie the roast and unroll on a cutting board. Salt the meat and spread the stuffing over the surface. Re-roll and tie. Salt the exterior, then return the rolled and stuffed roast to the skillet and brown on 3 sides before transferring it to a lightly oiled roasting pan. Pour in the wine and roast for 30 minutes in a preheated 425 degree F oven. Lower the heat to 350 degrees and roast until the internal temperature of the meat is 150 degrees, which will take between 60 and 90 minutes. Baste occasionally with the pan juices.

Remove from the oven, cover with foil and allow the roast to rest for 10 minutes. Meanwhile, deglaze the pan with 1/4 cup of water, then pour these juices into the heavy-bottomed pot in which you are going to prepare the sauce as directed below.

To serve, slice the roast into generous servings and drizzle each slice with some of the Balsamic Reduction Sauce. Sprinkle a handful of the chopped hazelnuts onto the sauce and around on the plate.

BEVERAGE THOUGHTS: Even though the pork is roasted with a dry white wine, my choice for drinking is a spicy, fruity Syrah, such as a Nuthatch Seven Hills Vineyard, because it compliments the spice of that sausage-flavored filling. A full, round and nutty brown ale, such as Rogue's Hazelnut Brown Nectar, is a lovely offering as well.

The well-fed pig

A few savvy local farmers have been supplementing their hogs' diets with hazelnuts. The resulting meat is sought after by regional chefs and sausage makers who appreciate the rich flavor a nut diet creates. It's a practice with a past that has spanned centuries and oceans. In Italy, the luscious Prosciuto di Parma comes from pigs that have thrived on chestnuts and whey. Spain's much-prized Iberico ham is the result of free-range hogs that have access to acorns.

And so, in an industry where commercial pork is mostly bred for leanness, the chops and roasts from a nut-fed pig produce an entirely different beast; one with just the right amount of marbling, which leads to exquisite flavor and juiciness.

Makes about 3/4 cup

1-1/4 cup balsamic vinegar

1/4 cup juice from deglazed pork roast pan (page 155)

4 tablespoons butter

Balsamic Vinegar Reduction Sauce for Stuffed Pork

Add the balsamic vinegar to the pot into which you have poured the cooking juices from the roast. Bring this to a boil. While the vinegar mixture is boiling, cut the butter into small chunks. After the mixture has been reduced by 2/3 (you will have about 1/2 cup left), add the chunks of butter one by one, stirring thoroughly after each addition. Do not add another chunk of butter until the previous chunk has thoroughly melted.

QuickTIP

Just about anything I bring off the grill is complimented by the nature of hazelnuts. So I've learned to garnish the platter with a handful of roasted hazelnuts just before bringing it to the table. It's a smooth move that hasn't really been done much. But it works, because the earthy-toasty character within the nut forms a rich layer of flavor—a bridge, if you will—between the freshly grilled meat and accompanying side dishes. An integrative measure like this steps up the quality of the meal as a whole.

Makes 6 servings

1 (3 rib) standing rib roast (about 7 pounds)

Olive oil

Salt and pepper

1 medium carrot

1 medium onion

3 stalks celery

1 tablespoon coarsely chopped fresh ginger

4 large cloves garlic, coarsely chopped

1/3 cup balsamic vinegar

1/3 cup Madeira (or dry sherry)

3/4 cup chicken broth (canned is okay)

3/4 cup beef broth (canned is okay)

2 teaspoons prepared horseradish

1/2 cup chopped roasted and
        skinned hazelnuts

1/4 cup butter (optional)

Prime Rib Roast with Balsamic-Madeira Au Jus

This is an exquisite offering. The hazelnuts truly are a remarkable layer of flavor, bringing a sophisticated crunch and toasty goodness. You won't be disappointed by this dish! Serve with Yukon Mashed potatoes, or baked potatoes, and some simple vegetable of the season, such as lightly steamed green beans or asparagus.

Remove the meat from the refrigerator 1 hour ahead of roasting so it can come to room temperature for even roasting. If the butcher hasn't done so, be sure to bind the roast with twine at two points (between the bones). If left untied the outer layer of meat will pull away from the ribeye muscle during roasting and overcook.

Preheat the oven to 450 degrees F.

Rub the beef with some olive oil, then season it throughly with salt and pepper on all sides. Place the beef on a roasting rack in a roasting pan, ribs down, fat side up. Put it in the oven and after 10 minutes reduce the temperature to 350 degrees. For medium-rare the roast will take about 90 minutes and a meat thermometer should read 125 to 130 degrees when you remove it from the oven. Its temperature will continue to rise another 5 degrees while it rests. For medium, the meat thermometer should read 135 to 140 degrees when the roast is ready to be removed from the oven.

While the beef is roasting, prepare the balsamic-Madeira au jus. Coarsely chop the carrot to measure about 1/2 cup and place it in the workbowl of a food processor. Repeat with the onion and celery, placing each chopped vegetable into the food processor along with the carrot. Add the fresh ginger and the garlic. Finely chop the vegetables using the pulse button on the food processor. Scrape the mixture into a bowl and set aside. In a medium-sized heavy-bottomed pot, over medium-high heat, bring the balsamic vinegar and Madeira to a boil. Simmer until it is reduced by half and has thickened. Add the chicken and beef broths, along with the finely chopped vegetables. Bring the mixture back to a boil, then reduce the heat to a simmer, cover, and cook until the vegetables are very soft and have almost dissolved into the broth. This will take about 30 minutes. Remove from heat and stir in the horseradish.

If you are beginning with whole raw hazelnut kernels, you can roast them in a small baking pan along with the roast; this will only take about 20 minutes, so keep an eye on them. When they're a rich golden brown and most of the skins have cracked, remove them from the oven and let them cool thoroughly, then remove the skins. Then chop them up and set them aside.

QuickTIP

Use raw hazelnuts (not roasted) for coating meats and fish before grilling, broiling, or frying. Roasted hazelnuts will burn before the meat or fish has had a chance to cook.

When the roast has reached the correct degree of doneness, remove it from the oven and let it stand for 10 minutes so its juices can redistribute evenly. Place it on a carving board. If you are lucky enough to have pan juices from the roast, then spoon off all the grease and pour the Balsamic-Madeira Aus Jus into the pan, stirring and scraping to dissolve all the cooked-on juices, then pour it back into the pot.

When ready to serve, bring the Balsamic-Madeira Au Jus to a boil. It's delicious as it is, but for an extra level of decadence—if you can stand the calories!—whisk in the 1/4 cup of butter, 1 tablespoon at a time. Keep the au jus hot until the beef is sliced and ready to serve.

To serve, slice the beef. Ladle a portion of the Balsamic-Madeira Au Jus onto the center of each plate. Sprinkle a handful of the chopped hazelnuts onto the sauce (and around on the plate here and there). Lay a serving of the prime rib on top of the sauce.

BEVERAGE THOUGHTS: The Del Rio Rogue Valley Syrah is a noble wine, and a dynamic choice to serve with this dish. It offers subtle layerings of berries and caramel. The touch of tannins and spicy hints of clove and pepper stand up to grilled beef and full-flavored stews. It's a dynamic pairing. For the beer lovers in the group, consider something with a bit of an edge to balance the richness in the beef, such as Ninkasi Brewing's Tricerahops Double IPA, or a finely-crafted amber ale, such as Full Sail's Original Amber Ale.

Jan's Marinated and Grilled Veggies
    (page 125)

Roasted Garlic Vinaigrette (recipe follows)

1 tenderloin of beef (4 to 4-1/2 pounds)

Salt and pepper

6 cups arugula, washed and thoroughly
    dried (use a lettuce spinner if you
    have one)

3 cups vine-ripened red cherry tomatoes,
    halved

3 cups vine-ripened yellow cherry tomatoes

QuickTIP

For a fast and fancy way to jazz up a platter of grilled steaks, combine dark-roasted chopped hazelnuts and Oregon Blue cheese and simply sprinkle on top of the steaks just as they come off the grill.

Tenderloin of Beef with Grilled Veggies, Arugula and Cherry Tomatoes in Roasted Garlic Vinaigrette

This makes a wonderful late-summer meal, when the tomatoes come straight out of a nearby garden and new-crop garlic is easily obtained. Perhaps you've noticed a recurring theme in my recipes: arugula and hazelnuts are a dynamic duo. If you want to introduce a starchy side dish to the plate, consider the Mashed Yukon Gold Potatoes with Caramelized Onions (page 129), or the Fingerling Potatoes (page 128).

About 2 hours before grilling the beef, prepare Jan's Marinated & Grilled Veggies, but substitute 1 cup of the Roasted Garlic Vinaigrette for the marinade. Add the 1 cup of hazelnuts, as directed, just before serving.

Remove the tenderloin from the refrigerator 30 minutes before grilling to allow it to reach room temperature for even cooking. Season it with salt and pepper, then grill over hot coals, turning once. For medium-rare the tenderloin will take about 20 to 25 minutes to cook and a meat thermometer should read 125 to130 degrees F when you remove it from the grill. Its internal temperature will continue to rise another 5 degrees while it rests. Allow it to cool a bit (for about 25 minutes) before serving. The tenderloin may be grilled up to 2 days ahead and refrigerated whole until you're ready to use it.

To serve, arrange a small handful of the arugula in the center of each dinner plate, then drizzle with some of the Roasted Garlic Vinaigrette. Cut the tenderloin into thin slices and arrange servings on each plate, on top of the arugula. Place the tomatoes in a bowl and toss with some of the vinaigrette, then divide them between the plates, arranging them alongside, rather than atop, the arugula. Place a serving of the Grilled Veggies & Hazelnuts on the other side of the plate, opposite the tomatoes. Serve additional vinaigrette at the table.

BEVERAGE THOUGHTS: All flavor components of this lovely meal—the beef, the arugula, the mellowed garlic, the roasted hazelnuts and vegetables—point toward a full bodied and fruity Pinot Noir. Some of my favorites from right around me in the mid-Willamette Valley include gems made by Tyee Wine Cellars, Lumos, Airlie (their Dunn Forest Vineyard, especially), Spindrift, and Belle Vallée.

3 heads of garlic, unpeeled

3 tablespoons extra virgin olive oil

2 teaspoons Dijon mustard

1/3 cup red-wine vinegar

1/3 cup balsamic vinegar

Salt and pepper

1-1/2 cups olive oil

Roasted Garlic Vinaigrette

Cut the top 1/4-inch off of each head of garlic (the stem end, not the root end). On a large square of foil, pour 3 puddles of olive oil, then plop each head down into one of the puddles, cut-side down. Loosely wrap the foil up around the sides of the garlic, leaving it open at the top. Roast the garlic in a 350 degree F oven for 30 to 45 minutes, or until very soft when pressed on the side. Unwrap the garlic heads and let them cool thoroughly for easier handling; reserve the foil with the olive oil to use in the vinaigrette. Squeeze the roasted garlic bulbs from each head. Add the bulbs to a blender or food processor and blend together with the mustard, vinegars, salt and pepper. With motor running, add the reserved olive oil from the foil, scraping as much of the cooked-on bits of garlic as you can into the blender.

Continue adding the remaining 1-1/4 cups of oil in a very thin stream and blend until the mixture is creamy and slightly thickened. This vinaigrette may be made up to one week ahead and chilled in a tightly sealed jar.

Four 6-ounce filet mignons (preferably
    of Angus beef), at room temperature
Salt and freshly ground black pepper
Hazelnut Hummus with Sautéed Shallots,
    Garlic and Carrots (recipe follows),
    warmed
Yukon Gold Potato chips (recipe follows)
Horseradish Sauce (recipe follows)
Roasted Tomatoes and Shallots
    (recipe follows)

Filet Mignon with Hazelnut Hummus and Homemade Yukon Gold Potato Chips

Hummus and beef? Sounds almost like a contradiction in terms, but I added depth to the al-ready-flavorful Freddy-Guys Hazelnut Hummus from Chapter 4 by puréeing it with sautéed shallots, carrots and garlic. By placing a serving of it beneath each perfectly grilled steak, the juices from the beef mingle with the hummus and form a third level of delicious flavor.

If you want to serve a crowd, consider roasting or grilling a whole tenderloin of beef instead of individual steaks, and then just slice right before serving and arrange onto individual plates so each diner gets some of the beef juices.

Don't be overwhelmed by the steps in this dish. Both sauces, as well as the home-fried potato chips and roasted tomatoes, can be prepared in advance, so timing is simple and stress-free.

Cook the steaks as desired, either over a hot charcoal grill or gas grill, or in a lightly buttered, heavy-bottomed frying pan over medium-high heat. Season the filets just before cooking with salt and pepper to taste. Grill for approximately 2 to 3 minutes on each side for medium rare, depending on how thick they are.

To serve, spread some of the hummus in the center of each plate. Place a hot fillet on top of the hummus. Top each steak with a handful of the warm potato chips. Accompany each serving with a spoonful of the Horseradish Sauce (contained, if possible, in small sauce dishes), and a serving of the Roasted Tomatoes and Shallots.

BEVERAGE THOUGHTS: I've enjoyed this dish with a Belle Vallée Rogue Valley Syrah. Its rich berry and plum character comes alive amidst the grilled beef, toasty-garlicky hummus, and caramelized home-fried Yukon golds. If you can get your hands on a Nuthatch Syrah, Walla Walla Valley, that would be most excellent as well. However, it's another case where you simply can't go wrong with a full-bodied Oregon Pinot Noir. An interesting craft beer would be an India pale ale, such as Ninkasi Brewing's Total Domination IPA, or a rich but refreshing amber ale, such as Widmer Brother's Drop Top.

3/4 cup peeled and chopped shallots

1/2 cup peeled and chopped carrot

4 cloves garlic, minced

3 tablespoons extra virgin olive oil

1/3 cup water

2 cups Barb's Hazelnut Hummus (page 64)

2 tablespoons ponzu sauce

1/4 teaspoon salt

1/4 teaspoon freshly ground black pepper

1/8 teaspoon cayenne

Hazelnut Hummus with Sautéed Shallots, Garlic and Carrots

Remember that fabulous Hazelnut Hummus in Chapter Four? Here's a really fabulous way to use it. I've enriched its flavor profile with the sautéed shallots, carrot and garlic, so it really works with beef and horseradish.

In a skillet, gently sauté the carrots, shallots and garlic with the olive oil over medium heat for about 2 minutes, stirring occasionally. Add the water, cover, and gently simmer until the carrots are very tender, about 6 to 7 minutes. Remove lid and continue cooking until the liquid has reduced and almost completely evaporated (there will be a bit of moisture remaining), without browning or scorching the vegetables. Remove from heat and cool.

Meanwhile, place Barb's Hummus in a blender jar, along with the ponzu sauce, salt, pepper, and cayenne. Scrape in the cooled vegetables (use a rubber spatula so that you get every bit of flavor from the pan) into the blender and purée until smooth. May be prepared several days ahead, covered, and refrigerated. To reheat, either bake, covered, in a 300 degree oven, or reheat in the microwave just until heated through.

Makes 4 servings as a garnish

3 cups vegetable oil for deep-frying
2 large Yukon Gold potatoes,
    cut into 1/8-inch thick slices
    (soaked in water until ready to fry,
    then patted dry on a clean kitchen
    towel)
Salt

Yukon Gold Potato Chips

These are really delicious alongside (or atop) a freshly-grilled steak. In fact, even though they're designed as a garnish, you might consider doubling the recipe and serving them as a bonafide side dish.

Heat the oil to 375 degrees F in a Dutch oven or large, heavy-bottomed pot (or deep fryer). Drop about half of the potatoes into the hot oil and cook, stirring with tongs to keep them cooking evenly and not sticking together, until golden brown. Remove this first batch with a slotted spoon and transfer them to paper towels to drain. Sprinkle with salt to taste. Repeat with the remaining potatoes. Keep warm in a low oven if serving immediately. May be made up to 24 hours ahead and gently re-heated.

Makes 1-1/2 cups

1/3 cup chopped celery
1/8 teaspoon paprika
3 tablespoons prepared "extra-hot"
    horseradish (not the "creamy" style)
1 tablespoon minced garlic
1-1/2 teaspoons fresh lemon juice
1 tablespoon ketchup
1 tablespoon Dijon mustard
1 tablespoon Worcestershire sauce
1-1/2 teaspoons red wine vinegar
3/4 cup good-quality mayonnaise
    (such as Best Foods/Hellmann's)

Horseradish Sauce

Combine all of the ingredients in a blender. Blend until smooth. Will keep, covered and refrigerated, for 2 to 3 weeks.

3 tablespoons extra virgin olive oil

4 Roma tomatoes, each cut into 6 wedges

2 garlic cloves, chopped

2 shallots, peeled and halved

4 sprigs of fresh thyme

10 fresh basil leaves (stack them together,
    roll them and then slice thinly
    into shreds)

Salt and freshly ground pepper

Roasted Tomatoes and Shallots

Preheat oven to 400 degrees F.

In a medium-sized roasting pan or baking dish, combine the olive oil, tomatoes, garlic, shallots, thyme, basil, salt, and pepper, tossing to coat the tomatoes with the olive oil. Roast until the tomatoes are soft but not falling apart, about 20 to 25 minutes. May be prepared earlier in the day and gently reheated.

Makes 6 servings

About 2-1/2 pounds flank steak
(see note below)

About 2 cups of an herbed vinaigrette
(see note below)

1 bunch fresh, young arugula leaves,
washed and stemmed (3 to 4 cups)

About 3/4 cup of shaved Parmesan

1-1/2 cups coarsely chopped darkly-roasted
and skinned hazelnuts

Good quality extra virgin olive oil
(see note below)

Kosher salt

Balsamic Glazed Cipolini Onions with
Pancetta, Hazelnuts and Rosemary
(page 119)

Mashed Yukon Golds
(page 129; omit the caramelized onions
in the recipe)

Green Beans with Hazelnuts and Thyme
(page 121)

Herbed and Grilled Beef with Green Beans, Hazelnuts and Thyme

Sliced and served on a bed of arugula with olive oil, kosher salt, darkly roasted hazelnuts and fresh-shaved Parmesan.

Marinate the flank steak in the vinaigrette for several hours.

When ready to cook, prepare a hot fire in a gas or charcoal grill. Cook the steak to desired degree of doneness. Remove from heat to a warm platter and allow to rest for about 5 minutes. Meanwhile, in a bowl, toss the arugula together with the Parmesan shavings, the hazelnuts, some olive oil and a sprinkling of Kosher salt.

NOTE ON HERBED VINAIGRETTE: Consider using the Hazelnut Vinaigrette (page 100) or the Dijon Vinaigrette (page 113), adding about a tablespoon of mixed fresh herbs, such as thyme, rosemary, and oregano. Alternatively, if you have a batch of Jan's Amazing Vinaigrette Base on hand (page 96), then combine 1 cup of it with 1 cup of extra virgin olive oil, along with a tablespoon of mixed fresh herbs, such as thyme, rosemary, and oregano.

On the other hand, for simplicity you could start with a commercial vinaigrette straight from the bottle, and jazz it up with the same collection of fresh herbs.

NOTE ON STEAK: For an even more elegant meal, consider using a beef tenderloin instead of flank steak.

NOTE ON OLIVE OIL: Use the fruitiest, most flavorful extra virgin olive oil you can afford, because it really can boost your offering to the sublime.

To serve, cut the flank steak into 1/4- to 1/2-inch thick slices (remember, for the most tenderness, cut the meat across the grain, and at a slight angle). On each plate, arrange a portion of the arugula mixture and then layer on a few slices of the steak. Accompany with the Mashed Yukon Gold Potatoes, the Balsamic Glazed Onions and Green Beans with Hazelnuts and Thyme.

BEVERAGE THOUGHTS: The Griffin Creek Merlot brings a lively essence of pepper and spice to the nose. One sip and the classic varietal flavors of red currant, rich plum and luscious blackberries tapdance on your palate. The tannins are relatively soft, but are sturdy enough to stand up to this richly flavored presentation for beef, be it the deelish flank steak or a great platter of juicy tenderloins. An interesting beer would be Rogue Ale's Captain Sig's Northwestern Ale, which brings a slightly citrusy-floral hop flavor that's tamed with a rich malt goodness that stands up beautifully to the meat.

Summer Vegetable Sauté

1 tablespoon butter

1 cup fresh corn kernels

1 cup blanched green beans or sugar snap
   peas (pick tender young ones)

2 tablespoons chopped red bell pepper

2 tablespoons chopped sweet onion

Salt and pepper to taste

Heat the butter in a skillet. Add the corn and sauté just until tender, about 3 minutes. Add the green beans (or snap peas), bell pepper and sweet onion and continue to sauté until the vegetables are heated through. Add salt and pepper and set aside.

2 (8-rib) racks of lamb

    (approximately 1-1/2 pounds each)

Salt and pepper

2 tablespoons extra virgin olive oil

1/2 cup Dijon mustard

3 tablespoons chopped fresh mint

3 tablespoons dry sherry

2 tablespoons firmly packed brown sugar

2 tablespoons chopped shallots

    or yellow onion

1 tablespoon chopped fresh garlic

1/2 teaspoon freshly ground black pepper

Hazelnut Hollandaise sauce (page 61)

1-1/2 to 2 cups of coarsely chopped

    darkly roasted and skinned hazelnuts

BEVERAGE THOUGHTS: A full-bodied Oregon Pinot Noir is not only a classic pairing with lamb and mustard, it's also dynamic. Enjoy!

Roast Rack of Lamb with a Mustard Glaze and Hazelnut Hollandaise

Hazelnut-flavored hollandaise sauce is a classic and a dynamic compliment to lamb. In this case, I'm actually calling for a beurre noisette, which in French, literally means "hazelnut butter." For a truly special occasion, this would be a marvelous choice. If your butcher won't French-trim the lamb, just follow my directions below.

Preheat the oven to 425 degrees F. Adjust the oven shelf to a lower-middle position and place a shallow roasting pan on the shelf to preheat. Remove and discard the fat covering from the meat portion of the racks, which is known as the cap. Remove any additional fat and membrane from the bones, scraping them as clean as possible. This is known as French-trimming and your butcher may agree to do this for you.

Season the lamb with salt and pepper. Heat the oil in a large, heavy-bottomed skillet over medium-high heat. Sear the lamb on both sides in the skillet. Remove the racks from the skillet and place them in the preheated roasting pan, meaty sides up, and the bones curving upwards.

Place the mustard, mint, sherry, brown sugar, shallots, garlic and black pepper in a blender or small food processor and blend until smooth. Divide this mixture between both racks, spreading it evenly over the top and sides of each portion.

For medium-rare the racks will take 12 to 20 minutes to cook and a meat thermometer should read 125 to130 degrees when they are removed from the oven. Cover with foil and allow to rest 5 minutes before cutting. The internal temperature will continue to rise another 3 to 5 degrees during this time.

While the lamb is roasting, make the Hazelnut Hollandaise; keep warm in the top of a double boiler over barely simmering water.

To serve, after the lamb has rested for 5 minutes, carve down between the ribs, producing individual chops. Each person will have 3 to 4 chops, which is plenty. Ladle a portion of the hollandaise sauce in the center of each plate, top with 3 or 4 of the chops and a sprinkling of chopped hazelnuts.

FABULOUS FISH

Since this book originates in wild Chinook salmon territory, why begin with anything else? With its exquisite, rich flavor, deep orange-red color and dense-yet-tender texture, wild chinook represents everything that's right with life in the Pacific Northwest. Farm-raised doesn't even come close in quality. So if you fancy yourself a salmon lover, getting your hands on a wild Chinook when it's available is a must. Even with the slightly heftier price tag attached.

After all, wild salmon are a prized commodity. From the Sacramento River drainage north throughout Oregon, Washington, British Columbia and Alaska, it wasn't long ago that these fish teemed in most of the west's coastal rivers. For eons, salmon have returned to these rivers, battling their way upstream to spawn and die; an annual rite that sustained bears, eagles and Native American tribes for generations.

But as any aware person living here knows, wild salmon are at risk. Their habitats are being altered or destroyed. They're also threatened through forced competition with hatchery-bred fish for spawning grounds and rearing habitat. When the two lines interbreed, future generations of wild salmon could be weakened through the perpetuation of bad genetics.

Take just one river, the Columbia. Back in 1805, when Lewis and Clark first witnessed the run, biologists estimate that at least 192 separate salmon and steelhead trout populations spawned in this vast river system, representing roughly 10 million to 16 million fish. Yet at the beginning of this new century, 67 of those populations are extinct, 36 are highly endangered, and 50 more are at risk.

So how does eating wild salmon help the wild salmon? For one thing, since wild salmon cost more per pound at the fish counter than "farmed" salmon, it proves that there's a market for them, which supports the fishermen willing to go out and catch them. And by keeping wild salmon in the market we're essentially keeping political pressure on society to protect and restore habitat needed for wild salmon runs.

Well, you don't need hazelnuts to enjoy salmon and all the other wonderful fish from this part of the world. But my, oh my, are you ever missing a bet if you don't take advantage of their combined culinary potential.

Salmon in Clarified Brown Butter with Hazelnut Sauce

Makes 4 servings

4 wild salmon fillets (about 5 ounces each)

Flour

1/3 cup clarified brown butter
(follow first steps in the
Hazelnut Hollandaise, page 61)

Salt and white pepper to taste

2 finely minced cloves garlic

1 tablespoon minced shallot

1/3 cup ground roasted and
skinned hazelnuts

Juice of 1/2 lemon

1/3 cup Madeira

1/2 cup fish stock, fish bouillon,
or chicken broth

1/2 teaspoon Dijon mustard

3/4 cup heavy cream

1 tablespoon Frangelico (hazelnut liqueur)

Dredge the salmon fillets in the flour. Heat the clarified brown butter in a large, heavy-bottomed skillet over medium-high heat, then brown both sides of the salmon fillets in the butter. Add salt and white pepper to taste.

When browned on both sides, add the minced garlic, shallots, ground hazelnuts, and the lemon juice. Cook until the garlic and shallots have softened a bit, about 30 seconds. Deglaze the pan with the Madeira and fish stock by scraping and dissolving all the cooked on bits of food.

When the salmon fillets are cooked through (another few minutes) to your preferred degree of doneness, remove them to a warm plate. Stir in the mustard and heavy cream and bring the sauce to a simmer, cooking until it reduces slightly and thickens. Add the frangelico and heat through for about 30 seconds. Drizzle the sauce over the fillets and serve.

NOTE ON CLARIFIED BROWN BUTTER: In French, a brown butter is called beurre noisette, which translates into "hazelnut butter." It brings an exquisite flavor to the fish. You make clarified brown butter the same way you'd make plain clarified butter, but you cook it for a longer period so that the milk solids have a chance to brown and produce a wonderful nutty flavor in the butter, even after the solids are strained off. The advantage of cooking with clarified butters is that they can be used at higher temperatures without scorching.

BEVERAGE THOUGHTS: This rich and succulent presentation for salmon, with the nutty, creamy sauce, is wonderful with a soft, medium-bodied Pinot Noir or a buttery, oakey Chardonnay. And I wouldn't hesitate for a minute to bring out my favorite hazelnut-friendly ale, Rogue's Hazelnut Brown Nectar.

QuickTIP

A quick way to jazz up a dinner of grilled or roasted salmon (or halibut, albacore, sturgeon, or ling cod), is to provide a side serving of Tomato-Ginger-Hazelnut Salad (page 185).

2 firmly packed cups fresh baby spinach

2 firmly packed cups fresh baby arugula

1 tablespoon butter or olive oil

1 cup chopped onion

1 teaspoon minced fresh garlic

1/2 cup coarsely chopped roasted
and skinned hazelnuts

3 tablespoons unseasoned dry bread crumbs

1/4 teaspoon salt

1/4 teaspoon freshly ground black pepper

Pinch of freshly grated nutmeg

3 ounces feta, crumbled

4 whole trout (about 5 ounces each),
dressed, heads and tail intact
or removed

1 tablespoon olive oil

Roasted Trout Stuffed with Arugula, Spinach, Hazelnuts, and Feta

Being somewhat neutral in flavor, trout benefits from this treatment. The stuffing adds flavor and moisture, while the high roasting temperature produces a crunchy exterior.

Preheat oven to 500 degrees F.

Arrange a lightly oiled rack that is large enough to hold all 4 trout in the bottom of a roasting pan. If you don't own such a rack, don't worry about it, just lightly oil the roasting pan.

Bring a large pot of salted water to a boil. Add the spinach and arugula and blanch just for 10 seconds. Remove from heat, drain, and plunge the greens into cold water to stop the cooking and set the color. When the spinach and arugula are thoroughly chilled, drain and squeeze the leaves to remove all of the moisture.

Melt the butter (or heat the olive oil) in a small skillet over medium heat. Add the onion and garlic, and sauté until soft and the onion is turning lightly golden, about 5 to 7 minutes; let cool.

Combine the cooled onion mixture with the spinach, arugula, hazelnuts, and breadcrumbs. Season with salt, pepper and nutmeg, and toss the mixture to combine well. Add the feta and toss again, just to distribute the cheese into the stuffing.

Stuff each trout with one-fourth of the spinach mixture. The fish should be plump without bursting with filling. Brush the outside of the fish lightly with olive oil, sprinkle with additional salt and pepper, and place on the prepared rack, or on the bottom of the pan .

Roast the trout in the preheated oven. (Alternatively, if you have a way to grill the fish using indirect heat, then place the prepared pan with the trout on your grill.) Cook until the flesh no longer springs back when gently poked at the thickest part, about 15 to 20 minutes. Remove from oven or grill and gently lift each fish from the pan and serve immediately.

BEVERAGE THOUGHTS: Consider a Pinot Blanc that is somewhat crisp, so that it cuts through and balances the feta, but with a soft finish, which would compliment the smokiness in the arugula.

1/2 cup finely chopped raw hazelnuts

1/2 cup shredded extra-aged Gouda

2 tablespoons chopped fresh chives,
     divided

1 tablespoon chopped fresh thyme

1 tablespoon chopped fresh Italian parsley

4 (6 to 8 ounces each) fresh halibut steaks

Salt and pepper to taste

About 4 tablespoons extra virgin olive oil,
     divided

Goat Cheese-Garlic Butter (recipe follows)

Mashed Yukon Golds with Caramelized
     Onions (page 129)

For garnish: 1/2 cup coarsely chopped or
     crushed roasted and skinned hazelnuts

Halibut with Hazelnut Crust of Gouda and Herbs with Mashed Yukon Golds with Caramelized Onions

Preheat the oven to 400 degrees F.

Combine the raw hazelnuts with the Gouda, 1 tablespoon of the chives, thyme, and parsley; set aside.

Season each halibut steak with salt and pepper. Warm a non-stick skillet over medium-high heat. Add about 2 tablespoons of the olive oil to the skillet. When the oil is hot, add the halibut and sear until golden brown on both sides.

Meanwhile, drizzle the remaining 2 tablespoons of olive oil into a shallow baking dish (approximately 9 x 13-inch). Transfer the browned fish to the dish. Sprinkle the hazelnut mixture evenly over the top of the fish and bake just until it is slightly firm to the touch, which will only take 5 to 8 minutes.

Remove the dish from the oven and top each steak with a dollop of the Goat Cheese-Garlic Butter.

To serve, place a serving of the mashed potatoes in the center of each plate and top with one of the halibut steaks. To garnish, sprinkle some of the coarsely chopped hazelnuts and remaining chives around the edge of each plate.

3 tablespoons softened butter

3 tablespoons goat cheese

2 teaspoons finely minced shallot

1 teaspoon finely minced fresh
     Italian parsley

1 finely minced clove of garlic

1/4 teaspoon finely minced fresh thyme

1/4 teaspoon finely minced fresh chives

1/4 teaspoon salt

Goat Cheese-Garlic Butter

Combine the butter, goat cheese, shallot, parsley, garlic, thyme, chives, and salt in a small bowl. Refrigerate until ready to use.

3 tablespoons Dijon mustard

2 tablespoons ponzu sauce

3 tablespoons melted butter

1 tablespoon honey

1/3 cup finely chopped lightly roasted
    and skinned hazelnuts

1/4 cup panko bread crumbs (or homemade,
    unseasoned dry bread crumbs)

1 tablespoon lightly toasted sesame seeds

About 1/8 teaspoon each salt and freshly
    ground white pepper

1 to 1-1/2 pounds of fresh halibut steak or
    fillets (skin and bones removed),
    rinsed and patted dry

About 3 cups of fresh baby arugula

1/4 cup freshly grated Parmesan cheese

1 tablespoon extra virgin olive oil

Hot Mustard Butter Sauce (page 184)

Mashed Yukon Golds with
    Caramelized Onions (page 129)

Additional chopped hazelnuts for garnish

Grilled Halibut Steaks with Dijon Mustard and Honey Topping on Hot Mustard Butter Sauce

Preheat a gas or charcoal grill to medium-high. Create a foil pan for the fish by folding two layers of heavy-duty foil into a rectangle (with a 1-inch rim all around) that is large enough to hold the pieces of fish.

In a small bowl, whisk together the Dijon, ponzu sauce, butter and honey; set aside. In another bowl, combine the hazelnuts, panko, sesame seeds, salt, and pepper.

Place the halibut in the center of the foil pan. Spread the mustard mixture on top of the fish, then sprinkle on the hazelnut topping, pressing it down into the mustard mixture so it will be anchored to the surface.

Place the fish on the grill, close, and cook until the halibut has just begun to turn opaque. Figure on about 10 minutes of cooking per inch of thickness. Remove to a warmed platter.

While the fish is grilling, place the arugula in a small bowl with the Parmesan cheese and drizzle on the olive oil, tossing to coat the greens evenly; set aside.

To serve, spoon a portion of the Hot Mustard Butter Sauce onto the center of each dinner plate, and top with a portion of halibut. Add a serving of the Creamy Mashed Potatoes on one side, and a serving of the Arugula on the other. Sprinkle the greens with a garnish of hazelnuts.

BEVERAGE THOUGHTS: This recipe has a lot of spice and richness to it that works beautifully with a dry-style Gewürztraminer or a Viognier. A fruity Southern Oregon Syrah, or a fruity, light-bodied Pinot Noir are lovely choices also. In the world of craft beers, consider anything from a light and slightly fruity pale ale, over to a richer and rounder brown ale.

1 cup Veri Veri Teriyaki sauce
    (made by Soy Vay; see note below)

1/2 cup dry sherry or extra-dry vermouth

1/3 cup fresh lemon juice

1 tablespoon chili garlic sauce
    (my favorite brand is Lee Kum Kee)

1/3 cup extra virgin olive oil

1-1/2 to 2 pounds fresh sturgeon
    (or other firm-fleshed fish,
    such as Pacific albacore or halibut)

About 2 tablespoons Dijon mustard

1/2 cup chopped roasted and skinned
    hazelnuts

Pacific Rim Mushroom Sauce (recipe follows)

Mashed Yukon Golds with
    Caramelized Onions

Lightly steamed French-cut green beans

Additional chopped hazelnuts for garnish

Grilled Sturgeon with Pacific Rim Mushroom Sauce

In a dish or re-sealable plastic bag large enough to hold the fish, combine the teriyaki sauce, sherry, lemon juice, chili garlic sauce, and olive oil. This can be prepared several days ahead and refrigerated until you are ready to marinate the fish.

Place the fish in the marinade, close the container and refrigerate for 3 to 6 hours.

Preheat the grill to 375 degrees F. While the grill is heating, form a foil pan using two layers of heavy-duty aluminum foil. Make the pan just slightly larger than the fish, with a 1-inch rim. Place the fish in the center of the pan. Spread its surface with the Dijon mustard, then sprinkle on the hazelnuts. Spoon some of the marinade on top, so that most of the hazelnuts are flavored with the marinade.

Place the fish on the grill, close the cover, and cook until the fish feels relatively firm to the touch, but is still tender—about 10 minutes per inch of thickness. Mid-way through the cooking, spoon a bit more of the marinade over the top and discard the rest. When the fish is done, remove the pan from the grill.

To serve, spoon about 1/3 cup of the Pacific Rim Mushroom Sauce into the center of each dinner plate. Top with a serving of the hot sturgeon, and add a serving of potatoes and a few green beans to the side. Garnish around the edges with a sprinkling of chopped hazelnuts.

ABOUT VERI VERI TERIYAKI SAUCE: This is a heavenly marinade produced by Soy Vay. It's only drawback is that it has become kind of expensive. My last purchase was about $6 for a 21 ounce bottle. But you are only going to use 8 ounces of that, which means you have a whole lot left over for other meals. Not convinced? No worries, use your favorite brand of teriyaki sauce and then, to bring it into the Veri Veri Teriyaki realm, goose the levels of fresh ginger and toasted sesame seeds.

BEVERAGE THOUGHTS: How about a Penner-Ash Viognier? That was my question. The answer, a resounding Yum! The Asian influences in the sauce hummed alongside this lovely white with its gentle pineapple, floral, peachy, tropical notes. With a bit of spice at the end. Another really delicious choice would be Gewürztraminer, which, when made well, is both spicy, citrusy (great with the sturgeon), and floral. There are several wineries here in the mid-Willamette Valley that make delicious ones: Lumos, Tyee, Airlie, Spindrift, and Namaste.

1 tablespoon hazelnut oil

1 tablespoon butter

1/4 pound finely minced mushrooms
    (I use my food processor)

1-1/8 cup Madeira

3/4 cup chicken broth

3 tablespoons rice vinegar

1-1/2 tablespoons tempura sauce
    (if unavailable, use ponzu sauce or
    regular soy sauce)

1 teaspoon chili garlic sauce

1/2 teaspoon instant dashi-no-moto

1-1/2 cups heavy cream

5 tablespoons unsalted butter

1-1/2 tablespoon all-purpose flour

1/2 teaspoon truffle oil
    (optional, but delicious!)

Pacific Rim Mushroom Sauce

This is an amazing sauce that is a fabulous companion to any number of firm-fleshed fish dishes you cook on your grill. Definitely the sturgeon, as noted above. But also grilled Pacific albacore and halibut. I served it to 150 diners at a Tyee wine dinner a few summers ago and it was a real show stopper. You'll be thrilled to have it in your repertoire. Granted, there are a few ingredients that are a little more challenging to run down, and there's the expense of the truffle oil. But, it is worthy of your time and attention.

In a heavy-bottomed pot, warm the oil and butter over medium-high heat. Add the mushrooms and cook until they have browned slightly and the liquid they release has cooked off.

Add the Madeira, chicken broth, rice vinegar, tempura sauce, chili garlic sauce and dashi no-moto. Bring to a boil, then reduce heat and simmer until reduced by half.

Whisk in the cream and continue simmering until reduced by one third; remove from heat.

In another heavy-bottomed pot, melt the butter over medium heat. Whisk in the flour and cook the mixture briefly, to remove the raw flour taste. Slowly whisk in the cream sauce, whisking constantly. Whisk in the truffle oil, if desired.

NOTE: The sauce may be prepared ahead and gently reheated. But don't add the truffle oil until you are reheating the sauce because its flavor is fragile and is greatly reduced by much heating.

ALTERNATIVES ABOUND: This sauce is equally great with grilled scallops, halibut, Pacific albacore, or any other firm-fleshed fish. It's also delicious with grilled chicken or pork tenderloin. If you don't have Madeira, consider substituting 3/4 cup of a dry sherry or dry vermouth. I've also used sake.

White Sturgeon—A Pacific Northwest Treasure

Unknown and underappreciated by many, the white sturgeon is another Pacific Northwest treasure, and a luscious fish to cook with. Particularly on the grill, its meaty-firm texture and gentle flavor make it the perfect choice for so many treatments, from a spicy marinade to a delicate butter sauce. It's an ancient species that is native to the Pacific Coast of North America. Although it cruises ocean waters, estuaries and freshwater rivers from Alaska to Baja, there had been only three river systems in which it is known to spawn: the Sacramento in Northern California, the Columbia, between Oregon and Washington, and the Fraser in British Columbia.

Unfortunately, its numbers have been decreasing. So the recent discovery of a sturgeon spawning ground in the Willamette River between Oregon City and the Columbia River is encouraging news for the struggling species. Good news for cooks, too.

Cooking Albacore

EVERY SUMMER-INTO-FALL, AS SCHOOLS OF ALBACORE are migrating from the coastal waters off Northern California toward British Columbia, local fishing fleets seize the opportunity to bring fresh catches of it ashore. Some weeks it's more challenging than others, because albacore prefer swimming in a water temperature range of 58 to 70 degrees F—even if they have to swim several hundred miles out to sea to find it. Only the larger fishing boats are able to follow, leaving the smaller vessels behind. For this reason, even in-season you can't always expect to find albacore in the market place. It all depends on where the preferred current is flowing. When it swings close, the albacore arrives fast and fresh in stores.

Cooking albacore is really pretty straightforward. First, be sure you're working with outstanding fish. It's gotta be fresh! Since albacore has a tendency to dry out quickly, all albacore cooks agree it should be cooked just until it becomes firm to the touch. Some like to leave the center pink, while others take it just slightly beyond that. It helps to know a little about the different cuts:

WHOLE LOIN: Each albacore has four wedge-shaped loins which radiate out from a central backbone. They taper in thickness, thinning as they approach the tail, and should be totally boneless. They're usually sold skinless, but sometimes one side still has the skin on. If so, cook it skin-side down. Whole loins are a delight to cook with. Think pork tenderloin, only juicier and more tender.

LOIN CUTS: Cross-cut sections of the loins. Like the whole loins, they are boneless and trimmed of the dark meat (which tends to have a stronger flavor).

STEAKS: Cross-cut sections of the fish, which includes the backbone and dark meat located near the backbone. The dark meat tends to be slightly stronger in flavor than the light meat, so you may want to remove it before cooking. The skin is typically removed before serving.

Some of my best summer grills have been centered around fresh, local, line-caught Pacific albacore. Whether loosely draped in foil and poached in wine, lemon, and herbs, or cooked straight over the coals after a brief stint in a teriyaki-style marinade, those exquisitely lean loins always turn out firm yet tender and flavorful.

For a more indirect approach to grilling, you could follow one of my evening delights from a while back. I fashioned a shallow roasting pan out of heavy-duty foil. While the grill was heating up, I finely chopped half a Walla Walla Sweet onion, half a rib of celery, about 6 plump mushrooms, a backyard tomato, and a fresh Serrano chile. I tossed all of those ingredients with some fresh corn kernels I'd just sliced off the cob, a bit of olive oil, a healthy pinch of salt, and an aggressive cranking of black peppercorns. I lay the albacore pieces in the center of the foil pan, rubbed them down with some olive oil, salt and peppered them, then arranged my little fresh salsa mixture all around the fish, letting a little of it hang out on top to flavor the tuna from all angles. After about 40 minutes of indirect heat, dinner was done.

At Harry's Fresh Fish in downtown Corvallis, Oregon, Harry Daughters will happily share his cooking tips with you. One of his tried-and-trues involves a basic marinade of soy sauce, sesame oil, olive oil and fresh ginger, which he says needs at least an hour in contact with a hefty chunk of albacore loin or kabobs (half an hour in the fridge, and half an hour at room temperature). His crowning glory is the addition of fresh peach quarters, skewered alongside the tuna and grilled to perfection.

Beurre Blanc Goes Pacific Rim—
The Ultimate Sauce for Albacore

BEYOND THOUGHTFUL COOKING, albacore tuna doesn't need any special treatment to be delicious. A simple grilling is most certainly an honorable and healthy way to prepare this seasonal delight.

But I tend to take this fish in the direction of the ocean from which it came, the Pacific—as in Pacific Rim cuisine. Something you'd encounter at Aqua Seafood Restaurant in downtown Corvallis, Oregon, which speaks to my own true passion when it comes to the merging of Asian-Hawaiian flavors.

Particularly in the context of albacore tuna.

Thanks to Aqua's owner, Corvallis chef and restauranteur Iain Duncan (Le Bistro, Aqua, Terzo, and Flat Tail Brewing), I've developed a few new and decadent approaches. It begins with a classic butter sauce, beurre blanc. For the uninitiated, beurre blanc is a reduction of white wine and/or vinegar and shallots into which a large amount of butter is whisked, one dollop at a time, until a rich, creamy-yet-tangy sauce is formed. The result? Heaven! Beurre blanc's zippy yet velvety character makes it a perfect compliment to grilled albacore.

For Duncan, that's merely a starting point. One time over coffee I asked him how everyday cooks could inject the same sort of Pacific Rim/Hawaiian regional influences into their nightly menus that he brings to Aqua. One approach, he advised, would be to incorporate a few Asian/Hawaiian elements into said beurre blanc. Shredded bits of fresh ginger, a drop of sesame oil, and a splash of soy sauce, for example. I have discovered this to be an exciting way to achieve Asian-influenced flavors in elegant style when working with albacore.

Two of my results can be found here, the Mustard Butter Sauce and the Spicy Black Bean-Garlic Butter Sauce. Both are spin-offs from a classic beurre blanc. And even though they're certainly rich, the idea is to use them sparingly, as an accent to the grilled or roasted albacore. If you add a third element, such as the Tomato Ginger Relish (also below), or a simple cucumber salad tossed with vinegar, chopped green onion and coarsely ground black pepper, then you lighten the dish even further.

Makes 4 servings

2 pounds of Pacific albacore

2 tablespoons olive oil

About 1/2 teaspoon salt

About 1/4 teaspoon freshly ground
black pepper

Spicy Black Bean-Garlic Butter Sauce
(recipe follows)

Summer Vegetable Sauté (page 169)

QuickTIP

A quick, easy, and flavorful way to coat a piece of fish, chicken, pork, or beef with chopped hazelnuts before cooking is to spread the surface with a mustard of choice, then roll it in a saucer of chopped hazelnuts. Two things happen: the hazelnuts won't fall off during cooking and the flavor adds a delightful bit of zoom to the meat. Remember to use raw nuts if the meat is to be roasted or grilled.

Grilled Albacore with Spicy Black Bean-Garlic Butter Sauce

I serve this with my Summer Vegetable Sauté and roasted potatoes (as pictured). It's also delicious with my Mashed Yukon Potatoes and Green Beans with Roasted Hazelnuts.

When ready to cook, prepare a hot fire in a gas or charcoal grill. When the grate has become hot, brush it with a bit of vegetable oil to keep the fish from sticking. Coat the albacore with the olive oil, then salt and pepper it on all sides. Place the albacore on the oiled grate over the hot fire, close the grill and cook for about 3 minutes per side (if cooking a portion of a whole loin, as opposed to steaks, you should cook it on 3 or 4 sides), or until the fish is just becoming firm and turning opaque when prodded with a fork. Do not overcook; for "medium-rare," the inside should still be pink; for "medium," the inside should just be turning to gray.

To serve, spoon a portion of the black bean sauce onto the center of each dinner plate. Place a serving of the albacore on top of the sauce, then arrange a serving of the potatoes on one side and the beans on the other. Drizzle a little more sauce over the albacore and serve immediately.

OTHER OPTIONS: If you want to marinate the albacore before grilling, use Jan's Teriyaki Marinade (page 184).

BEVERAGE THOUGHTS: This is another case where a dry-but-fruity Gewürztraminer is a heavenly choice. Lumos makes a lovely one, as do Airlie and Spindrift Cellars. A soft-style Pinot Blanc would also bring balance and depth to the meal.

1 tablespoon olive oil

1 teaspoon toasted sesame oil

1 tablespoon finely minced sweet onion

1 teaspoon peeled finely shredded
     fresh ginger

2 teaspoons chili garlic sauce

1 teaspoon ponzu sauce
     (or regular soy sauce)

1 teaspoon black bean garlic sauce

3/4 cup dry white wine

1 tablespoon heavy cream

1/2 cup unsalted butter, cut into
     1/2-inch chunks

Spicy Black Bean-Garlic Butter Sauce

Heat the olive oil with the sesame oil in a heavy-bottomed, medium-sized skillet over medium high heat. Add the sweet onion and ginger and sauté for 1 minute. Stir in the chili-garlic sauce, ponzu sauce, black bean garlic sauce, and the wine. Simmer until reduced by half, which will take about 5 minutes. Whisk in the heavy cream and bring to a boil. Remove from heat. The sauce may be prepared to this point up to 24 hours ahead; cover and refrigerate.

When ready to serve, complete the sauce: First, bring it to a simmer over medium-high heat. Turn the heat to low, then gradually whisk in the chilled pieces of butter, one or two at a time. Keep whisking steadily until all of the butter has been incorporated. Keep the sauce over very low heat (or in the top of a double boiler set over hot water) or the sauce will eventually separate.

Makes 4 to 6 servings

2 to 2-1/2 pounds fresh albacore loin

Jan's Teriyaki Marinade (recipe follows)

1/4 cup butter, cut into 4 chunks

Hot Mustard-Butter Sauce (recipe follows)

**Tomato-Ginger-Hazelnut Salad
     (recipe follows)**

BEVERAGE THOUGHTS: A dry-but-fruity Gewürztraminer is a heavenly choice. Lumos makes a lovely one, as do Airlie and Spindrift Cellars. A soft-style Pinot Blanc would also bring balance and depth to the meal.

Foil-Grilled Albacore with Hot Mustard-Butter Sauce and Tomato-Ginger-Hazelnut Salad

This is my more decadent approach to a simple teriyaki grill. You could cut back on the butter, and it would still be delicious.

Combine the albacore and Jan's Teriyaki Marinade in a dish or re-sealable plastic bag. Refrigerate for at least 1 hour, up to 3 hours; remove 30 minutes before grilling.

When ready to cook the fish, create a foil pan for the fish that is large enough to surround everything and partially enclose the top. Spread open the foil. Remove the albacore from the marinade and place it in the center of the prepared pan. Pour 1/2 cup of the marinade over the fish. Pour the remainder of the marinade, which you will boil before serving, into a pot.

Distribute the four chunks of butter around the sides of the fish, then snuggle the foil up and around the fish, leaving the top open so the fish will poach but not steam over the grill (or in the oven). Cook over hot coals (or in a 375 degree F oven) until the fish is just cooked through, which will take about 30 to 40 minutes, depending on how thick the loin is. Spoon the butter-sauce over of the fish several times during cooking.

Towards the end of the cooking process, bring the reserved marinade to a boil in the pot, then reduce the heat and simmer for 5 minutes. Remove from heat and let cool slightly while you deal with the grilled albacore. Serve the boiled marinade in a small bowl alongside the albacore for people to spoon over their fish as desired.

DIRECT GRILL ALTERNATIVE: For a stronger grilled approach, eliminate the foil pan and simply cook the marinated albacore directly over hot coals or on a gas grill with the cover closed. Brush the fish with some of the marinade during cooking. Serve with the boiled marinade as described above.

SPICY ALTERNATIVE: For an extra special dinner, consider making the Spicy Black Bean-Garlic Butter Sauce (page 182) to serve alongside this dish.

Jan's Teriyaki Marinade

Makes about 2-1/2 cups of marinade, enough for about 2-1/2 pounds of albacore loin

1 cup Veri Veri Teriyaki sauce
(made by Soy Vay—
see note on page 176)
1/2 cup dry sherry or extra-dry vermouth
1/3 cup fresh lemon juice
1 tablespoon chili garlic sauce
(my favorite brand is Lee Kum Kee)
1/3 cup extra virgin olive oil

In a dish or resealable plastic bag large enough to hold the albacore loin, combine the Veri Veri Teriyaki sauce, sherry, lemon juice, chili garlic sauce, and olive oil. This can be prepared several days ahead and refrigerated.

Hot Mustard-Butter Sauce

Team this rich and flavorful butter sauce with the Tomato-Ginger Hazelnut Salad above for a dynamic approach to grilled albacore. The sauce is a spin-off from a classic French butter sauce, beurre blanc.

Makes about 1-1/3 cups of sauce, enough for 2 to 3 pounds of grilled Pacific albacore

2 tablespoons prepared Chinese mustard
(I use Beaver brand "extra hot")
2 tablespoons ponzu sauce
(or regular soy sauce)
1/2 cup dry white wine
1 tablespoon rice vinegar or
white wine vinegar
1-1/2 tablespoons minced shallot
Pinch of ground white pepper
3 tablespoons whipping cream
1/2 cup chilled unsalted butter,
cut into 32 pieces (cut the cube lengthwise into quarters, then cut cross-wise
to produce 32 chunks)

In a small bowl, whisk together the mustard and the ponzu sauce; set aside (you'll be adding it to the butter sauce at the very end of cooking).

In a small pot, combine the wine, vinegar, shallots, and white pepper. Bring to a boil and simmer until it is reduced to about 4 tablespoons (this will only take about 5 or 6 minutes). Whisk in the cream and boil just until it begins to thicken and reduce slightly, about 1 minute. Set the reduction aside until just before serving (refrigerate if delaying more than 1 hour).

When ready to finish the sauce, bring the reduction to a boil. Turn the burner to low, then whisk in the chilled pieces of butter one or two at a time. Keep whisking steadily until all of the butter has been incorporated. Keep the sauce over very low heat (or in the top of a double boiler set over hot water) or the sauce will separate. Whisk in about half of the reserved mustard-ponzu mixture. Taste and then add more of the mustard mixture as desired.

2 cups diced tomato

1/3 cup chopped green onion

1/3 cup minced Walla Walla Sweet onion
(or other sweet onion)

1/4 cup chopped roasted and
skinned hazelnuts

2 tablespoons peeled, minced fresh
ginger root

2 tablespoons mirin (sweet rice wine)

1-1/2 tablespoons black sesame seeds

1-1/2 tablespoons toasted white
sesame seeds

1-1/2 teaspoons coarsely ground
black peppercorns

1 teaspoon salt

1 teaspoon nam pla (fish sauce; optional)

Tomato-Ginger-Hazelnut Salad

Team this fresh tomato-rich salad with the Mustard-Butter Sauce for a dynamic approach to grilled albacore.

Combine the tomatoes, green onion, sweet onion, hazelnuts, fresh ginger, mirin, sesame seeds, ground peppercorns, salt, and nam pla (if using). This can be prepared up to 6 hours ahead (but don't add the hazelnuts until just before serving); cover and refrigerate.

Grilled Albacore in Honey-Soy Marinade with Roasted Hazelnut Slaw

Makes 4 to 6 servings

About 2 pounds of albacore (a portion of a
whole loin, loin cuts, or steaks)

About 1/2 cup orange juice

1/4 cup soy sauce

2 tablespoons peeled and grated
fresh ginger

1 tablespoon honey (or brown sugar)

1/4 cup olive oil

Salt and freshly ground black pepper

Roasted Hazelnut Slaw (page 109)

BEVERAGE THOUGHTS: It's the Roasted Hazelnut Slaw that drives this selection because the slaw brings such exciting elements to the dish, from the toasty nuts to the smoky bacon. With that in mind, I always reach for a lovely Southern Oregon Syrah, which brings a bit of spice, fruit, and soft tannins to the table. Of course, a medium-bodied, fruity Pinot Noir would be lovely too. And if a white wine is needed, consider a barrel-aged Chardonnay to compliment the earthy qualities in the dish. Of course, you'll also want to save some of that Rogue Ale Toasted Hazelnut Brown Nectar that's IN the Roasted Hazelnut Slaw to pour at the table.

This is a spin-off from the approach Harry Daughters likes to do at Harry's Fresh Fish in downtown Corvallis, Oregon. It can be an end unto itself, or a great starting point for any of the butter sauce recipes in this book. The Roasted Hazelnut Slaw is the perfect sidekick: a warm and savory melange of tender-crunchy cabbage, smoky bacon and roasted hazelnuts. You can make it ahead and reheat it gently in a skillet right before serving.

Place the albacore in a dish or re-sealable plastic bag. Combine the orange juice, soy sauce, fresh ginger, honey and olive oil and pour over the tuna. Refrigerate for several hours to marinate.

When ready to cook, prepare a hot fire in a gas or charcoal grill. Brush the grate with a bit of vegetable oil. Ideally, you should use a special grill grate designed with narrower slots or holes in it for fish and cut up vegetables, but because albacore is so firm, it will do pretty well on a regular grate.

Remove the albacore from the marinade and drain slightly. Place the albacore on the grill and cook for about 3 minutes per side (if cooking a portion of a whole loin, you should cook it on 3 or 4 sides), or until the fish is just becoming firm and turning opaque when prodded with a fork. Do not overcook; for "medium-rare," the inside should still be pink; for "medium," the inside should just be turning to gray. Remove from heat and let the albacore sit for about 5 minutes to compose.

To serve, arrange a serving of the Roasted Hazelnut Slaw on the plate, just off-center. Follow with a portion of the albacore, resting partially on top of the slaw. To the side, add a serving of either fingerling potatoes (page 128), or Mashed Yukon Gold Potatoes (page 129) with a garnish of grilled mushrooms and green onions, as described under "Tasty Option", if desired.

TASTY OPTION: Marinate some mushrooms and whole green onions along with the albacore. Grill them in a perforated vegetable grilling pan or improvised foil pan while grilling the albacore.

1-1/4 pound scallops (either bay or
    sea scallops will work)

2 teaspoons Italian seasoning

1/4 teaspoon salt

1/4 teaspoon freshly ground black pepper

8 ounces orzo pasta

2 tablespoons olive oil, divided

1 teaspoon chopped fresh garlic

1/2 pound sugar snap peas, trimmed

1/2 cup chopped lightly roasted and
    skinned hazelnuts, divided

1 tablespoon basil-flavored oil
    (or olive oil with a dollop of pesto
    swirled into it)

Scallops with Hazelnuts and Snap Pea Orzo

This is a great last-minute meal that's really very special. Use very fresh scallops, or scallops that have only been thawed for a few hours.

Rinse the scallops and dry well. Sprinkle the herbs, salt and pepper evenly over the scallops; set aside. Cook the orzo according to package directions, then drain and set aside in a covered pan.

Heat 1 tablespoon of the olive oil in a large skillet over medium heat. Sauté the garlic gently for a minute or so, just to soften, then add the sugar snap peas and 1/4 cup of the hazelnuts. Continue cooking just for another few minutes to heat them through. The peas should maintain their brilliant green color and a bit of their crunch. Spoon them into the pot with the orzo to stay warm.

Re-coat the skillet with the remaining tablespoon of oil and sauté the scallops over medium-high heat for about 2 minutes on each side until opaque and just barely cooked through and lightly browned.

To serve, place the scallops on a plate with the orzo mixture and drizzle a little basil-flavored oil over them. Sprinkle with the reserved 1/4 cup of chopped hazelnuts.

OTHER OPTIONS: With this basic preparation in hand, consider some of the more lively options. For instance, once the scallops have cooked, deglaze the pan with a little of the wine you're serving with the meal, along with a splash of heavy cream. Then, when plating the dish, drizzle around the edges with a simple balsamic sauce that is made by whisking together equal amounts of ponzu sauce, balsamic vinegar, melted butter and ketchup.

BEVERAGE THOUGHTS: This simple, straightforward dish shines bright next to a Lumos Dry Style Gewürztraminer, which actually comes through with a lot of complexity in fruit and spice. Also, an Oregon Pinot Gris that has a nice balance of tropical/citrus/fruit is a nice pairing. These scallops would also be delicious with an aromatic, relatively light wheat beer, such as Pyramid's Haywire Hefeweizen, or Widmer's classic Hefeweizen.

3 tablespoons butter

3 cups sliced mushrooms (about 1/2 pound)

2 cups sliced celery

1-1/2 cups chopped onion

About 1-1/2 teaspoons fresh dillweed, chopped (or 3/4 teaspoon dried dillweed)

3/4 teaspoon salt

1/4 teaspoon white pepper

2 tablespoons Pernod (an anise-flavored liqueur)

2 tablespoons capers, rinsed and drained

1 pound bay scallops, rinsed and drained

1-2/3 cups half and half

1 pound of fettuccini pasta (preferably spinach or herb-flavored)

About 2 tablespoons melted butter

1/4 cup coarsely chopped roasted and skinned hazelnuts

QuickTIP

Hazelnuts roasted in browned butter are great over squash ravioli.

Scallops and Mushroom Sauté with Buttered Fettuccini and Hazelnuts

This is a simple dish for mid-week entertaining! But like I've said before, you can't skate on freshness. Make sure that your scallops are very, very fresh, or have only been thawed for a few hours. There are so many complimentary elements in this dish I don't know where to start. The mushrooms love the hazelnuts and the scallops. The scallops are in good company with the dillweed and Pernod, and the capers just make everything livelier.

Melt the butter in a large skillet and sauté the mushrooms, celery, and onion until the onions are soft and the mushrooms have released their liquid, about 5 minutes. Add the dill, salt, pepper, Pernod and capers and continue cooking until the liquid is almost evaporated. Add the scallops and continue cooking until they begin to turn opaque, about 1 minute. Add the cream and cook until it reduces by about 1/2 and the mixture thickens, about 5 minutes; adjust seasonings.

Meanwhile, cook the fettuccini according to package directions in a large pot of boiling water. Drain, then toss with the butter to coat. Toss again with the hazelnuts before serving.

To serve, on each of four dinner plates, place a serving of pasta, then top with a portion of the scallop mixture. Serve immediately.

NOTE: Pernod is an essential ingredient in this recipe. The faint licorice flavor is a delicious compliment to scallops. Finely chopped fennel leaves or bulb, which also have a faint licorice flavor when cooked would also work.

BEVERAGE THOUGHTS: The earthy qualities within this dish, from the mushrooms to the fennel to the hazelnuts, all work beautifully with medium to full-bodied Oregon Pinot Noirs. Wheat beers are excellent choices for balancing the richness of a cream sauce, but a medium-hopped pale ale with a smooth malt balance, such as Rogue's Juniper Pale Ale, would also be a nice choice.

Makes 6 servings

1 pound rock shrimp, peeled,
    deveined, rinsed, dried

1 tablespoon finely chopped fresh rosemary

1 tablespoon finely chopped Italian parsley

1/4 cup extra virgin olive oil

3 cloves garlic, peeled and finely minced

1 Walla Walla Sweet onion, with separate
    layers cut into 1-inch squares

Salt and freshly ground black pepper
    to taste

Bamboo skewers

Creamy Guacamole (recipe follows)

1 cup Romesco Sauce (page 57)

Grilled Rock Shrimp with Romesco Sauce and Creamy Guacamole

Here's a wonderful use for my romesco sauce. I love rock shrimp because of their unique flavor and texture, which is a cross between a lobster and a crawfish. If you can't get your hands on rock shrimp, however, you can certainly substitute another shrimp or even bay scallops.

In a re-sealable plastic bag or in a bowl, combine the shrimp with the rosemary, parsley, olive oil and garlic. Marinate the mixture for 30 minutes. Preheat the grill to medium-high. While the grill is heating up, thread the shrimp onto the bamboo skewers, alternating with the pieces of sweet onion. Arrange the skewers onto a platter, then brush each one with another dose of the marinade. Season the shrimp and onions with salt and pepper.

Grill the shrimp over the hot coals until done, turning once. This will take about 3 to 4 minutes, depending on the size of the shrimp.

To serve, while the shrimp are grilling, place a portion of the Creamy Guacamole on each of 6 dinner plates. On top of the guacamole, add a portion of the romesco sauce. When the skewers come off the grill, place them onto the plates, on top of the sauces.

BEVERAGE THOUGHTS: This is a delightful, sitting-on-the-deck-in-summer sort of dish. And what goes so beautifully with it is a light, fruity Pinot Noir. Another option to consider would be a soft Pinot Gris that's not too acidic. An amber ale would also bring a nice balance to the dish without overpowering the shrimp.

Makes about 1-1/2 cups

2 ripe Haas avocados

Juice of 1 lime

2 tablespoons sour cream

1 tablespoon bottled salsa

About 1/2 teaspoon salt

Creamy Guacamole

Place the avocados, lime juice, sour cream, salsa and salt into a blender or food processor and blend until smooth and creamy. Scrape the mixture into a small bowl and cover the surface with plastic wrap to keep it from turning brown. Refrigerate up to 2 hours (beyond that you're risking that it will discolor).

CHAPTER **8**

Sweets

From toffies and tortes to caramels and cookies, it's hard to go wrong when hazelnuts are part of the formula.

There's something startlingly perfect about chocolate coated hazelnuts. Even around here—smack dab in the middle of hazelnut country—folks are anything but blasé with the concept. In our own household, a gift bag of Wayne and Joann Chamber's CCH's has the life span of a, well, let's just say I have MY cut of them and my husband has HIS.

But beyond chocolate coatings, hazelnuts are simply wonderful in all sorts of confections. It gets back to their inherent toasty-sophisticated-complex character, which compliments so many styles of sweet cookery. From toffies and tortes to caramels and cookies, it's hard to go wrong when hazelnuts are part of the formula.

Hazelnuts, Chocolate and Pinot

YOU KNOW IT WHEN IT'S RIGHT— combinations in which the whole becomes greater than the sum of the parts. Like cookies and milk; bacon and eggs; sweet corn and butter. Some of these are natural progressions along the same flavor spectrum. Others start out at opposite ends, but from the moment their essences meet, it's magic. Like a big ol' juicy slab of prime rib and a sinus-blowing scoop of horseradish. Putting those two together seems a little demented. But someone did. And in so doing, confirmed one of life's most fundamental facts: opposites attract. Take ketchup and scrambled eggs. Oil and vinegar. Berries and cream. Chocolate and Pinot Noir.

Pinot and chocolate. The natural. It's so easy one hardly knows where to begin. Starting with chocolate, you could go with a simple solid chunk. Nothing wrong with that. Or a simple chewy-chocolaty brownie, or a fluffy dollop of chocolate mousse. Or a wedge of chocolate cheesecake. They and most of their relatives are all in love with Pinot, and Pinot loves them.

So your job is to kick it to a new level. And how do you do that? Surprise, surprise—throw in the hazelnut, gently and richly roasted. Now you have a natural bridge between the chocolate and the wine, the sweet and the savory, brought elegantly together by the sweet-yet-earthy nut. You have synergy, and synergy tastes great!

Of course, when it comes to confections and wine, it's reasonable to consider wines that are sweeter in nature than the classic, dry Pinot Noir. Pinot ports, for example, are a very hot and very delectable commodity these days in Oregon. And what I like about them, when they're made properly, is their complexity. They're sweet, yes. But the sweetness is tempered by a rich flavor blast of fruit, spice, oak, and so much more.

I've learned to trust the palate of wine professional Maggie Crawford, manager and co-owner of Grand Vines Wine Shop and Bistro in downtown Salem, Oregon. She got her wine chops in Southern California's wine market, but Oregon has been her home for almost two decades now and the wine industry has benefitted from her transfer. "We make more ports than ever before here in Oregon," says Maggie. But when it comes to pairing with food, you have to know what style of port you're dealing with. In general, she says, it's tawny ports versus ruby ports. "Tawny ports tend to be nutty and brown-sugary in nature, so they go better with hazelnuts, and cheeses. They also go well with some chocolates. Not every chocolate. But definitely nutty chocolate."

On the other hand, continues Maggie, "the ruby ports tend to be fruitier and cherry-esque. So they will go better with fruit desserts. Really, unless the label literally says "tawny," most of the ports we make in Oregon are ruby-like. Partly because they're made from a lighter grape than normal port is made from. Most ports in Oregon are made from Pinot Noir.

"So they tend to be fruitier. They also tend to be a bit lighter. There are people that do make tawny ports, however. David Hill, for one, makes a really nice, true tawny. It's made out of Pinot noir, but the style is a tawny."

I've noted that Eola Hills Cabernet port is also a tawny style. And in fact, it's my ultimate pairing for my favorite candied hazelnut recipe, Grandma Aden's Candied Filberts (page 196).

But I wondered about the late harvest Oregon wines, like the late harvest Gewürztraminer. "Well," says Maggie, "Gewürz' being a little spicy, and Riesling being a little more fruity, along with late harvest Viogniers, those tend to go better with non-chocolate sweets. But really, they're okay with nuts. Think hazelnut tortes, or hazelnut biscotti. Or hazelnut shortbread."

And hazelnuts with poached pears, I add.

"Yes, so things with fruit, obviously. And blue cheese. But then again, it depends on what you do with the blue cheese. Do you have a fruit compote with it? Are you putting hazelnuts next to it? Or are you putting flavored hazelnuts into it? Those are the questions to ask when you're figuring that out."

"So just like with meats, you know, if the meat's heavy and strong, you want a full-bodied wine with it. If it's lighter meat, then it's usually more important to consider what you're doing with it. A lemon-dill sauce, as opposed to something tomatoey on fish, changes what you're going to serve with it dramatically."

Hazelnuts and Holiday Cooking

FOOD WRITERS DON'T GENERALLY DEAL WITH EARTH-SHATTERING ISSUES. But food does bring people together. Which is why a lot of life's problems are solved while sitting around the dinner table. Or around a simmering Christmas Eve crab pot with a brother you don't see nearly enough. Or over a cup of tea with your mother.

And, of course, there's also the evocative element of food. How simple things like baking shortbread or sipping a single-malt scotch can kindle images of beloved people from our past, or reaffirm long-forged ties with our contemporaries during holiday gatherings. This has led my family to make great efforts over the years to get our hands on Grandma Roberts' gum drop cookie recipe, to perfect Grandma Skinner's griddle scones, and to ensure that the McMillan chutney was being made according to my Great Aunt Meg's finicky standards. So a few Decembers ago, when I got an email from a reader in search of a family recipe, I decided to get in on the hunt. I knew what it would mean to her to recover that recipe.

Marcia Stille of Lake Oswego, Oregon, wanted to recreate the candy coated hazelnuts that her grandmother used to make. In her note, Marcia said that her search had begun "during two post-funeral family gatherings this past spring, (when) we cousins were reminiscing about the old world family foods we used to enjoy during the holidays, and the family patriarch, my 90-year-old uncle from Spokane, was avidly quizzing each of us to see if anyone had that recipe for candied filberts."

Marcia had provided a terrific description of the treasured recipe: "It was something simple that my grandmother kept in her head and involved covering roasted filberts with a light, subtle, buttery, brown-sugar type of coating and, I think, roasting them a second time. The coating did not make the nuts clump together the way a caramely coating would, and the finished coating was not chewy or hard but more on the dry, un-sticky side. The nuts stayed separate, and the coating enhanced their natural flavor and aroma rather than overpowering them."

"Needless to say," she concluded, "eleven grateful cousins (none of whom seem to have inherited Gram's talent in the kitchen) and two elderly uncles would be thrilled to be able to eat these treats again."

I poured through old cookbooks and Googled "candied filberts," but was getting nowhere. The breakthrough came via a phone call to friends Wayne and Joann Chambers. As second generation hazelnut growers, they live, eat and breathe hazelnuts. If anybody had bumped into this particular nutty confection it would be the Chambers.

"Let me check with Wayne's cousin," said Joann. From that inquiry, two recipes arrived in the mail. One of them struck me as a contender, so I headed into the kitchen to give it a test run.

In an email back to Marcia, I told her that I was possibly on the right track. "As you suspected, the recipe for the batch in question was really straight-forward. After roasting and rubbing off the skins, the nuts are roasted again on a baking sheet in a puddle of Karo light syrup and butter, with a sprinkling of salt. They're stirred several times during the roasting. The finished nuts have a light glaze on them as you described and don't stick together."

I mailed off a batch for her to taste, fingers crossed. Her response was swift: "Dear Jan...Thank you so very, very much for the delicious hazelnut treats! They arrived in excellent shape...and I have been sneaking a few every chance

I get. They are perfect! On behalf of the entire family (all of whom will soon be making their own batches), I thank you for all your help...Thank you for giving this part of our grandmother back to us! We are all more grateful than you can imagine..."

But I can imagine. Particularly during the holidays. At a time of year when we are all teetering on the edge of chaos there is many a household that will forgo making and sharing whatever recipes define their family. And that's a shame. You see, if I had one wish for the holidays, it would be to travel back in time to sit at one more family dinner surrounded by my loud, lively, and oh-so-loving relatives now gone. And with that impossibility as my goal, the very least I can do is make the food that had meaning to us then and share it with those who mean the world to me now. If in so doing I perpetuate just a fraction of the love and nurturing that enveloped me during my youth, well, then my wish will not have been entirely in vain.

1 tablespoon butter

1/4 cup light corn syrup

Popcorn salt

3 cups lightly roasted and skinned hazelnuts

BEVERAGE THOUGHTS: If you serve these wonderful nuts with the Eola Hills LBV Cabernet Sauvignon Port your guests will think you're brilliant. It's that delicious a pairing. Honest! If you can't get your hands on that particular port, then at least use a tawny style port (rather than a ruby port), which compliments the toasty-caramely nature of these treats.

Grandma Aden's Candied Filberts

This is the recipe that Marcia Stille asked me to find for her. It's like the one her Grandma Aden in Wilsonville, Oregon used to make and send to Marcia in Bend where she lived with her family. Now that the recipe has been revived, it has been appreciated by an even wider audience. A few years ago, says Marcia, "I was taking a graduate course at Portland State University and students were required to prepare and share with our classmates a special family food from our culture. I'm sure you've guessed by now what mine was—everyone just loved them and the story they came with."

Of course, to be fair, Wayne Chambers pointed out to me that in the Chambers household, these would be called "Auntie Helen's Candied Filberts." I'm mindful of that. In fact, if your family adopts them, you should feel free to call them whatever you want.

Even without a link to the past, these are a wonderful treat to make, especially during the holidays—both as gifts and to have on hand when friends drop by.

Preheat oven to 350 degrees F.

Place the butter in the center of a rimmed baking sheet and warm briefly in the oven. When the butter has melted, remove it from the oven and stir in the corn syrup. Then add the skinned hazelnuts. Sprinkle lightly with salt and, using a wide spatula or dough scraper, stir the nuts around in the syrup/butter mixture to evenly coat the nuts and spread them into a flat layer.

Roast the nuts for 20 to 30 minutes on the center rack of the oven, stirring them around every 5 to 7 minutes so they remain evenly coated with the syrup. The overall roasting time needed will vary depending on your oven, so just be watchful.

While the nuts are roasting, spread a large sheet of waxed or parchment paper on a cutting board. When the nuts have reached a lovely golden brown, remove them from the oven and scrape them out onto the paper, quickly spreading them out so they don't touch each other for the most part. Allow them to cool and then break them apart as desired into single nuts or clusters.

The nuts should be stored at room temperature in an airtight container, in which they can be kept for several weeks. Their crunchiness and flavor will continue to develop for the first 24 hours, so it's best to prepare them at least a day in advance of when they will be needed.

Makes 3 cups

1/4 cup butter (1/2 stick)

1/2 cup firmly packed golden brown sugar

2/3 cup light corn syrup

5 teaspoons orange extract

1/4 teaspoon salt

3 cups lightly roasted and skinned hazelnuts

BEVERAGE THOUGHTS: Well, since these candied nuts are the kissing cousins to the previous recipe, you can be sure that the Eola Hills LBV Cabernet Sauvignon Port is still a truly delicious pairing. Beyond that, a tawny style port (rather than a ruby port), would compliment the toasty-caramely nature of these treats. I'd also bring out a David Hill Muscat Port, with flavors of orange and dried apricots, plus spice and caramel that compliment the nut so well.

Margaret's Orange Glazed Hazelnuts

It was my mother's brilliant idea that I should make an orange variation to Grandma Aden's Candied Filberts. "Why?" I asked her. "I don't know. I just think that the flavor combination would be excellent."

She was so very right. The gentle orange backdrop mingles beautifully with the toasty caramely flavor in the nut, producing a rich experience. I also made them slightly more "candied" than the recipe for Grandma Aden's. Enjoy, Mom!

Preheat the oven to 350 degrees F.

In a heavy-bottomed medium-sized pot, over medium-high heat, melt the butter with the brown sugar and corn syrup. Bring the mixture just barely to a boil, then remove the pot from the burner and stir in the orange extract and salt. With a silicon spatula, stir in the hazelnuts, making sure that they all get evenly coated with the syrup.

Scrape the nuts and all of the syrup onto a rimmed baking sheet, spreading the nuts out into a single layer. Roast for 20 to 30 minutes on the center rack of the oven, stirring the nuts around every 5 to 7 minutes so they remain evenly coated with the syrup. The overall roasting time needed will vary depending on your oven, so just be watchful. As the syrup gets thicker, it will bubble and foam around the nuts. Just keep stirring and spreading them out in a single layer after each stir.

While the nuts are roasting, spread a large sheet of waxed or parchment paper on a cutting board. When the nuts have reached a lovely golden brown and the syrup is thick and clinging to them, remove them from the oven and scrape them out onto the paper, quickly spreading them out so they don't touch each other for the most part. Allow them to cool and then break them apart as desired into single nuts or clusters.

The pieces should be stored at room temperature in an airtight container, in which they can be kept for several weeks. Their crunchiness and flavor will continue to develop for the first 24 hours, so it's best to prepare them at least a day in advance of when they will be needed.

Roasted Hazelnut Toffee

Like most forms of candy-making, toffee construction can certainly go awry if you don't pay attention. But this is a fabulous recipe that produces an outstanding gem, with very little risk of failure. Just make sure you use a candy thermometer. Amongst my legion of taste-testers during the making of this cookbook, my hazelnut toffee produced the most requests for more.

Makes 4-1/4 pounds of toffee
(100 pieces measuring 1 x 2 inches)

1 pound (4 sticks) butter (see note)

1 cup granulated sugar

1 cup firmly packed golden brown sugar

1 tablespoon light corn syrup

1/4 cup water

2-1/2 cups raw hazelnuts, coarsely chopped

2 teaspoons vanilla extract

1/4 teaspoon salt

16 ounces semi-sweet chocolate
(either chips, or squares that have been
broken into chunks)

2 cups chopped dark-roasted and `
skinned hazelnuts

Grease one large (12 x 17- inch) rimmed baking sheet or two smaller (10 x 15-inch or less) ones with butter. If you're lucky enough to have a kitchen equipped with a marble slab, then use it instead of the baking sheet(s). Grease it the same way.

Melt the pound of butter in a large, heavy-bottomed pot over medium heat on a wide-diameter burner. While the butter is melting, combine the granulated sugar, brown sugar and corn syrup. Add this mixture to the melted butter, along with the water. When the sugars have dissolved, increase the burner setting to medium high, stirring with a flat-edged wooden spoon. Attach a candy thermometer to the pot and cook the mixture, stirring constantly to keep it from scorching. When the temperature reaches 240 degrees F, add the nuts and continue stirring. At 260 degrees, reduce the burner setting to medium-low and continue cooking and stirring occasionally, until the toffee reaches 300 degrees ("hard crack").

Remove the pot from the burner and stir in the vanilla and salt, stirring quickly because the toffee will become quite thick at this point. Scrape it out onto the prepared baking sheet(s) or marble slab, spreading it out to a thickness of about 1/4 to 1/2 inch. A silicon spatula is the best tool for spreading the sticky toffee.

"Well, I should think you'd have a recipe that you could eat right away!"

My husband, Steve, on being told that hazelnut toffee needs about 24 hours to reach its full flavor potential. Of course, he'd just downed two pieces and was eying a third.

Allow the toffee about 5 minutes to set up, then distribute the chocolate pieces evenly over the surface. The heat from the toffee will melt them. While it's still soft, gently even out the layer of chocolate and then sprinkle it with the roasted and chopped hazelnuts.

At this point, you can refrigerate the toffee until it is cold and hard. Or you can just let it cool to room temperature over several hours or overnight. Once the toffee is very firm, it can be broken into smaller, irregular-sized pieces. I like the irregularity of the pieces that are derived this way. However, if you want the pieces to be broken into uniform shapes just score the toffee slab appropriately before layering on the chocolate.

NOTE: I use salted butter, but if you use unsalted butter instead, increase the amount of salt in the recipe from 1/4 teaspoon to 1 teaspoon.

3 cups granulated sugar

1 cup light corn syrup

1/2 cup water

3 cups raw hazelnuts

1 tablespoon butter

1 teaspoon salt

2 teaspoons baking soda

Sheri's Filbert Brittle

Good friend Sheri Albin always makes peanut brittle in mid-December. Then she and hus-band Rod hop in the car the week before Christmas, making sweet deliveries to lucky friends and family. One year I supplied her with some new-crop hazelnuts to see if her wonderful brittle recipe could make the leap from peanuts to hazelnuts. Turns out it could. We quickly ate the evidence, and it was heavenly! Sheri's recipe is straightforward, but does require some brute strength at the end when the salt and baking soda are stirred in to the molten candy. She always enlists Rod.

Grease a cookie sheet with cooking spray, oil or butter; set aside.

In a medium-sized heavy-bottom pot, heat the sugar, corn syrup and water over medium-low heat, stirring constantly, until the sugar has dissolved. As the sugar is dissolving, brush down the sides of the pot with a pastry brush dipped in cold water to remove all sugar crystals (any that remain will cause unwanted crystallization).

Insert a candy thermometer, increase the temperature to medium and continue cooking until the candy temperature reaches 280 degrees F (soft crack). Stir in the hazelnuts and continue cooking to 300 to 310 degrees (hard crack). Remove from heat, then add the butter and stir well until dissolved. Add the salt and stir well. Finally, add the baking soda, stirring well (it will bubble and foam!).

Quickly spread the brittle out onto the prepared cookie sheet and let cool.

Once it has cooled, break it into pieces and store in an air-tight container to prevent the surface from becoming sticky.

The Evolution of a Caramel:
Mother Peach's Caramels Meet the Oregon Hazelnut

ONE YEAR MY FORMER EDITOR at the Oregonian newspaper's FOODday section, Ginger Johnston, gave me a box of Mother Peach's Caramels for Christmas. She knew that those candies would mean a lot to me because they're made by a former home economist at The Oregonian, Cheri Swoboda. Cheri's been selling her amazing caramels for over 25 years, all the while with the Mother Peach's label. No caramel that I've ever had compares to the creamy-smooth-yet-chewy-buttery-brown-sugary perfection found in a Mother Peach's caramel.

None.

As I nursed my special stash along in the weeks after Christmas, I found myself in the delightful post-lunch habit of unwrapping one of those treasures and pressing its surface into a bowl of roasted and chopped hazelnuts. Just for a nosh. Turns out, the flavor combo of the caramelized sugar and butter and smoky-toasty-nutty hazelnut is exquisite. It's hard to describe why. It just is. So one night I thought, "You know, I'm just going to have to come up with a caramel recipe as close to Mother Peach's as I can get so I can create my own caramel-hazelnut confection for the book." Without giving away her secret recipe, Cheri generously shared some important tricks of the trade, plus a few guidelines on how to develop a good recipe.

The recipe below is what came of that effort. I'm very pleased and I think you will be too. They are now a part of my Christmas Treat repertoire. And in fact, when I shared some with the Hazelnut Marketing Board administrator, Polly Owen, her thoughts ran along the same lines. "Oh my goodness!" she said. "I would definitely make these for some really good friends!"

 And so I did.

Word came from hazelnut grower Dave Buchanan: "It's deadly! You know what I usually like about caramel is you take a little bite and sort of just suck it. But with these hazelnuts, you just want to take a BIG bite and eat it all at once!" Which validated a complaint from Dave's wife Margy about a week after the last delivery. "There's something wrong with these caramels," she harumphed. "They keep disappearing!"

At the Griesmeyer household, John got in similar trouble from Debbie when he ate all four of the samples I had dropped off. "Well, I ate my first two and then Debbie's just were still there on the counter. I gave her a couple of days, then I ate one more. Then, the next day, her last one was still there, so I ate it too."

That very afternoon, Debbie got home from work and said, "Where are those caramels that Jan left us?"

"Boy was I in trouble," said John.

Now I have the problem of naming this confection. I've had lots of suggestions from tasters. Margy and Dave started with "Divorce Court Caramels," since Margy had some trouble getting her share. Then Margy left a stash under Dave's pillow when she went on a trip and "Divorce Court" became "Love Bites." Those two pretty much bracket the emotional range of what I've gotten so far. For now, I think I'll just stick with something pretty relationship-neutral until my tasters, who are clearly less evolved than Polly Owen, have time to adjust to temptation.

*Makes 3-1/4 pounds of caramels
(about 64 individual pieces measuring
1 x 2 inches...a very generous amount,
even for Dave Buchanan!)*

**1-1/2 to 2 cups very coarsely chopped
(a mixture of halved and coarsely
chopped) dark-roasted and skinned
hazelnuts**

1-1/2 cups granulated sugar

**1-1/2 cups firmly packed
golden brown sugar**

1 cup (2 sticks) butter

1 cup half & half

1 cup heavy cream

1 cup light corn syrup

1/2 teaspoon salt

1 teaspoon vanilla

Jan's Hazelnut Caramels

Lightly coat a 9 x 13-inch pan with cooking spray, then line it with parchment paper as follows: cut two rectangles of parchment paper, one measuring 9 x 22 inches, and the other measuring 13 x 18 inches. Lay the 9 x 22-inch piece in the pan, parallel to its long axis, so the excess drapes evenly over each end of the pan. Spray the center of this piece of parchment with cooking spray (so the top sheet will stick to it), then press the other sheet of parchment down on top, orienting it crosswise. Now there will be a few inches of paper hanging over each side of the pan, making it easy to lift the caramel out in one whole slab when it's time to cut it into pieces. Pour the hazelnuts into the prepared pan and spread them out evenly.

In a heavy-bottomed 4-quart saucepan, combine the granulated sugar, brown sugar, butter, half & half, heavy cream, light corn syrup and salt. Cook over medium heat, stirring occasionally until the butter and sugars have melted and the mixture comes to a gentle boil. This will take about 15 to 20 minutes.

At this point, insert a candy thermometer and continue cooking and stirring occasionally until the temperature reaches between 243 and 245 degrees F. This will take at least another 20 minutes, but I've had batches that have taken up to 40 minutes. The timing varies due to the amount of moisture in the butter, for one thing. Don't rush it! (That's the advice of Mother Peach's creator, Cheri Swoboda).

Remove from heat immediately and stir in the vanilla. Using two very thick potholders if your saucepan lacks insulated handles, pour the hot caramel evenly into the prepared pan on top of the chopped nuts. Let it cool completely. If it's going to be more than two or three hours before you cut the caramel into pieces, cover the surface with another piece of parchment, then cover the entire pan with a piece of foil, crimping the corners so that the foil will help keep the caramel from being exposed to air, which will make the surface of the caramels sticky.

When ready to cut, lift the slab of caramel from the pan using the excess parchment paper as handles and place it on a cutting board. Spray a large knife (or kitchen shears) with nonstick cooking spray. Cut the caramel into desired shapes. Wipe the blade and re-spray as necessary (I don't usually need to do this more than once or twice). To keep the caramels from sticking together, immediately wrap them in twists of waxed paper or food-grade cellophane.

Making Perfect Caramels—Tips from Mother Peach

START WITH QUALITY INGREDIENTS such as butter, not margarine, and have the sugar lump-free. When ready to start, have all ingredients measured. Use a large heavy duty pot, as caramel can splatter as it boils. It's important to wear long sleeves to protect your arms and glasses to protect your eyes. Use a long handled wooden spoon, as the mixture boils to 245 degrees F ("firm ball" stage) and you don't want the spoon melting. I feel a candy thermometer is a must. I often use two thermometers to check for complete accuracy. If you don't reach the correct temperature, the mixture won't set up, and if you overcook, it will burn. Use medium heat to avoid scorching. Stirring constantly results in a creamy, smooth caramel. Color and shine are two important things to look for. The mixture will be heavy and dull looking when first mixing all ingredients together.

As it boils and reaches the firm ball stage, you will notice it's easier to stir (more fluid) and the color is a golden brown with a shine. Each of my 2-pound batches takes about 15 to 20 minutes to stir. Once the firm ball stage (245 degrees) is reached, immediately take it off the stove and pour it into the prepared pan. Caramel sets up quickly.

In evaluating recipes, I look at the list of ingredients and the instructions. If the recipe is easy to read with clear instructions, that's a plus. I enjoy an introduction to the recipe from the cook with hints. You feel like that person is cooking with you in the kitchen. If a recipe calls for salt, be sure and use it. My recipe does call for a small amount and it adds to the balance of flavors.

8 ounces dried black Mission figs
(see note below)

2/3 cup all-purpose flour

2 tablespoons unsweetened cocoa powder

2 teaspoons freshly grated orange zest

1/2 teaspoon ground cinnamon

1/8 teaspoon ground cloves

1 cup roasted and skinned hazelnuts

1 cup whole, roasted almonds
(see instructions for roasting hazelnuts)

2/3 cup granulated sugar

1/2 cup honey

Back Country Panforte

Chock-full of toasty hazelnuts and almonds, luscious dried figs and thick, golden honey, this is a trail treat that pairs fabulously with that after dinner scotch. And because it's sturdy in nature, it gets high grades in the transportability department too. It's also an energizing mid-afternoon snack, enjoyed at the upper-most end of an alpine day hike. You can make several batches in late November so that you'll have it on hand for gifts (consider it a sophisticated "fruit cake") or to tuck into your backpack for winter hikes and ski trips.

Preheat the oven to 300 degrees F.

Butter and flour a 10-inch springform pan and set aside. If you don't have a springform pan, line a 10-inch round or square baking pan with heavy-duty foil (or parchment), then butter and flour the foil. The foil will help you lift the baked panforte from the pan after it's cooled.

Trim the tiny stem end from each dried fig. Slice the figs into very thin pieces, at least 6 per fig; set aside.

In a large bowl, combine the flour, cocoa powder, orange zest, cinnamon, and ground cloves.

Coarsely chop the hazelnuts and almonds. By "coarsely chop" I mean simply cut each nut into 2 or 3 pieces. Naturally, during the chopping some fragments will wind up smaller, but that's okay. The idea is just to have a preponderance of fairly large nut pieces in the finished panforte. Add the nuts and the prepared figs to the flour mixture and toss thoroughly to evenly coat the fruit and nuts; set aside.

Pour the sugar and honey into a small, heavy-bottomed saucepan and stir gently to combine. Scrape the sides of the pan with a silicon spatula to remove any honey and sugar crystals. Now set the pan over low heat. Without stirring, let the mixture heat up so the sugar can begin to dissolve. Increase the heat to medium and continue cooking without stirring. The syrup will become quite foamy as it boils. Do NOT stir the mixture. Hook a candy thermometer to the side of the pan and continue to let the mixture boil without stirring until the thermometer reaches between 240 and 245 degrees, which is the soft ball stage in candy-making terminology.

Remove the syrup from the heat and immediately stir it into the flour/fruit/nut mixture. The mixture will firm up immediately, but keep stirring to make sure the syrup is evenly distributed throughout. Transfer the batter to the prepared pan. Moisten your fingers with tap water and use them to press the thick-and-sticky mixture evenly into the pan.

Bake in the preheated oven until the mixture puffs slightly and releases a wonderful toasty aroma, about 35 minutes. At this point, the panforte will be soft and sticky when prodded with a dull knife. Remove from oven and allow to cool on a rack at room temperature. Once the panforte has cooled thoroughly, wrap it tightly in plastic wrap and store in a cool, dry place. It will keep for months.

Traditionally, panforte that has been baked in a round pan is cut into wedges. But for backpacking or hiking purposes, I prefer to cut the round into thirds, then cut each third into 1/2-inch wide bars.

NOTE ON FIGS: I found mine in the bulk foods section of a natural foods grocery store. Wherever you go, if the black Mission variety isn't available, but another type is, go ahead and substitute.

BEVERAGE THOUGHTS: A sip of Belle Vallée's Pinot Noir Port, made in Corvallis, Oregon entirely from Willamette Valley grapes, delivers a cascade of flavors from raisin and black cherry, to candied orange peel, with a toasty, caramely, hazelnut finish. Of course, there's also the more direct route: your favorite scotch! Then there's David Hill's white port, the Muscat Port, which mirrors the panforte with its cloves, cinnamon, dried apricots and orange. Imperial stout is another beverage traditionally served with fruitcake-like desserts, and a very nice one from Oregon is Rogue Ale's XS Russian Imperial Stout, which has garnered international attention in the last few years.

Classic combos

Chocolate with hazelnuts is a classic combo. Throw our region's berries into the mix—especially the velvety-cool raspberry—and the experience is utterly elegant.

Makes about 2 cups

1 cup lightly roasted and skinned hazelnuts

3/4 cup granulated sugar

3 tablespoons light corn syrup

3 tablespoons water

1 teaspoon orange zest

1/4 teaspoon salt

Hazelnut Fairy Dust (Praline Powder)

Handing out jars of this magical dust at Christmas is a brilliant maneuver. Made from pulverizing a roasted hazelnut brittle into glistening dust, you will be amazed at the number of uses you find for it. Ramp up desserts by folding it into whipped cream for garnishing pies, or sprinkling it between layers of cake or into creamy custards. The possibilities are endless.

Lightly grease a cookie sheet and set aside. Warm the roasted hazelnuts by placing them on a rimmed ungreased baking sheet in a 250 degree F oven for 10 minutes. Turn off the oven, remove the nuts, and pour them into a small oven-proof bowl; return the bowl to the oven to stay warm. You could leave the nuts on the baking sheet, but I find it easier to pour them into the candy mixture from a bowl.

Combine the sugar, corn syrup, and water in a small heavy-bottomed saucepan. Bring the mixture to a boil over high heat. After boiling starts, wipe down any sugar crystals on the sides of the pan with a wet pastry brush. Boil the syrup until it begins to turn a light caramel color, at which point it will register between 320 and 340 degrees on a candy thermometer. Remove from heat and quickly add the orange zest and salt, mixing quickly but thoroughly. Add the warmed nuts and stir the mixture quickly (it hardens up fast!), then pour it onto the lightly greased cookie sheet and spread it out with a wooden spoon or silicon spatula.

You've just made hazelnut brittle. Yum! But don't stop there. Cool the brittle completely, then break it into small pieces. Working in batches, grind it to a fairly fine powder in a food processor or blender. Operate the machine intermittently to avoid over-heating the material, which could cause it to clump.

Store the Fairy Dust in an airtight container. This magical mixture will keep several months at room temperature, and even longer in the freezer. If it is chilled or frozen, allow it to come to room temperature before opening the container. This will keep it from absorbing moisture.

Makes over 3 cups sauce

1 pound semisweet chocolate,
   cut into very small chunks,
   or your favorite chocolate chips

1-1/3 cups heavy cream

5 tablespoons butter, softened
   and cut into chunks

3 tablespoons hazelnut flavored syrup
   (see note)

3/4 cup coarsely chopped roasted
   and skinned hazelnuts

"Did you know that roasted hazelnuts with chocolate chips makes a great snack?!"

My husband, Steve, in response to:
"Hey! What happened to all the
chocolate chips???!"

Jan's Special Chocolate Truffle Sauce with Roasted Hazelnuts

This has been a favorite specialty of mine for many years. NOBODY suspects just how easy and fast it comes together. In no time flat, I have a decadently rich and chocolaty topping for bowls of ice cream. It makes a great hostess gift during the holidays, which I jazz up by presenting it in a lovely jar with a colorful homemade label. The recipe can easily be doubled or tripled.

Slowly melt the chocolate, without stirring, in a double-boiler arrangement (page 36). This will take about 20 minutes.

When the chocolate has melted, pour the cream into a small, heavy-bottomed saucepan over medium-high heat and warm just until the cream is steaming and small bubbles have formed around the edges. If it actually boils, it's not a tragedy, but remove it from the burner immediately.

Remove from heat and immediately pour it over the melted chocolate, stirring constantly. Don't be alarmed when the chocolate seizes up. Just keep stirring gently with a flat wire whisk or a wooden spoon until the chocolate relaxes, softens up and ultimately blends into the warm cream. Keep the vessel positioned over the hot water to keep the temperature at the melting point. Once the chocolate is smooth and creamy, stir in the butter a few chunks at a time and continue stirring until the mixture is well blended and smooth. Stir in the hazelnut syrup and the chopped hazelnuts; stir well.

Pour the sauce into clean, dry jars, making sure not to drip water into it from the bottom of the vessel as you do so. Allow to cool completely before screwing on the lids. Refrigerate the sauce, at which point it will become firm.

To serve, scoop out the sauce as needed and soften for use by warming at low power in the microwave or in a pan on the stove.

ALTERNATE SERVING METHOD: Sneak it out of the fridge and just lick it off a spoon, baby!

NOTE ON HAZELNUT FLAVORED SYRUPS: These are typically sold in the coffee and tea aisle of a supermarket since the syrups are used to flavor beverages.

1/2 pound white chocolate,
  broken into small chunks

3/4 cup heavy cream

1/2 cup granulated sugar

Pinch of salt

2 tablespoons unsalted butter

1/2 cup coarsely chopped roasted
  and skinned hazelnuts

1 to 2 tablespoons hazelnut-flavored
  liqueur, such as Frangelico, if desired

White Chocolate Sauce with Roasted Hazelnuts

Another fabulous gift idea for the holidays. Darkly roasted hazelnuts have a rich, toasty and ruggedly robust flavor profile. Just the ticket when dealing with white chocolate, which can be too sweet for its own good. A fantastic sauce over dark, bittersweet chocolate ice cream.

Grate the white chocolate in a food processor, then pour it into a large bowl and set aside.

In a small heavy-bottomed saucepan, combine the cream with the sugar, butter and salt. Set the pot over low heat and bring the cream almost to a boil (don't let it boil), stirring frequently, until the butter has melted and the sugar has dissolved. Pour the very hot liquid into the bowl of chocolate and stir constantly until all of the chocolate has melted and the sauce is thick and smooth.

Stir in the hazelnuts and, optionally, the hazelnut-flavored liqueur. Pour the sauce into clean jars and allow to cool completely before screwing on the lids. Refrigerate the sauce, at which point it will become firm.

To serve, scoop out the sauce as needed and soften for use by warming at low power in the microwave or in a pan on the stove. Stir the sauce once or twice as it warms. If it becomes too thick, add a little more cream.

Makes about 40 cookies

5 or 6 ounces of a good quality semi-sweet
    chocolate in small pieces,
    or chocolate chips
3/4 cup (1-1/2 sticks) butter, softened
3/4 cup granulated sugar
1-1/3 cups all-purpose flour
1 cup finely chopped roasted and
    skinned hazelnuts
Beyond Peerless Red Raspberry Preserves
    (recipe follows)

Crank up the flavor

To crank up the celebration factor of any hazelnut-style cookie or dessert, consider serving it with an adult-styled coffee, spiked with Rogue Ale's Hazelnut Spice Rum. For a bit of sweetness, add a splash of Frangelico, a hazelnut liqueur, and top it with a fluffy dollop of whipped cream, sprinkled with some Hazelnut Fairy Dust (page 206).

Hazelnut Shortbread Wafers with Raspberries and Chocolate

This is an extra-special shortbread cookie treat that I created one February day for my sons and husband. I wanted it to be decadently delicious for sure, but also beautiful to behold. An offering of love. Sweets for my sweeties. This is what I came up with. Now it's a family treasure.

Preheat oven to 375 degrees F. Grease 2 cookie sheets and set aside.

Slowly melt the chocolate, without stirring, in a double-boiler arrangement (page 36). This will take about 20 minutes.

While the chocolate is melting, cream together the butter and sugar with an electric mixer until light and fluffy. Stir in the flour and hazelnuts (dough will seem grainy). Roll out the dough on a lightly floured surface to 1/8- to 1/4-inch thickness. Cut into rounds using a 2-inch cookie cutter. Using a spatula, transfer the rounds to greased cookie sheets. Bake in the upper third of a 375 degree F oven for about 9 minutes, just until wafers begin to brown around the edges. Wafers should cool for at least 10 minutes before being moved to a wire rack (or cool completely on the baking sheet). When cool, place a 1/2-inch dollop of jam in the center of each wafer. Spread the jam out to a diameter of about 1 inch.

Transfer the melted chocolate to a re-sealable plastic bag, tilting the bag so that the chocolate flows to one corner. Cut a tiny tip from the chocolate-filled corner. Using the plastic bag like a pastry bag, invert the tip over your cookies and drizzle the chocolate in a lacy pattern on each cookie. The chocolate will firm up in about 10 minutes.

BEVERAGE THOUGHTS: This special cookie is a delicious treat that is happy around a glass of milk, cup of tea, or mug of coffee to be sure. But for after dinner, I'd definitely encourage you to offer a lovely dessert wine, such as Harris Bridge Vineyard's Sarah's Stories Pinot Gris dessert wine, or your favorite ruby-style port, which would embrace the raspberry character of the cookie. Beer and cookies is another winner in my book that would work with a wide range of styles, from a fruity pale ale or soft and round wheat beer, to an amber ale.

4 heaping cups red raspberries
    (make sure that about 1/3 cup of the
    berries are slightly under-ripe)
3-1/4 cups granulated sugar
    (1 pound, 6 ounces)
1/3 cup strained fresh lemon juice
1 teaspoon butter

Storing preserves

For long-term storage at room temperature, ladle the hot preserves into 1 hot canning jar at a time, leaving 1/4-inch headspace. Wipe the jar rim with a clean, damp cloth. Attach lid. Fill and close remaining jars. Process in a boiling-water canner for 10 minutes (at 1,000 to 3,000 feet, process for 15 minutes; 3,000 to 6,000 feet, for 20 minutes; above 6,000 feet, for 25 minutes).

Beyond Peerless Red Raspberry Preserves

This is the jam I make to use on my Hazelnut Shortbread Wafers. In my library of cookbooks a favorite is "Fancy Pantry" by Helen Witty. For anyone interested in the art of preserving, it's a valuable and inspirational book, filled with delicious ways to capture the harvest. One of Witty's best jam recipes is called Peerless Red Raspberry Preserves. I began sharing it with readers in my preserving column back in the early 90's. Each season I would fine-tune it a bit, adding a dab of butter to reduce foaming, increasing the cooking time slightly to guarantee a gel, tweaking the condition of the berries (if you add a handful of slightly under-ripe ones, which is where more natural pectin resides, you'll achieve a firmer gel). But because the basic technique—a brief, fast boil in a wide, shallow skillet—is the key to the recipe's success, I have always striven to give credit where credit is due. Thanks Helen! And all the benefactors of the gallons of preserves I've given away all these years thank you too.

If you are planning to store your jam at room temperature, wash 4 half-pint canning jars and keep them hot on a towel-lined cookie sheet in a low oven until ready to fill and process in a boiling water canner. Prepare lids as manufacturer directs. If you plan to store your jam in the refrigerator, any clean jars or food grade plastic containers with lids will work just fine.

Sort fresh berries, discarding any that are soft, moldy, or otherwise suspect. Rinse them and drain them well. Stir the berries, sugar, and lemon juice together in a bowl, using a rubber spatula. Let the mixture stand, stirring gently once or twice, until the sugar has dissolved, about 2 hours (many times I let it sit all day in the refrigerator, or overnight). Do not reduce the amount of sugar called for in this recipe because it aids in the gelling.

Scrape the mixture into a large skillet or sauté pan. Add the butter. Bring it to a boil, stirring constantly with a straight-ended wooden or silicon spatula, and boil it rapidly for 7 minutes. If you have a candy thermometer and want to be absolutely sure that you're going to obtain a gel, then cook the jam until the thermometer registers 220 degrees F. Remove from heat.

The butter helps reduce foam, but if some foam remains after you've removed the skillet from the burner and let the jam settle for about 10 seconds, just skim it off.

For storage in the refrigerator, ladle hot preserves into clean jars or plastic food grade containers. Attach lids and allow to cool before transferring to the refrigerator, where the jam will keep for ages— 24 months and beyond, actually!

Makes about 5 cups custard, which makes 6 desserts using 8-ounce ramekins, filling each one with about 6-1/2 ounces of custard. You can use smaller or larger ramekins as desired

3 cups heavy cream

1/3 cup milk

6 large egg yolks

1/8 teaspoon salt

3/4 cup plus 1 tablespoon granulated sugar

1 teaspoon vanilla extract

Superfine sugar for caramelized topping

1/2 cup finely chopped roasted and skinned hazelnuts

BEVERAGE THOUGHTS: Harris Bridge Vineyard Pinot Gris Dessert Wine is a fitting finale. That, or any slightly toasty-sweet dessert wine that finishes with a slight edge to balance the sweetness in the crème brûlée.

Jan's Crème Brûlée with Caramelized Hazelnut Topping

Here's your chance to wow your guests with a little torch work to caramelize the tops of their desserts. Just remember to sprinkle on the hazelnuts AFTER the torching, or you'll wind up with sprinkles of charcoal.

Combine the cream and milk in a heavy-bottomed medium-sized saucepan. Heat over medium heat until the mixture just barely begins to boil, then remove immediately and set aside.

In a bowl, whisk together the egg yolks with the salt and granulated sugar.

At this point, you'll combine the yolk mixture with the cream. First, temper the eggs by whisking a ladle of the hot cream into them. Keep whisking and repeat with 2 or 3 more ladles of hot cream. Now whisk the tempered egg mixture into the hot cream.

Set the pot of custard in a bowl of ice water for about 30 minutes to cool, stirring occasionally. Stir in the vanilla extract.

Cover and refrigerate for up to 2 days, if desired.

When ready to bake, preheat the oven to 325 degrees F. Pour the desired amount of custard into your ramekins.

Place the filled ramekins in a baking pan (or 2 pans, depending on how many cups you're using) and fill the pan with enough hot water to reach halfway up the sides of the ramekins. Bake for 35 to 55 minutes, or until the middles of the custards quake just a bit when you move the pan and the custards are not quite set. Remove the cups from the pan and allow to cool for one hour on the counter. Then cover and refrigerate for at least 4 hours to chill thoroughly, but no more than 24 hours before serving.

When ready to serve (or up to 2 hours ahead if you don't want to do it at the last minute), sprinkle each custard with a tablespoon of superfine sugar and proceed with your torch! As you complete the caramelization of each surface, while it is still molten (do NOT test for this with your fingertip), sprinkle on about 1 tablespoon of the chopped hazelnuts. Bon appetit!

1/2 cup (1 stick) unsalted butter, softened

1 cup firmly packed golden brown sugar

4 tablespoons dark molasses

1 large egg

2-1/4 cups all purpose flour

1-1/2 teaspoons baking soda

1/2 teaspoon salt

2 teaspoons ground ginger

2 tablespoons grated fresh ginger root

1/2 cup chopped crystallized ginger
     (see note)

1/2 cup finely chopped roasted and
     skinned hazelnuts

About 36 whole hazelnuts,
     lightly roasted and skinned

BEVERAGE THOUGHTS: Well, it's a cookie, so again, milk, tea, and coffee are not out of the question. Even sparkling wine would be playful against the ginger. But any number of dessert wines, particularly ones with caramel or roasted nut flavors would be delicious too. Rogue's Hazelnut Brown Nectar would speak to the nuttiness in this cookie, while standing up to the ginger. And Pyramid's Audacious Apricot Ale, with its apricot fruity forwardness and smooth malty finish would also be a fun choice.

Foley Station Triple Ginger Snaps with a Hazelnut Back

Whenever we're about to start a big hike into the Wallowas (Oregon's answer to the Swiss Alps!), we generally spend a night in La Grande. On such stop-overs, we always plan a visit to Foley Station, where no matter what time of day, the food is always creative and smashing, thanks to the restaurant's owner/chef Merlyn Baker.

Okay, so the Hazelnut Back portion of this recipe was my idea, not Chef Baker's. But I wanted to find a way to use his delightful cookie recipe in this book, and the hazelnuts really do contribute. And Baker did give it his approval. The original recipe (without hazelnuts) is my son Brandon's FAVORITE cookie. In fact, he's the one who suggested I try to talk Baker out of it several years ago. True to form, Baker didn't disappoint. So Brandon and I have been able to duplicate this marvelous treat ever since. It would be a dynamite offering for the ginger-hazelnut lovers on your gift list.

Using an electric mixer, cream the butter and brown sugar together until smooth and fluffy. Add the egg and molasses, blending well.

In a separate bowl, combine the flour, baking soda, salt, and ground ginger. Blend the flour mixture with the grated fresh ginger, crystalized ginger, and chopped hazelnuts, then blend with the butter mixture. Chill the dough for about 1 hour.

When ready to bake, preheat the oven to 350 degrees F.

Portion the dough for cookies of desired size (Chef Baker recommends 1/4-cup scoops) onto a lightly greased baking sheet, leaving 2 inches between each one. Press a whole hazelnut into the center of each cookie, then sprinkle each one with the sugar reserved from chopping the crystallized ginger (see following note). Bake for 10 to 14 minutes, depending on the size of the cookies and the desired level of crispness.

NOTE ON CRYSTALLIZED GINGER: Look for crystalized ginger in well-stocked bulk food sections and Asian markets. To easily chop, sprinkle the ginger with some granulated sugar while chopping to keep it from sticking to your knife, then sift the ginger out of the sugar. Reserve the sugar to coat the cookies before baking.

Makes 3 dozen cookies

1-1/2 cups all-purpose flour

1-1/2 cups coarsely chopped raw hazelnuts

3/4 cup shredded sweetened coconut

3/4 cup butter (1-1/2 sticks)

3/4 cup light corn syrup

3/4 cup firmly packed golden brown sugar

2 teaspoons vanilla extract

1/2 cup miniature semisweet chocolate chips

Hazelnut Hill

At Hazelnut Hill just south of Corvallis, Oregon, Rob and Sally Hilles can roast 50 pounds of hazelnuts in 5 minutes in their fluid-bed coffee roaster. No oils or butters are used in the process. Just very hot and lively airflow. Picture a giant hot air popcorn popper and you can understand the sort of jostling taking place in that chamber— it's enough to scrape the skins right off the nuts as they reach the precise temperature required for a consistent roast.

Roasted Coconutty Crisps

These are packed with coconut-nutty flavor. You start with raw hazelnuts so they have plenty of time to roast in the oven without getting overdone.

Preheat oven to 375 degrees F. Grease 2 cookie sheets and set aside.

In a medium bowl, combine the flour, hazelnuts, and coconut and set aside.

In a medium-sized saucepan, combine the butter, corn syrup and brown sugar. Heat the mixture over medium-high heat, just until it comes to a boil, stirring occasionally. Remove from heat and stir in the vanilla. Stir in the flour mixture, then stir in the chocolate chips, mixing well to evenly distribute all of the ingredients.

Drop rounded teaspoons of the dough onto the well-greased cookie sheets, leaving 2 inches between each cookie. Bake for 8 to 10 minutes, or until the mixture spreads out and bubbles. Remove from oven and let the cookies cool for 1 minute on the pan to set, then transfer to a cool, flat surface with a metal spatula. Cookies will be soft until they cool completely. Then they're crispy!

Makes 16 bars
(each measuring about 2 x 2 inches)

HAZELNUT BUTTER CRUST:

1-1/2 cups flour

1/3 cup ground raw hazelnuts

1 cup firmly packed light brown sugar

3/4 cup butter (1-1/2 sticks), softened

HAZELNUT TOPPING:

2/3 cup firmly packed light brown sugar

2/3 cup light corn syrup

2 eggs

1/4 cup butter (1/2 stick), melted

1 teaspoon vanilla

1/4 teaspoon salt

1-1/2 cups chopped raw hazelnuts

Hazelnut Butter Crust Bars

These are decadently delicious! And very rich, so a little goes a long way. When I created them, I was thinking about pecan pie and how I wanted my filling to provide a similar "take no prisoners" sort of experience. The crust is a shortbread style: buttery, sweet, and more cookie-like than flaky.

Preheat oven to 350 degrees F.

For the Hazelnut Butter Crust: In a food processor, or in a bowl using an electric mixer, combine the flour, hazelnuts, brown sugar and butter. Blend just until crumbly and beginning to hold together. Scrape the mixture into an ungreased 9-inch square pan. Press the mixture firmly and evenly into the bottom of the pan. Bake until lightly browned, about 20 to 25 minutes. Remove from oven.

Meanwhile, for the Hazelnut Topping: In a medium bowl, combine the brown sugar, light corn syrup, eggs, butter, vanilla and salt. Mix well. Stir in the hazelnuts.

When the crust has browned and been removed from the oven, let it stand for 5 minutes (to firm slightly), then gently spread the egg mixture over the surface of the partially cooked crust. Return to oven and bake until the top layer has set and is a rich golden brown, about 45 to 50 minutes. Remove from oven and cool completely on a rack before cutting. Store the bars in an airtight container.

 BEVERAGE THOUGHTS: A sip of scotch or your favorite whiskey really balances the sweet richness in this treat. A tawny port would be another route. And, of course, the Eola Hills LBV Cabernet Sauvignon Port or the David Hill Pinot Noir Port—with their toasty, nutty, caramely personalities, would be exquisite. Rich, but exquisite.

Makes 12-16 servings

1 Hazelnut Butter Crust (page 214),
    baked and cooled in a springform pan

FOR THE CHOCOLATE TRUFFLE FILLING:
16 ounces semi-sweet chocolate chips
1 cup heavy cream
5 tablespoons butter,
    cut into about 20 pieces

FOR THE CHOCOLATE GLAZE:
3 tablespoons butter, melted
2 tablespoons unsweetened cocoa powder
3 tablespoons milk or half & half
1/4 teaspoon vanilla extract
1-1/4 cups sifted confectioner's sugar

Double Trouble! Chocolate Truffle Tart with Hazelnut Crust

I had this vision: What if I layered my chocolate truffle sauce over a rich and buttery hazelnut crust, then smeared on an extra chocolate glaze, followed by a blanket of darkly roasted chunks of hazelnut? How would that turn out, I wondered? Well, the answer came at the end of a very long day. And even though by the time I finished making this masterpiece it was 11 pm on a week night, we dove in. "Wowie!" we said. Sure, there would be some tweaking involved with the construction concept. My first run-through had involved an 8-inch square pan, because I thought that I was aiming for a bar-cookie sort of creation. Negotiating those servings out of the pan turned out to be too messy, but boy, could I tell this baby had promise. Ultimately, it came down to the use of a springform pan, which made cutting far more graceful——if you're into elegance, like at a dinner party or something. Of course, if you're strictly gunning for the incredible taste experience it provides (Damn the mess, full speed ahead!), and don't have access to a springform pan (that's a two-piece arrangement involving a round base with a removable sidewall), then by all means, stick with the 8-inch square pan and just hack away at this awesome confection.

Preheat the oven to 350 degrees F.

Prepare the hazelnut crust as described in the Hazelnut Butter Crust Bar recipe (page 214), pressing the crumbly mixture into the bottom of a 10-inch springform pan. Bake in the preheated oven until the crust turns golden and appears cooked (it will still be very soft, however), about 30 minutes. Remove from the oven and set aside to cool.

Once the crust has cooled, prepare the chocolate truffle filling. Slowly melt the chocolate, without stirring, in a double-boiler arrangement (page 36). This will take about 20 minutes.

When the chocolate has melted, place the cream in a small, heavy-bottomed saucepan over medium-high heat, and warm just until the cream is steaming and small bubbles have formed around the edges.

Remove from heat and immediately pour it over the melted chocolate chips. Don't be alarmed when the chocolate seizes up. Just keep stirring gently with a flat wire whisk or a wooden spoon until the chocolate relaxes, softens up and ultimately blends into the warm cream. Keep the vessel positioned over the hot water because this will help keep the temperature at the melting point. Once the chocolate is smooth and creamy, stir in the butter, 2 or 3 pieces at a time and continue stirring until the mixture is well blended and smooth. There may be a few little chunks of chocolate that don't completely melt, but that's okay.

Lift the vessel of truffle sauce away from the hot water and wipe its outer sides with a towel so that no water will drip into the sauce when you tip the vessel to pour it out. Pour the sauce onto the surface of the cooled crust, scraping out every last drop with a rubber spatula. Smooth it out evenly, then set aside to cool for about 30 minutes. Then place the pan in the refrigerator to cool completely and set firmly.

Once the truffle sauce has set firmly, prepare the chocolate glaze. In a small bowl, whisk together the melted butter and the cocoa powder. Add the milk and vanilla extract and continue whisking. Finally, whisk in the confectioner's sugar. If the mixture seems too thick (it should be thin enough to drizzle from a spoon), whisk in a little more milk or half and half.

Spread the chocolate glaze over the surface of the tart, spreading it evenly out to the edge. Return the tart to the refrigerator to set the glaze. The tart may be served chilled or at room temperature. It's up to you. It will be softer if stored at room temperature, but it isn't a food safety issue.

TIP: If you want to get out in front of any Double Trouble Chocolate Truffle Tart cravings, go ahead and make the Hazelnut Butter Crust ahead of time—heck, make two or three—and then freeze. When ready to construct the tart, simply pop a frozen tart shell back down into the springform pan and assemble the rest of the recipe. Quick and delicious.

BEVERAGE THOUGHTS: For such a rich, chocolatey confection, Grand Marnier is always a winner, because the orange essence within this heavenly liqueur really sings in tune with the chocolate. But a tawny-style port is a lovely sidekick as well. Two Oregon favorites are Eola Hills LBV Cabernet Sauvignon Port Style wine, and David Hill's Pinot Noir Port. There's also Abacela's port, from Southern Oregon. Abacela grows five Portuguese varietals in their own vineyards specifically to create this estate port in a fruity and extra-rich ruby style that thrives in a chocolate environment. Of course, because of the flavor bridge of hazelnuts in the crust, this dessert also gets along very well with a big full-bodied Oregon Pinot Noir. So keep that in mind.

Pairing dessert wines

When pairing dessert wines with desserts, it's not exactly as cut-and-dried as you might think. Both components bring varying levels of acidity that affect their compatibility. From the wine end, a rich and nutty tawny port is less acidic than a late harvest Gewürztraminer. From the dessert side of things, think chocolate truffle versus lemon tart.

Pairing a sweet low acid wine (such as the tawny port) with a tangy dessert, or a low-acid dessert (such as a Crème Brûlée) with a high acid wine makes the tangier partner taste sour.

5 large egg whites, unbeaten

1 pound powdered sugar

1 pound ground roasted and skinned
    hazelnuts (about 3-1/4 cups)

1 tablespoon vanilla

McDonald Family's Hazelnut Macaroons

This is a family favorite of Wilsonville-area hazelnut growers Jill and Peter McDonald. Says Jill: "I've used this recipe from the kitchen of Peter's mother for many years. The macaroons don't look like anything fancy, but it's that hazelnut TASTE! One of my simplest, most reliable, useful, long-time favorites. Goes well with any fruit or ice cream. Always served with a good cup of Lapsang at teatime by Lady McDonald."

Mix together the egg whites, sugar, hazelnuts and vanilla with a spoon. Do not beat. Hold in the refrigerator for several hours to blend flavors and "relax" the mixture.

When ready to bake, preheat the oven to 325 degrees F.

Place a sheet of parchment on a baking sheet. Using a teaspoon or melon-baller, scoop the dough into about one-inch balls and place them on the parchment. Flatten each ball a bit with fingers or the base of a damp glass. There should be about 2 inches of space between the cookies. Bake for about 15 to 20 minutes, just until they are barely browned around the edges. Do not overcook, as they're nicer chewy. They will spread out but should still have a slightly soft interior and be light brown on the bottom.

Cool thoroughly on cooling racks before storing in an airtight container. They freeze well. Extra uncooked dough can be frozen; thaw before baking.

BEVERAGE THOUGHTS: Who am I to second guess Lady McDonald? Lapsang tea it is. Of course, for an after dinner nosh, don't overlook one of Scotland's more popular adult beverages.

Makes about 45 biscotti

4 cups all-purpose flour

1 tablespoon baking powder

1/2 teaspoon salt

1-1/2 cups chopped roasted and
    skinned hazelnuts

1 cup dried cherries

1 cup butter (2 sticks), softened

1-1/2 cups granulated sugar

4 large eggs

1/4 cup Frangelico (hazelnut liqueur)

2 teaspoons grated orange zest

2 teaspoons vanilla extract

1-1/2 pounds semisweet (or bittersweet)
    chocolate, coarsely chopped

Unsweetened cocoa powder (optional)

BEVERAGE THOUGHTS: Well, biscotti have traditionally been something to serve with a glass of wine, so why not bring out the chocolate-friendly Pinot Noir? For a beer, I would definitely lean toward something rich and malty, like Rogue's Shakespeare Oatmeal Stout.

Chocolate-Dipped Hazelnut-Cherry Biscotti

Preheat the oven to 325 degrees F. Lightly grease a cookie sheet.

In a medium-sized bowl, combine the flour with the baking powder, salt, hazelnuts and cherries; set aside.

In a large bowl, cream together the butter and sugar until light and fluffy. Beat in the eggs, one at a time, just until blended. Stir in the Frangelico, orange zest and vanilla. Stir the flour mixture into the butter mixture, and continue stirring until the flour is well incorporated.

Divide the dough into 4 equal parts. Form each portion of dough into a log measuring about 9 inches long and 3 inches in diameter. Gently transfer each log onto the baking sheet, leaving plenty of room between them for even baking.

Bake for 25 minutes in the preheated oven, until a pale golden brown. Remove from oven (but don't turn the oven off) and cool the logs on the baking sheet for 15 minutes. Using a sharp or serrated knife, cut the still-warm logs crosswise and diagonally into 1/2-inch thick slices. Arrange the slices cut side down on the baking sheet. Bake the biscotti for 10 minutes, then turn each one over and continue baking until light golden brown, about 10 more minutes. Remove from oven and transfer the biscotti onto cooling racks.

While the biscotti are cooling, slowly melt the chocolate, without stirring, in a double-boiler arrangement (page 36). This will take about 20 minutes. Dip one side of each biscotto into the melted chocolate to a depth of about 1/4 inch. After allowing excess chocolate to drip off, place the biscotti, chocolate side up, on baking sheets. Refrigerate until the chocolate is firm (about 30 minutes).

If desired, you can give the chocolate coating a dusting of cocoa powder. To do so, dip a pastry brush into the cocoa, then lightly brush the cocoa over the chilled chocolate.

These biscotti can be made ahead and stored in airtight containers at room temperature for about 1 week. For longer term storage, up to 2 or 3 months, pack them into re-sealable plastic bags and freeze.

1-3/4 cups all-purpose flour

1/2 cup instant nonfat dry milk powder

1 teaspoon baking soda

1 teaspoon ground cinnamon

1/4 teaspoon salt

1-3/4 cups quick-cooking oatmeal
   (not instant)

1 cup finely chopped dried figs
   (or other dried fruit that has been
   chopped into 1/4-inch pieces)

1 cup coarsely chopped roasted and
   skinned hazelnuts

Hazelnut and Fig Jar Cookies

This is a great kid activity, assembling the ingredients for a make-ahead cookie mix, one layer at a time into quart size canning jars. Attach a tag explaining how to use the mix and give away to lucky friends and family members.

To assemble the mix, combine the flour, skim milk powder, baking soda, cinnamon and salt in a small bowl. Spoon this mixture into the bottom of a quart canning jar. On top of that, spoon on the oatmeal, then add the layer of dried figs, and finally, the layer of hazelnuts. Attach the lid.

CREATE A GIFT TAG FOR EACH JAR WITH THE FOLLOWING INSTRUCTIONS:

Preheat oven to 350 degrees F.

In a large bowl, cream together the butter and brown sugar until light and fluffy. Beat in the vanilla, then stir in the thoroughly drained crushed pineapple. Add the contents of the cookie mix and stir until thoroughly combined.

Drop rounded teaspoons of dough about 2 inches apart onto a lightly greased baking sheet. Bake in the preheated oven until golden brown, about 12 to15 minutes. Using a spatula, remove the cookies from the baking pan to cool on a cooling rack. Makes about 2 dozen large cookies.

To make a batch of Hazelnut and Fig Jar Cookies, you will need:

1/2 cup (1 stick) butter, softened

1 cup firmly packed brown sugar

1/2 teaspoon vanilla extract

1 (14 ounce) can crushed pineapple, well drained

1 jar of "Hazelnut and Fig Jar Cookie Mix"

River Brownies and Hazelnuts

IN THE PLANNING STAGE OF ANY OUTDOOR ADVENTURE, when a fellow trekker takes the river brownie pledge, there's no question what you'll be getting: a big pan of chocolaty gooey-rich and decadent finger food.

Unlike plain ol' fudge brownies—which are perfectly fine in their own right and place—river brownies come laden with all sorts of hidden treasures. Chunky islets of chocolate, shoals of roasted hazelnuts and almonds, riffles of caramel or peanut butter. Anything that will provide an extra boost of energy to hurl you further along the stream or up the mountain or over the granite scree. Gorp on steroids. And so much the better to go with those three ounces of scotch you've tucked into your pack for after dinner!

Such additives are what set river brownies apart from other sweet delights. The trick, however, is to create something that's decadent to be sure, yet harbors enough restraint to allow one-handed management in case you're other hand is preoccupied with a canoe paddle or fishing rod or trekking pole.

It's difficult to predict how far any given pan of river brownies will go, because part of the deal is NOT cutting them into tidy little servings. River brownies are designed to service outdoor appetites, and part of the delight is in carving off scrumptious blocks sized according to the degree of need you've worked up.

Some river rats guard their recipes. But most of my friends share. Which is how I've compiled such a sturdy collection. Each one takes me back to a specific spot in the wilderness. One friend's creation places me amongst a stand of towering firs alongside Oregon's deep blue, silently rushing McKenzie River.

And then there's the Metolius River, and the late spring adventure spent delving below its surface. We'd donned dry suits and diving masks so we could peer into the crystalline depths of the Blue Pool where a school of redband trout were loafing. At the end of an exhilarating hour in that cold, cold water, it was Chris's Double Shot Espresso Brownies that fueled our recovery from the shivers.

Every June I gather my river brownie recipes in anticipation of great adventures yet-to-come. Here are three of the best. Enjoy, and Happy Trails!

Makes 24 2-inch brownies

24 ounces semisweet or bittersweet
    chocolate, chopped

1 cup (2 sticks) butter, cut into chunks

6 large eggs

2 cups granulated sugar

1 tablespoon vanilla extract

1-1/2 cups all-purpose flour

1 teaspoon baking powder

1/4 teaspoon salt

1 cup chopped roasted and skinned
    hazelnuts

Classic River Brownies

Starting with a rich-and-chocolaty brownie batter made from scratch, there are many directions that you can take this recipe. Mostly, it's about adding "stuff." Stuff that is both tasty and nutritious. Hazelnuts and extra chunks of chocolate are always at the top of the list. In fact, I don't consider them optional, because of their energy-boosting potential, as well as the extra layer of flavor they provide.

Preheat the oven to 350 degrees F. Butter a 9 x13-inch baking pan and set aside.

Slowly melt the chocolate and the butter, without stirring, in a double-boiler arrangement (page 36). This will take about 20 minutes.

In a large bowl, whisk (or use a hand-held mixer) together the eggs and sugar. Fold in the melted chocolate mixture and vanilla extract. In a separate bowl, whisk together the flour, baking powder and salt, then fold into the chocolate mixture, along with the hazelnuts, until just combined.

At this point, if you're adding any ingredients from the "Extra Additions" list below, stir them in, then scrape the batter into the prepared pan. If you're going with the "peanut butter cup option" then scrape half of the prepared batter into the baking pan. Arrange the peanut butter cups upside down onto the batter, spacing them evenly in rows. Push the cups down into the batter slightly, then top with the remaining batter and gently spread smooth.

Bake in the preheated oven on the center rack just until a toothpick inserted into the center comes out with just a few moist crumbs, about 40 to 50 minutes. Remove from oven and allow to cool completely before cutting.

Extra additions (select 2 or 3): 1 cup peanut butter chips or butterscotch chips, 1/2 cup sweetened flaked coconut, 1/2 cup raisins, 1 cup chopped peppermint bark (either commercially-made or home-made) or coarsely chopped Andes Creme de Menthe thins (the ones in the green foil wrappers), 1 cup chocolate-covered peanuts.

PEANUT BUTTER CUP OPTION: This takes16 miniature chocolate-covered peanut butter cups, foil wrapping removed. If you choose this variation, you'll need to be more discriminating about adding any ingredients from the first "extra additions list" because the brownies would tend to be too rich and prone to falling apart in hand.

1 package Super Moist German Chocolate
    cake mix (do not follow directions
    on the box)

2/3 cup evaporated milk (divided)

3/4 cup (1-1/2 sticks) melted butter

1 cup coarsely chopped roasted and
    skinned hazelnuts

12 ounces chocolate chips

50 good quality caramels
    (cellophane wrappers removed)

Mary's River Brownies

Hazelnut grower, co-owner of Tyee Wine Cellars, good friend, and fellow adventurers Margy and Dave Buchanan have a tried-and-true favorite which came about during their river-rafting adventures. Challenging rapids, lazing in stream pools and hot springs, and huddling close to campfires would always leave them "refreshed, invigorated, and hungry." Mary Catt Sturgis, special friend since the hallowed halls of junior high, was their designated river brownie chef. And it's her namesake creation that gave them that extra bit of oomph, whether tackling an extra-tough set of rapids at the end of the day or one last campfire song before hitting the sack.

Preheat the oven to 350 degrees F.

Butter a 9 x13-inch glass baking dish.

In a large mixing bowl, stir the cake mix together with 1/3 cup of the evaporated milk and the melted butter. The batter will be very thick. Spread half of the batter into the baking dish. Cover with hazelnuts and bake for 5 minutes in the preheated oven. Meanwhile, roll the remaining batter into a 9 x 13-inch rectangle between two sheets of waxed paper and freeze for a few minutes to make it even firmer.

Remove the partially-cooked brownies from the oven when the time is up and layer on the chocolate chips. Combine the caramels with the remaining 1/3 cup of evaporated milk, then melt in a microwave oven and spread over the chocolate chips.

Remove the lightly frozen batter from the freezer and peel off the top sheet of waxed paper. Invert the dough onto the top of the caramel sauce and peel off the second sheet of waxed paper. Return the pan to the oven and continue baking for 25 to 30 minutes until the batter is set but still relatively moist. Remove from oven and cool completely before cutting and removing from the pan.

3/4 cup (1-1/2 sticks) softened butter,
   divided

3 oz unsweetened chocolate

3/4 cup granulated sugar

1/4 cup instant espresso powder
   (or instant coffee), divided

2 large eggs

1 teaspoon vanilla extract

1/2 cup coarsely chopped roasted
   and skinned hazelnuts

1/2 cup all purpose flour

1-1/4 cups confectioner's sugar

2 to 3 tablespoons Kahlua
   (or other coffee-flavored liqueur)

1/3 cup semi-sweet chocolate chips

Additional coarsely chopped hazelnuts
   (optional; see note below)

Espresso River Brownies

My friend Chris Peterson shared these coffee-flavored wonders during a wonderful weekend on the Metolius River in Central Oregon. The intense coffee flavor compliments the smoky-toasty flavor of the hazelnuts.

Preheat oven to 350 degrees F.

Butter a 8 or 9-inch square pan.

Combine 1/2 cup of the butter (cut into chunks) with the unsweetened chocolate in a 3-quart saucepan. Stir often over low heat until melted and smooth. Remove from heat and beat in the sugar, 3 tablespoons of the espresso powder, eggs and vanilla until well blended. Stir in the hazelnuts, then stir in the flour just until incorporated.

Pour the batter into the cake pan. Bake in the preheated oven until the center is just set (20 to 25 minutes). Allow to cool completely in the pan on a rack for about an hour.

In a bowl, combine the remaining 1/4 cup of butter and the remaining 1 tablespoon of espresso powder with the confectioner's sugar and 2 tablespoons of Kahlua. With an electric mixer on medium speed, beat the mixture until smooth and fluffy, adding up to 1 more tablespoon of Kahlua. Spread evenly over the top of the cooled cake.

Place the chocolate chips in a small re-sealable plastic bag. Microwave on full power for 15-second intervals until the chips are completely melted. Squeeze the melted chocolate into one corner of the bag. Clip off about 1/4 inch of the corner and drizzle the chocolate over the brownies. Chill until the chocolate is firm.

NOTE: If you want to pack these brownies along on an adventure, then consider covering the frosting and chocolate drizzles with an additional 1/2 cup of chopped hazelnuts, which will keep the brownies from being too messy!

Spring into Summer with Rhubarb

A couple of planting seasons ago, my young neighbor figured out a universal truth as we hunkered down in front of his freshly-sown lettuce seeds: come Spring, the world takes off in all directions representing greenness and life; then, before you know it, "you've got salad!"

It's an encouraging thought that our winter-weary palates can be tantalized by the fresh tastes of Spring-into-Summer produce. We've waited months upon months for the exquisite sight and flavor of such Northwest specialties as asparagus, wild mushrooms, sugar-snap peas, and rhubarb.

The latter, rhubarb, can be traced back to pioneer days. Root balls of this hearty "pie plant" came west with the settlers over the Oregon trail, and did so well here—particularly in the fertile soil and kindly climate of the Willamette Valley—that it grew into a serious commercial crop. In fact, of the five states growing rhubarb commercially, Oregon leads the pack in production, so there's plenty of reason to celebrate its arrival every spring in the Oregon marketplace.

Our most popular variety, Crimson Crown, possesses the rich, ruby color preferred by consumers and processors nationwide. Look for stalks that are firm, bright and glossy, and if you're not going to use them immediately, simply wrap them in a damp paper towel and refrigerate in an airtight container, which will usually ensure freshness up to 2 weeks.

For longer storage, my method of choice is freezing, since it's as simple as "chop-and-toss." Chop into chunks, then toss into freezer bags and freeze. Another plus is that frozen chunks of rhubarb can be used in most recipes calling for fresh, without altering the formula. So, fresh or frozen, it cooks down to a velvety sauce in no time, making an exceptionally delicious sweet tart with little fuss, and providing the hearty backbone to a homemade chutney in under thirty minutes.

7 cups diced rhubarb

1-3/4 cups granulated sugar

1-1/3 cups all-purpose flour, divided

1 teaspoon ground cinnamon, divided

1 teaspoon ground nutmeg, divided

1/4 teaspoon salt

2 tablespoons water

1 cup firmly packed brown sugar

1 cup old-fashioned rolled oats
    (not "instant")

1/2 cup chopped raw hazelnuts

3/4 cup (1-1/2 sticks) butter, softened

Rhubarb and Hazelnut Crisp

One of its most remarkable qualities is that it takes so little fussing to turn rhubarb into any number of simple, tasty offerings. No peeling, pitting, coring or stemming. Simply cut the lovely red stalks into chunks and proceed with your recipe. If you can wield a chef's knife and boil water, then you're 10 minutes away from rhubarb pudding or rhubarb sauce. You spend more time than that picking through the basil in preparation for your special pesto concoctions.

Preheat oven to 375 degrees F.

Butter a 13 x 9 x 2-inch baking dish.

Toss the rhubarb with the granulated sugar, 1/3 cup of the flour, 1/4 teaspoon of the cinnamon, 1/4 teaspoon of the nutmeg, the salt and the water. Spread the rhubarb mixture into the baking dish.

In a small bowl, combine the brown sugar with the oats, hazelnuts, and remaining cinnamon, nutmeg and flour. Cut in the butter and mix until a crumbled consistency is achieved. Sprinkle this topping over the rhubarb, making sure it drops down into and around the fruit.

Bake for about 30 to 45 minutes or until the rhubarb is tender and the topping is golden. Serve warm, at room temperature, or chilled, with cream or vanilla ice cream.

BEVERAGE THOUGHTS: Trying to pair rhubarb with any type of wine can be a challenge. But the Tualatin Estate semi-sparkling Muscat Frizzante brings a lot of fruit and fun to this dessert, and is really a lovely compliment.

4 cups 1-inch diced rhubarb

1/4 to 1/2 cup granulated sugar

2 tablespoons water

Simple Rhubarb Sauce in the Microwave

When local rhubarb is coming on strong at the farmers' markets, consider this sauce for a sweet and speedy topping to serve over a vanilla ice cream and hazelnut sundae. It freezes well, so make a lot of it!

Combine the ingredients in a microwave-safe bowl. Cover and microwave on HIGH until the rhubarb is tender, about 3 minutes, turning and stirring once. Purée the mixture in a blender or food processor, adding more sugar if desired.

This sauce will keep in the refrigerator for several days. For long-term storage, pour into freezer containers, leaving about 1 inch headspace, cover and freeze.

1 cup chopped raw hazelnuts

1/2 cup granulated sugar

6 tablespoons softened butter, divided

1 teaspoon ground cinnamon

1-1/2 cups firmly packed golden
    brown sugar

1 large egg

1 cup plain low-fat yogurt

2 cups all purpose flour

1 teaspoon baking soda

1/2 teaspoon salt

1 pound rhubarb, cut into 1-inch chunks

Rhubarb Cake with Sugared Hazelnut Topping

Preheat oven to 350 degrees F.

Butter a 13 x 9-inch baking pan.

Prepare the topping by combining the hazelnuts and sugar with 2 tablespoons of softened butter and the cinnamon in a small bowl; set aside.

For the cake, beat together the brown sugar with the remaining 4 tablespoons of softened butter and the egg until well blended. Beat in the yogurt. In another bowl, combine the flour with the baking soda and salt, then add to the butter and sugar mixture; stir just to blend. Fold in the rhubarb and spread the batter into the prepared pan. Sprinkle on the hazelnut topping.

Bake for 35 to 40 minutes, until the center springs back when gently pressed.

BEVERAGE THOUGHTS: Beyond coffee, tea, and espresso, a smooth tawny port would be complimentary to the rhubarb and nuts.

1-1/2 cups old-fashioned rolled oats
   (not "instant")

3/4 cup all-purpose flour

2 cups firmly packed golden
   brown sugar, divided

1 cup coarsely chopped lightly roasted
   and skinned hazelnuts

3/4 cup (1-1/2 sticks) butter,
   chilled and cut into 12 pieces

3 pounds apples (consider using 2
   different varieties), peeled, cored,
   and cut into eighths to measure
   about 10 cups

1-1/2 teaspoons ground cinnamon

Pinch of salt

Grated zest of 1 orange
   (optional, but delicious!)

Autumn Apple Crisp

Just about the time I'm in the mood for apple crisp, on come the new-crop Oregon hazelnuts. Their toasty-sweet character contributes grandly to the crisp and sugary topping on the apples.

Preheat the oven to 350 degrees F.

Lightly butter an 9 x 13-inch (or thereabouts) baking dish.

Place the oats, flour, 1-1/2 cups of the brown sugar and the hazelnuts in a food processor, and process briefly to blend the mixture. Add the butter and, using short pulses, process until the ingredients are mixed. Be careful not to over-mix. You want to maintain the texture of the oats and the nuts. The mixture will be dry-looking.

In a large bowl, combine the apples, the remaining 1/2 cup brown sugar, and the cinnamon, salt, and orange zest. Toss until well mixed.

Layer the apple mixture in the baking dish. Cover it evenly with the oat topping, patting it gently into place. Bake in the center of the oven until the topping is golden and the fruit is bubbling, about 45 minutes. Remove the dish and either serve the apple crisp hot or let it cool to room temperature.

Strawberries and Hazelnuts

HAZELNUTS PAIR BEAUTIFULLY WITH MOST FRUITS OF THE PACIFIC NORTHWEST. Pears and peaches, of course. And raspberries? Well, hazelnuts and raspberries do produce amazingly elegant results when brought together. But in the course of the annual harvest cycle, the first fruit to consider is the strawberry, because it's season hits its stride in early June. Indeed, there are those who cheerfully endure the downside of a soggy Northwest spring only because they know that when rainbows finally appear, the pots at their ends will be filled with sweet, juicy, Oregon strawberries.

James Beard knew about Oregon strawberries. He talked often of the wild ones that grew along the coast near his boyhood town of Gearhart. They were so small that it took hours to gather enough to satisfy one's appetite. But they were so good that nobody minded. He said they were filled with a sugary, wild essence that lingered on his palate and filled him with a nostalgia that stayed with him even into his later years.

So even though gallons and gallons of Oregon strawberries have already passed through my life, the season should never be taken lightly. Not when it's so frustratingly short. Not when for every fresh, sweet, succulent Oregon strawberry there are dozens and dozens of road-weary imitations to contend with the rest of the year.

There's an art to expressing appreciation for such precious bounty. One of my favorite ways is Chocolate Dipped. Admittedly, there are a few people who would no sooner dip a strawberry in chocolate than they would gild a lily. But for every one of them, there must be twenty of us who get absolutely goofy in the presence of such primal temptation.

Indeed, it's the kind of homemade confection that will make you an instant success at parties. Just check out any summer potluck where there's an abundance of desserts. Even if they're the last to appear, chocolate-covered strawberries are always the first to disappear.

To create such a treat, select only beautiful specimens: no bruises or imperfect caps and stems. Since they deteriorate quickly, plan on using them within one or two days of purchase. Until the dipping begins, store the berries in a shallow pan lined with paper towels. Cover with more paper towels and plastic wrap to hold in a little moisture. Don't wash them until just before use. And then give them another light pat with a paper towel before allowing them to come in contact with the melted chocolate.

Now, you may encounter some culinarily jaded souls who need an extra boost to make the chocolate-covered strawberry experience as special as it was the very first time. This is where my first recipe comes in. It's an original Chocolate Covered Strawberry creation I call "Jan's Killer Berries Supreme."

Makes enough coating for about
2 dozen strawberries

1-1/2 pints fresh strawberries,
    the pretty caps and stems intact

 12 ounces semi-sweet chocolate,
    in 1/4-inch chunks

1 tablespoon vegetable shortening

2 tablespoons butter, cut in 8 pieces

1/2 cup (1 stick) butter, softened

3 cups confectioner's sugar

1 tablespoon milk

2 teaspoons hazelnut or almond extract

1/2 cup finely chopped darkly roasted
    and skinned hazelnuts

Jan's Killer Berries Supreme with Hazelnut Filling

These are the ultimate chocolate-covered berries. Their one and only professional gig was many years ago at Corvallis' first Grace Center Strawberry Jubilee, which was the reason I created them in the first place.

Rinse the berries gently, leaving stems and caps on. Pat completely dry with paper towels. Store on paper towels to absorb any oozing juice until ready to use.

Slowly melt the chocolate with the vegetable shortening and 2 tablespoons of butter without stirring, in a double-boiler arrangement (page 36). This will take about 20 minutes.

Meanwhile, cream together the 1/2 cup butter and sugar. Beat in the milk, hazelnut or almond extract, and hazelnuts. This will form a stiff dough.

Now pinch off small portions of the dough and pat out on your hand into thin round pancakes (do this quickly or the dough will begin to melt). Place a berry in the center of a pancake and form the dough up around the berry, making sure the upper portion of the berry and the leaves remain exposed. If possible, chill the strawberries at this point so the chocolate will harden quickly around the hazelnut dough without melting the dough.

Dip the chilled dough-covered strawberries in the melted chocolate, to within 1/4-inch of the top of the dough mixture (in other words, leave a rim of the dough exposed for the prettiest presentation) and place on a waxed paper-lined cookie sheet. Chill. Remove from cookie sheet when the chocolate has hardened and place in a covered container in the refrigerator. Berries are best when served within 24 hours. After that, they begin to ooze berry juice but they still taste wonderful!

Yields 18 to 20 chocolate-covered
strawberries

18 to 20 perfect strawberries
    (good color, no soft spots,
    beautiful green caps and stems)
8 ounces semi-sweet chocolate
    (broken into 1/4-inch pieces)
1 cup finely chopped roasted
    and skinned hazelnuts

Just Chocolate-Covered Strawberries on a Hazelnut Bed

When you're in a hurry, here's the quick-but-effective approach to chocolate-coating your berries. Keep in mind that even though chocolate-covered strawberries are a culinary end unto themselves, you shouldn't overlook their garnishing potential. They will quickly jazz up the top of a chocolate layer cake or bowl of vanilla ice cream. Ditto for chocolate mousse, or a platter of cookies.

Rinse the berries gently, leaving stems and caps on. Pat completely dry with paper towels. Store on paper towels to absorb any oozing juice until ready to use.

Slowly melt the chocolate, without stirring, in a double-boiler arrangement (page 36). This will take about 20 minutes.

While the chocolate is melting, spread the hazelnuts out on a platter to form a bed on which you will place the dipped strawberries.

Once the chocolate has melted, remove the pan from the heat. Holding a strawberry by its stem end, dip it into the chocolate two thirds of the way up towards the stem. Set the berry down on the bed of hazelnuts. Repeat with the remaining berries. Place the platter in the refrigerator so the chocolate can firm up. When you pick up a strawberry, your first bite will be a triple-header of fruit, chocolate and nut. Wowie!

BEVERAGE THOUGHT: Sparkling wine, hello!

Makes 3 to 4 servings

**1 pint good quality strawberries,
  pretty caps and stems intact**

About 1 cup of sour cream

About 1 cup of golden brown sugar

**1/2 cup finely chopped darkly
  roasted and skinned hazelnuts**

Don's Strawberries with a Twist

Strawberries dipped in sour cream and brown sugar. What could be more simple? I learned this wonderful and easy trick from my brother many years ago when he was still in college. I think it must have been one of his most impressive ways to woo a date. Over the years, I started zooping up the brown sugar with roasted hazelnuts for an even richer layering of flavors.

Rinse the berries gently, leaving stems and caps on. Pat completely dry with paper towels. Store on paper towels to absorb any oozing juice until ready to use.

Arrange the strawberries on a platter or in a beautiful bowl. Place the sour cream in a small, attractive bowl. In a matching (or at least coordinating) bowl, combine the brown sugar with the hazelnuts.

Place all of the components in the middle of the table and simply encourage the diners to take a strawberry, and while holding it with the stem end, dip it in sour cream and then dip the sour cream end into the brown sugar mixture. Yum! Thanks Don!

BEVERAGE THOUGHT: Again...sparkling wine.

QuickTIP

Darkly roasted hazelnuts are great additions to hand-cranked ice cream. But to keep the nuts from getting soggy in the freezer, do what the professionals do: coat them in chocolate first.

Oregon's Own Berry—A Gift to the World

The Marionberry, of course. Bold, purple and proud, it's a unique contemporary variety of blackberry that was introduced in Oregon in 1956, after years and years of cross-breeding. The path that plant breeders traveled to obtain this particular berry was circuitous, to say the least, but the creation of the Marionberry began with the pairing of a blackberry with a raspberry, which produced a Loganberry. Many different crossings sprang from the Loganberry, and ultimately two of those breeds—the Chehalem and the Olallie—were crossed to produce the Marionberry.

The Oregon Raspberry and Blackberry Commission proudly boasts that the Marionberry is the most widely planted blackberry variety in the world. It's named after Marion County, where it was first produced. The fruit is medium to large, round in cross section and longer than wide. Compared to evergreen blackberries, they have smaller seeds, are juicier and have an intense, rich "earthy Cabernet" flavor with a dark purple color. Their superior flavor makes them ideal for baking and their large, sturdy structure holds up well in everything from cobblers to preserves.

**The equivalent of 2 (8 or 9-inch)
    rounds of sponge cake**

Raspberry jam

2 cups fresh raspberries

2 cups fresh Marionberries

**1 (8 or 10-ounce) can crushed pineapple,
    drained**

**1-1/2 cups coarsely chopped roasted
    and skinned hazelnuts**

**1/2 cup whole or halved roasted and
    skinned hazelnuts (for garnish)**

1/2 to 3/4 cup dry sherry, or to taste

1/2 cup brandy

**Optional liquor: about 1/4 cup
    Grand Marnier**

Soft custard (recipe on next page)

1 cup heavy cream, whipped

McMillan Raspberry and Marionberry Trifle
with Candied Hazelnuts

This is one of my favorite ways to enjoy the fruits of summer. Layer after delectable layer of sponge cake, fresh fruit, soft custard and whipped cream, generously laced with sherry, brandy, and perhaps even a splash of Grand Marnier if you're feeling extravagant. I learned how it's composed from my mother, Margaret. All of our Clan McMillan women have known how to make it. It seemed like all festivities in my youth ended with a Trifle. And the older I got, the deeper down into the bottom layers I was allowed to scoop (which is where all the liquor ends up, of course!). Mom will still make one at the drop of a hat. And she never cheats on the custard. Always from scratch. Never out of a box.

Restaurants rarely get this right because it's simply not cost-effective to include the amount of custard, fruit and liquor necessary to achieve sinful perfection.

Cut horizontally through each sponge cake (a serrated knife works best) and gently lay the halves open. Spread the bottom half of each cake with raspberry jam, then replace the top halves, creating jam sandwiches. Cut these sandwiches into 1- or 2-inch cubes.

Layer the bottom of a large bowl with a 3-quart capacity (preferably a lovely crystal or glass bowl so the beautiful layers will show) with half of the cake-and-jam cubes. Next, spread about 2 cups of the berries over the cubes, and then half of the crushed pineapple over the berries. Sprinkle on half of the chopped hazelnuts.

Combine the sherry, brandy and (optionally) Grand Marnier in a measuring cup with a pouring spout. Drizzle half of this liquid (or less, depending on your taste) over the mixture, then spoon on about half of the warm custard. Begin layering again, starting with the cake-and-jam cubes, then the remaining liquor, and ending with the custard (you may not use all of the custard, depending on the size of your bowl.) Refrigerate the trifle at this point for at least 4 hours, and preferably overnight.

Before serving, spread on the whipped cream and garnish the top with fresh berries and the whole or halved hazelnuts. To serve, scoop into individual dessert dishes. Be sure to scoop all the way down through the dessert for each serving, because that's where all the juices end up.

SOFT CUSTARD SAUCE:

4 eggs

1/2 cup sugar

1/4 teaspoon salt

4 cups milk

SOFT CUSTARD SAUCE: In the top of a double boiler, beat the eggs. Mix in the sugar, salt and milk. Stir the mixture over hot water (this can be done directly on the burner if you use a heavy-bottomed pot and are careful not to get the mixture too hot), stirring constantly until it begins to thicken. When the custard is thick enough to coat the spoon, remove from heat and stir in 2 teaspoons vanilla extract. Makes about 4-1/2 cups custard. Use while warm, or gently re-heat before using if making ahead.

ABOUT SPONGE CAKE: Sponge cake is not fun to make from scratch, so I've always managed to find bakeries willing to supply me with the undecorated sponge layers. Any of the suggested substitutes (angel food, chiffon or pound cake) simply don't produce perfection.

BEVERAGE THOUGHTS: Since there's already a lot of alcohol going on in this dessert, you might think enough is enough. But you'd be wrong. This is such a special creation, why not introduce just one more interesting alcohol note? In this case, Adelsheim's rendition of a classic ice wine, their Deglace of Pinot Noir, is made from 100 percent Pinot Noir grapes. So it brings a lot of fruit to the palate. There's some wonderful berry, orange blossom and nectarine flavors with a sweet hit that is balanced by a natural acidity that keeps it on the interesting side of edgy. Just what you want for a dessert that already is loaded with brandy, sherry, and maybe even Grand Marnier. Yahoo!

Makes 4 servings

MARIONBERRY SAUCE:

1 quart frozen Marionberries, thawed

3/4 cup granulated sugar

2 tablespoons cornstarch

Pinch of salt

DUMPLINGS:

1 cup sifted flour

1-1/2 teaspoons baking powder

1/2 teaspoon salt

1/4 cup granulated sugar

2 tablespoons butter or margarine

1/2 cup milk (more if needed)

1/2 teaspoon vanilla

Good quality vanilla ice cream

Coarsely chopped darkly roasted
   and skinned hazelnuts

The McAdams Family Dumplings with Marionberry Sauce

From Lake Oswego friend Cheryl Taylor, this is a wonderful dessert featuring the Marionberries grown on her folks' farm in Lebanon, Oregon. Cheryl tries to freeze enough quart containers of the berries each summer to guarantee dumpling hits throughout the year. Give yourself a treat...try this recipe.

To prepare the sauce, drain the juice from the whole Marionberries. Combine the sugar, cornstarch, and salt with the juice in a medium saucepan. Stirring constantly, bring the mixture to a boil and simmer gently until it thickens. Fold in the whole berries and simmer gently while preparing the dumplings.

To prepare the dumplings, sift together the flour, baking powder, salt and sugar. Cut in or rub in the butter. Add the milk and vanilla to this mixture, stirring to make a thick batter (however, if it seems too thick, add a little bit more milk). Drop by spoonfuls into the boiling sauce, then cover and steam the dumplings gently in the sauce for 20 minutes (do not lift the cover during the steaming process). Serve the dumplings and sauce warm with good-quality vanilla ice cream and a handful of the darkly roasted hazelnuts.

 BEVERAGE THOUGHTS: This is a delight with Abacela's very fruity and rich ruby-style port. You could also serve one of the many ice wines that are being produced in the state from such wonderful grapes as Gewürztraminer and Viognier.

Makes 4 servings

2 cups Marionberries, or other caneberry,
    such as blackberries, Loganberries,
    or raspberries
Granulated sugar to taste
2 cups vanilla ice cream, softened
6 tablespoons orange-flavored liquor
    (such as Grand Marnier or Cointreau)
1 cup heavy cream, whipped
Whole berries for garnish

Berries Romanoff

Gently smash the berries with a potato masher or the back of a spoon, leaving about one-third of the berries whole. Sprinkle with granulated sugar to taste. Place the ice cream in a large bowl, then stir to soften and smooth it out. Reserve one cup of the berries and stir the rest into the softened ice cream, along with the liqueur. Gently fold in the whipped cream. Quickly divide the reserved cup of berries among 4 dessert glasses (clear glass is the most elegant because you will be able to see the layers). Spoon the cream mixture into the glasses, top each serving with one or more whole berries and serve.

BEVERAGE THOUGHT: This is another one that is particularly elegant with a bit of the bubbly.

2-1/2 cups all purpose flour

1 cup granulated sugar

1/4 teaspoon salt

1 teaspoon baking powder

1 teaspoon baking soda

1 cup chopped roasted and
   skinned hazelnuts

1-1/2 cups fresh cranberries

Grated zest of 2 oranges

2 eggs, beaten

1 cup buttermilk

3/4 cup vegetable oil

FOR TOP OF CAKE:

1 cup orange juice

1 cup granulated sugar

Whipped cream, optional

Orange Cranberry Torte

When two of Corvallis' finest citizens, Maria and Charlie Tomlinson, owned the Harrison House Bed and Breakfast, guests were treated to some of Maria's best breakfast fare. One of her favorites was this flavorful torte, which was from her childhood. At the B & B, its nutty, citrus and berry character was in harmony with most of their egg dishes. And because the cake improves with age, it's a convenient choice to keep on hand for last minute guests.

Preheat oven to 350 degrees F.

Generously butter a 16-inch tube pan.

In a medium-sized bowl, combine the flour, sugar, salt, baking powder, and baking soda. Stir in the nuts, cranberries and orange zest. Combine the eggs, milk and vegetable oil and add this mixture to the flour/fruit mixture and stir until blended.

Pour the batter into the tube pan and bake for 1 hour. Allow to stand until partially cool, then remove from pan and place on a rack centered over a wide dish.

Combine the orange juice and sugar. Heat in a microwave (or over a burner) until the sugar dissolves. Pour this icing over the cake. Collect the icing that has dripped onto the dish and spread it over the cake again. Tilt the cake in all directions so the orange-sugar glaze evenly coats all sides.

Wrap the cake in aluminum foil. Refrigerate for at least 24 hours (or up to 2 weeks or more). Serve in slices with or without whipped cream.

2 cups dried figs, quartered

1-1/2 cups chopped roasted
and skinned hazelnuts

3/4 cup coarsely chopped crystallized
ginger (about 4 ounces; see note)

3/4 cup golden raisins

1/2 cup dried currants

1/2 cup bourbon or rum

2 tablespoons grated orange zest

1 tablespoon grated lemon zest

1 cup all-purpose flour

1-1/2 teaspoons baking powder

1/2 teaspoon nutmeg
preferably freshly grated)

1/2 teaspoon ground allspice

1/4 teaspoon ground cloves

1/2 cup (1 stick) unsalted butter, softened

1 cup finely packed dark brown sugar

2 eggs, room temperature

Hazelnut Holiday Cakes with Figs and Ginger

These ginger-spiced cakes improve and mellow over time and will keep up to 2 weeks if tightly wrapped and stored at a cool room temperature.

In a large bowl, combine the figs, hazelnuts, crystalized ginger, raisins, currants, bourbon or rum, orange zest, and lemon zest. Allow to stand at least 2 hours at room temperature, stirring occasionally.

Position a baking rack in the center of the oven and preheat to 275 degrees F. Generously butter four 5-1/2 x 3 x 2-inch loaf pans. Line bottoms with waxed paper. Butter the papers, then dust with flour, tapping out the excess.

Sift together the flour, baking powder, nutmeg, allspice and cloves into a medium bowl. Using an electric mixer, cream the butter with the sugar in a large bowl until light and fluffy. Add the eggs one at a time, blending well after each addition. Mix in the dry ingredients, then the fruit and nuts with the liquid in which they have been soaking.

Divide the batter among the prepared pans; smooth tops. Set the pans on a baking sheet and bake until a cake tester inserted in centers comes out clean, about 1 hour and 45 minutes.

Cool the cakes in the pans for 15 minutes, then unmold and cool completely on racks. Wrap tightly in plastic, then in foil. Allow to mellow 5 days before serving (or giving).

NOTE: Look for crystalized ginger in well-stocked bulk food sections and Asian markets.

1-1/2 cups finely diced fresh rhubarb,
     or 2 cups frozen sliced rhubarb
2 cups all-purpose flour
1 tablespoon baking powder
1/4 teaspoon salt
1/4 teaspoon ground cinnamon
1 egg
1/2 cup firmly packed golden brown sugar
3 tablespoons red currant jelly
1 cup milk
4 tablespoons butter, melted
1 teaspoon vanilla extract
1/2 cup chopped roasted
     and skinned hazelnuts

Rhubarb Hazelnut Muffins

If you are using frozen rhubarb, spread it on the counter for about 5 minutes until it is thawed enough to finely dice.

While the rhubarb thaws, heat oven to 375 degrees F.

Lightly grease a standard 12-muffin pan or line with paper or foil baking cups, or coat with nonstick spray.

In a large bowl, combine the flour, baking powder, salt and cinnamon. In a medium-sized bowl, whisk together the egg, brown sugar, and currant jelly until smooth (the jelly will not completely dissolve). Whisk in the milk, butter, and vanilla. Stir in the hazelnuts and finely diced rhubarb. Pour over the dry ingredients and gently fold in with a rubber spatula just until the dry ingredients are moistened.

Scoop the batter into muffin cups. Bake 20 to 30 minutes, or until light brown and springy to the touch in the center. Turn out onto a rack and cool at least 15 minutes before serving.

1 cup all-purpose flour

3/4 cup whole wheat flour

2 teaspoons baking powder

1/2 teaspoon baking soda

1/2 teaspoon salt

1/2 cup granulated sugar

1/3 cup unsweetened dark cocoa powder

2 teaspoons instant coffee powder

1 large egg, lightly beaten

2 large egg whites, lightly beaten

1 cup milk

2 teaspoons vanilla extract

3 tablespoons hazelnut oil
   (or substitute canola oil)

1 cup chopped raw hazelnuts, divided

Hazelnut-Chocolate Muffins

As you've figured out by now, hazelnuts and chocolate are one of my favorite combos. A few roasted hazelnuts sprinkled on top, combined with hazelnut oil in the batter, give these muffins a heavenly dose of nuttiness. If you don't want to go to the extra expense of using hazelnut oil, you can certainly substitute canola oil. The nut flavor just won't be as pronounced.

Preheat the oven to 400 degrees F.

Lightly grease a standard 12-muffin pan or line with paper or foil baking cups, or coat with nonstick spray.

Combine the flours, baking powder, baking soda, salt, sugar, cocoa powder and coffee powder in a medium-sized bowl. In a separate bowl, whisk together the egg with the egg whites, milk, vanilla and oil. Scrape the egg mixture into the flour mixture, stirring just until the dry ingredients are moistened, about 20 strokes. Fold in 1/2 cup of the nuts.

Spoon the batter into the muffin cups, dividing the batter evenly. Sprinkle the remaining 1/2 cup of nuts over the tops of the muffins. Bake for 15 to 20 minutes, or until lightly browned and springy to the touch in the center. Turn out onto a rack and cool at least 15 minutes before serving.

Makes about 2-1/2 cups

3/4 cup high-quality Dutch process cocoa

1 cup granulated sugar

1/4 teaspoon salt

1/2 cup hot water

3/4 cup (1-1/2 sticks) unsalted butter, softened

1/2 to 1 teaspoon vanilla extract

1 cup finely chopped darkly roasted and skinned hazelnuts

Hazelnut Buttercream with Chocolate Syrup

This keeps for months in the fridge and is handy to have available when you want to frost a batch of cupcakes, cement two pieces of shortbread together, or layer a sheet cake with something sweet and decadent.

Combine the cocoa, sugar and salt in a heavy-bottomed saucepan. Gradually whisk in the hot water, then place the pot over medium heat and continue stirring until the sugar has dissolved. Remove the pot from the burner and set aside to cool.

Cream together the butter and the vanilla with an electric mixer until light and fluffy. With the mixer running, gradually add the cooled chocolate mixture, continuing to beat just until everything is combined.

Whisk in the nuts, then scrape the mixture into a clean, dry storage container, cover tightly and refrigerate. Keeps for about 2 months.

Serves 1

1 tablespoon firmly packed brown sugar

1 tablespoon finely chopped darkly
    roasted hazelnuts

Fresh orange juice

1-1/2 ounces Stoli Vodka

3/4 ounce Godiva Dark

3/4 ounce Frangelico

Ice

Chocolate Hazelnut Martini with Brown Sugar and Hazelnut Rim

This scrumptious drink is the creation of Mark Rowland, the talented bar manager at 101, a popular Corvallis, Oregon restaurant. There are plenty of chocolate martinis floating around in the world. Some are too sweet, others just not very inspired. This one, however, is refreshingly decadent yet decadently refreshing. One of Mark's most unique departures from the usual preparation is his method for rimming the glass. Instead of the usual drizzles of chocolate that harden on the edge of the glass and are near-impossible to nibble off without putting the fragile barware at risk, Mark's approach is easy to enjoy, not to mention deliciously interactive.

First prepare the rim of a well-chilled martini glass: Combine the brown sugar and hazelnuts and spread the mixture into a saucer wide enough to accommodate the width of the glass rim. Pour orange juice into a second saucer to a depth of about 1/4 inch. Dip the rim of the martini glass into the orange juice and let it air dry for about 10 seconds to become a bit sticky. Then dip it into the brown sugar mixture, making sure that both the inside and outside of the rim are well coated. Set the glass aside in a refrigerator until ready to use.

Pour the vodka, Godiva Dark and Frangelico into a cocktail shaker. Add ice and shake well to chill, then strain into the prepared martini glass and serve immediately.

CHAPTER **9**

Pacific Northwest
Celebrations

Pick a theme. Put it all together. Throw a party. It really does come down to that. Here are some sample menus to help you figure out your own festivities. Most of the recipes can be found in this book, and are referenced by page number. But I'm also including a few that are so basic you won't have any trouble finding them elsewhere, probably in your own recipe files.

A Simple Crab Feast!

OREGON'S COMMERCIAL CRAB SEASON begins on December 1st and continues through August 14th. The peak harvest, however, occurs during the first eight weeks of the season, with up to 75 percent of the annual production landed during this period. So those early weeks are prime Crab Feast time. Here's how to acquire the guest of honor:

THE NUMBER ONE BEST WAY TO BUY CRAB: Dungeness crab is never better than when it has just come from the sea. A live crab fresh from its habitat is in the ideal state for cooking. If you fancy a trip to the coast, then drop by your favorite bay front where the crab boats are dropping off their loads. Many skippers sell direct on the dock. Short of those circumstances, all crab buying, cooking and eating involve some compromise. Which leads to...

THE SECOND BEST WAY TO BUY CRAB: Buying crabs kept alive in saltwater tanks is a close second. Some inland fish markets have them.

THE THIRD BEST WAY TO BUY CRAB: Cooked crab is your final option, but it's a frustrating one because you can get burned from a quality point of view if the crabs aren't fresh. Find a place where they cook their live crabs right there on the premises, so you know they're fresh. But steer clear of places that can't tell you where—or even when!—their crabs were cooked. When buying cooked crab, don't be shy. Smell it! There should not be a fishy odor.

How many people per crab? The general rule around our house is two people per crab, unless the crab is smaller than 1-1/2 pounds, at which point, you should play it safe and have one crab per person. Plus, I always throw in one extra crab "for the pot." There is no shortage of delectable uses for leftover crab, and you deserve the perk for hosting the party.

My preferred approach to cooking crabs is to drop them into a couple gallons or more of boiling salted water (4 heaping tablespoons of salt per gallon of water), then when the water returns to a boil, cook for 20 to 30 minutes, depending on their size. After cooking, clean a crab by removing the back shell, rinsing out the viscera and pulling off the gill filaments (these will be very obvious to you when you get around to doing it).

Once cool enough to handle, pull all of the legs from the body, and, using anything that can be viewed as a kitchen mallet—such as a metal ice cracker or steel meat tenderizer, or a (washed) regular hammer—tap the legs in several spots to crack the shells for easy removal of the meat. Pile the cracked legs and bodies into big bowls and set them on the table along with some empty bowls to collect discarded shells. For the uninitiated, demonstrate how the pointy end of a claw can be used to pry meat from the far reaches of legs and body cavities.

SINCE THIS IS A REALLY SIMPLE CRAB FEAST (nothing wrong with that!), then besides fresh and crunchy artisan bread, and a great big green salad, consider having the following sauces for dunking and drizzling, and call it good.

~ Tomato-Pesto Mayonnaise for Crab (page 115)

~ Buttery Cocktail Sauce (page 115)

~ Classic Louis Dressing (page 114)

Tyee Wine Cellars

MARGY AND DAVE BUCHANAN, Corvallis-area hazelnut growers and owners of Tyee Wine Cellars, throw a crab feed every January for about 100 fun-loving folks who show up for the crab, grilled oysters, and some rollicking ambiance. Ties and stuffy attitudes are checked at the door. It's been a tradition for almost 20 years.

Sometimes I'm in on the menu plotting—at least in an opinion capacity. Margy will very often try out the year's salad or appetizer course on a few of us die-hard guinea pigs...er, friends. So it's been easier to plan my own crab menus. Straightforward appetizers that tantalize the palate without overwhelming the appetite are the ticket. And salads that go beyond simple tossed greens into the realm of specialty greens and seasonal veggies, with delectable dressings that don't fight with the sweet and mild nature of the Dungeness crab. The crab is the main dish, after all!

Pacific Northwest Crab Feast Menu A Festive Approach!

FIRST COURSE

A Trio of Spreads with Crostini: [page 77-78]

*Mushroom Hazelnut Pâté
Oregon Three-Cheese Ball with Hazelnut Coating
Muffuleta Garlic-Olive Relish*

Tyee Estate Pinot Noir

...

SECOND COURSE

Fresh-cooked Dungeness Crab

Buttery Cocktail Sauce [page 115]

*Salad of Baby Greens with
Roasted Sweet Peppers and Mushrooms*

Balsamic Vinaigrette with Sweet Honey Mustard
[page 111]

Good Quality Artisan Bread

Lumos Pinot Gris, Rudolfo Vineyard

...

THIRD COURSE

*Double Trouble! Chocolate Truffle Tart
with Hazelnut Crust* [page 215]

Belle Vallée Pinot Noir Port

Spring Wine Dinner Menu

FIRST COURSE

Oregon Pacific Shrimp Cocktail
with Tomato-Pesto Mayonnaise [page 115]

Del Rio Viognier, Rogue Valley

...

SECOND COURSE

Leeks Braised in Butter and Sherry Au Gratin
[page 116]

Tyee Wine Cellars Estate Gewürztraminer

...

THIRD COURSE

Chicken Skewers with Savory Hazelnut Crust [page 81]

King Estate Signature Viognier

...

FOURTH COURSE

Grilled Sturgeon with Pacific Rim Mushroom Sauce
[page 177]

Sugar Snap Peas with Garlic and Hazelnut Oil
[page 118]

Mashed Yukon Golds with Caramelized Onions
[page 129]

Lumos Gewürztraminer,
Temperance Hill Vineyard

...

FIFTH COURSE

Rhubarb and Hazelnut Crisp [page 225]
with French Vanilla Ice Cream

Soter Vineyards Sparkling Brut Rosé

Summer Wine Dinner Menu

FIRST COURSE

Bruschetta [page 85] *with Backyard Tomatoes,*
Hazelnut Aillade [page 63]
Pesto Dollops, and Balsamic Vinegar Essence [page 67]
Belle Vallée Syrah, Rogue Valley

...

SECOND COURSE

Grilled Prawns with Romesco Sauce [page 79]
Adelsheim Elizabeth's Reserve Pinot Noir

...

THIRD COURSE

Mushroom Bisque with Leeks and Hazelnuts [page 89]
Herbed Croutons
Lange Estate Winery Pinot Noir

...

FOURTH COURSE

Grilled Wild Chinook Salmon with
Balsamic Vinegar Essence [page 67]
Creamy Corn, Baby Leeks and Pancetta
Tyee Pinot Gris

...

FIFTH COURSE

New York Style Cheesecake with Marionberry Coulis

Harris Bridge Sarah's Stories Pinot
Gris Dessert Wine

Autumn Wine Dinner Menu

FIRST COURSE

*Scallops and Mushroom Sauté with
Buttered Fettuccini and Hazelnuts* [page 188]

Airlie Vineyards Dunn Forest Pinot Noir

...

SECOND COURSE

*Creamy Gazpacho with
Fire-Roasted Sweet Corn Kernels*

Eola Hills Lodi Old Vine Zinfandel

...

THIRD COURSE

*Salad of Fuji Apples, Baby Greens and Roasted
Hazelnuts With Sweet Honey Mustard and Hazelnut
Oil Vinaigrette* [page 111]

Eola Hills Wolf Hill Chardonnay

...

FOURTH COURSE

*Grilled Albacore with
Spicy Black Bean-Garlic Butter Sauce* [page 182]

Green Beans with Hazelnuts and Thyme [page 121]

Mashed Yukon Golds with Caramelized Onions [page 129]

Lumos Gewürztraminer, Temperence Hill

...

FIFTH COURSE

Jan's Crème Brûlée with Caramelized Hazelnut Topping
[page 211]

*Eola Hills LBV Cabernet Sauvignon
Port Style Wine*

Winter Wine Dinner Menu

FIRST COURSE

*Melted Manchego Cheese on Crostini
with Grilled Aidells Apple Sausage Chunks*

Terra Vina Sangiovese

...

SECOND COURSE

Mushroom Bisque with Leeks and Hazelnuts [page 89]

*Arbor Brook Vineyards
Vintner's Select Pinot Noir*

...

THIRD COURSE

*Dungeness Crab Meat on Mixed Salad Greens
with Fresh Lemon*

Hazelnut Vinaigrette [page 100]

King Estate Domaine Pinot Gris

...

FOURTH COURSE

*Filet Mignon with Hazelnut Hummus and Homemade
Yukon Gold Potato Chips* [page 129]

Belle Vallée Cabernet Sauvignon

...

FIFTH COURSE

*Chocolate Hazelnut Martini with Brown Sugar and
Hazelnut Rim* [page 244]

December Wine Dinner for Really Good Friends

FIRST COURSE

Three-Cheese Tart with Parmesan-Hazelnut Crust and Baby Greens

Dressed in Pear Vinaigrette [page 86]

Pheasant Court Vice (Viognier Late Harvest)

...

SECOND COURSE

Mushroom Bisque with Leeks and Hazelnuts [page 89]

Lumos Pinot Noir, Five Blocks

...

THIRD COURSE

Spinach Salad with Brown Sugar Vinaigrette and Roasted Hazelnuts [page 101]

Oregon Blue Cheese Crumbles

Airlie Winery Marachal Foch

...

FOURTH COURSE

Prime Rib with Balsamic-Madeira Au Jus [page 157]

Del Rio Syrah, Rogue Valley

...

FIFTH COURSE

McMillan Raspberry and Marionberry Trifle with Candied Hazelnuts [page 235]

Margaret's Orange Glazed Hazelnuts [page 197]

Elk Cove Vineyards Late Harvest Riesling

Wine Touring in the Willamette Valley

SOME TRADITIONS—even when they're highly treasured—aren't sustainable. For a core group of my friends, my husband, and I, the one we finally had to let go of was the annual post-Thanksgiving tour of wineries. At least as a dedicated gang of high-spirited, wine-sipping, cheese-chomping pals.

It was a precious 6-year window when we could plot the annual 3-hour hiatus without conflicts from children finally old enough to want their own hiatus (from us!). So that was the time we earmarked for touching down together before the chaos of December slammed into us.

In the years that followed, the tradition became unwieldy. As empty-nesters, we were adapting to grown children returning for the long weekend. Schedules no longer meshed gracefully.

But the time spent roving the back roads of the Willamette Valley together, tasting the local wine and catching up on the lives of the local winery folk is something we all look back on with fondness. We'd arrive home with trunks full of wine and treasures, our spirits soaring from a strong dose of friendship and Oregon outdoor beauty.

Some of us still like to plot an excursion at some point during the Friday, Saturday and Sunday after Thanksgiving when most of the state's wineries open their doors. And a picnic basket filled with sandwiches or soup only heightens the experience.

Now we're more likely to have our grown children along—young adults who have decided that getting to know wine and parents are worthy pursuits. Which, come to think of it, has all the makings of a new tradition.

Thanksgiving Weekend
Wine Touring Menu

Potato Cheese Soup with Hazelnut Cheese Crisps
[page 90]

*Foley Station Green Olive and Hazelnut Pesto
with Crostini* [page 79]

*Lumos Winery Gewürztraminer,
Temperance Hill*

Coq au Vin

Eola Hills Reserve Lodi Petite Syrah

Grandma Aden's Candied Filberts [page 193]

Eola Hills LBV Cabernet Sauvignon Port

Fireside Après Ski
Wine Menu

Red Onion and Blue Cheese Spread [page 76]

Red Grapes and Toasted Baguette Rounds

*Eola Hills Vin d'Epice—
Late Harvest Gewürztraminer*

Mushroom Hazelnut Pâté [page 77]

Tyee Barrel Select Estate Pinot Noir

*Corn Bisque Garnished with
Pacific Shrimp and Bacon Crumbles*

Belle Vallée Syrah, Rogue Valley

Oregon's Vibrant
Craft Breweries

HOPS GROW REALLY WELL HERE in the Willamette Valley. In fact, such abundance is most certainly behind Oregon's vibrant craft beer industry. The city of Portland alone has more breweries than any other city in the world. In 2009, the count was 38. Craft brewers in other states dream of a future in which 10 percent of the draft beer poured in local pubs would be the brew of local artisans. In Oregon, that figure is almost 40 percent and climbing. So it's no surprise that beer dinners abound. There's so much delicious brew to work with.

If you're planning a multi-course feast with beer accompanying every course, start with beers that are lighter and lower in alcohol and end with the richer, heavier beers. Also, since beer creates a feeling of fullness, pour small portions for most courses; about 4 ounces each, for the appetizer, soup, and salad courses; about 6 to 8 ounces for the main course; and 4 to 6 ounces for the dessert course.

In the same facility near the Oregon State University campus where hazelnut germplasm is stored, the nation's largest collection of hop genetic material resides as well.

Spring Craft Beer Menu

FIRST COURSE

Dungeness Crab Meat with Hot Mustard-Butter Sauce

Rogue Ale Mairfest Lager

…

SECOND COURSE

Coconut Ginger Shrimp and Jasmine Rice with Lime
and Roasted Hazelnuts [page 146]

Ninkasi Brewing Total Domination IPA

…

THIRD COURSE

Warm Mushroom and Baby Greens Salad with
Hazelnuts and Extra-Aged Gouda
and Hazelnut Vinaigrette [page 100]

Ninkasi Brewing Tricerahops Double IPA

…

FOURTH COURSE

Grilled Butterflied Leg of Lamb

Steamed Asparagus

Fingerling Potatoes, Pan Roasted with Herbs [page 128]

Rogue Ale Dry-Hopped St. Rogue Red

…

FIFTH COURSE

Double Trouble! Chocolate Truffle Tart
with Hazelnut Crust [page 215]

Ninkasi Brewing Oatis Oatmeal Stout

Summer Craft Beer Menu

FIRST COURSE

Bruschetta with Tomato, Bacon, Arugula, Hazelnut
and Oregon Blue Topping [page 85]

Rogue Ale Hazelnut Brown Nectar

…

SECOND COURSE

Gazpacho Garnished with Fire-Roasted
Sweet Corn Kernels

Rogue Ale Juniper Pale Ale

…

THIRD COURSE

Roasted Polenta with Best Ever Balsamic Sauce
[page 126]

Widmer Brothers Drop Top Amber Ale

…

FOURTH COURSE

Grilled Halibut Steaks with Dijon Mustard
and Honey Topping on Hot-Mustard Butter Sauce
[page 175]

Bend Brewing Company Outback Old Ale

…

FIFTH COURSE

Strawberry Shortcake

Rogue Ale Mocha Porter

Autumn Craft Beer Menu

FIRST COURSE

Steamer Clams Cooked in Garlic and Beer

Widmer Hefeweizen

...

SECOND COURSE

Roasted Hazelnut Slaw [page 109]

Rogue Ale's Hazelnut Brown Nectar

...

THIRD COURSE

*Potato Cheese Soup
with Hazelnut Cheese Crisps* [page 91]

Deschutes Green Lakes Organic Ale

...

FOURTH COURSE

*Tenderloin of Beef with Grilled Veggies,
Arugula and Cherry Tomatoes
in Roasted Garlic Vinaigrette* [page 160]

Fresh Sweet Corn on the Cob with Butter

*Southern Oregon Brewing Company
Whoop Shed Red Ale*

...

FIFTH COURSE

Mocha Cheese Cake with a Caramel Sauce

Chateau Rogue First Growth Dirtoir Black Lager

Winter Craft Beer Menu

FIRST COURSE

Dungeness Crab Crostini in Lemon and Herb Sauce
[page 80]

*Fresh Greens Tossed with Raspberry-Poppy Seed
Vinaigrette* [page 104] *and Candied Hazelnuts* [page 104]

*Bridgeport's Stumptown Tart Ale
(A Belgian Framboise Style Ale infused
with Oregon Red Raspberries)*

...

SECOND COURSE

Roasted Hazelnut Cakes [page 128]

Full Sail American Pale Ale

...

THIRD COURSE

*Coconut Shrimp and Jasmine Rice with Lime and
Roasted Hazelnuts* [page 146]

Rogue Ale Morimoto Soba Ale

...

FOURTH COURSE

Grilled Pork Chops

*Yukon Gold Mashed Potatoes
with Caramelized Onions* [page 129]

Steamed Broccoli

Deschutes Brewery Jubelale

...

FIFTH COURSE

Hazelnut Butter Crust Tart [page 214]

Deschutes Black Butte Porter

Fireside Beer Menu

FIRST COURSE

Oregon Dukkah [page 54]
with Fruity Extra-Virgin Olive Oil and Olive Bread

Deschutes Mirror Pond Pale Ale

...

SECOND COURSE

Mushroom Bisque with Leeks and Hazelnuts [page 89]

Deschutes Brewery Cinder Cone Red

...

THIRD COURSE

*Spinach and Pears with Candied Hazelnuts and
Raspberry-Poppy Seed Vinaigrette* [page 103]

Full Sale Original Amber Ale

...

FOURTH COURSE

*Raclette with Assorted Sausages, Mustards, Potato and
Cornichon Pickle*

Deschutes Green Lakes Organic Ale

...

FIFTH COURSE

Foley Station Triple Ginger Snaps with a Hazelnut Back
[page 212]

Full Sail Wassail

THE FOOD

Hazelnut Marketing Board

503-678-6823
www.oregonhazelnuts.org

The HMB is the go-to source for everything related to the Oregon hazelnut industry. It's also a great jumping off point for locating sources for all variations on hazelnuts, from raw and roasted to chopped, chocolate covered, seasoned, and ground into luscious hazelnut butter. There are even sources for obtaining hazelnut shells, which have become a popular ground cover within the landscaping industry.

You can also obtain copies of "Oregon Hazelnut Country—The Food, the Drink, the Spirit" through HMB. I'll be posting lots of book-related information on their website, so visit it as often as you can for updates on cooking demonstrations, TV and radio appearances, and even fabulous new recipes that came along too late to make it into the first edition of the book.

Freddy Guys Hazelnuts

503-606-0458
www.freddyguys.com

Barb and Fritz Foulke operate a completely vertical hazelnut business, from orchard to a wide range of raw, roasted and flavored kernels. Product is available (retail and wholesale) through their website and at regional farmers' markets. If you visit the website, be sure to watch the videos of their hazelnut harvesting and processing operations.

Not only are they the only producers of hazelnut oil in Oregon, it is the best I have ever tasted.

Hazelnut Hill

27681 Nutcracker Lane
Corvallis, OR 97333
541-754-5657
www.hazelnuthill.com

Rob and Sally Hilles' gift store and website are the retail outlets for another vertical hazelnut operation. They feature a wide variety of hazelnut products produced in their own plant using nuts from their own orchards. Dried fruits and other nuts are available as well. They have gift packages, or you can assemble your own using their boxes, which ship beautifully. In the store, you can taste different varieties of hazelnuts, and even enjoy hazelnut ice cream treats.

Holmquist Hazelnut Orchards

9821 Holmquist Road
Lynden, WA 98264
360-988-9240
www.holmquisthazelnuts.com

Mother Peach's Homemade Caramels

P.O. Box 25071
Portland, OR 97298-0071
503-297-2600
www.motherpeachcaramels.com

These are the caramels I patterned my wonderful hazelnut caramels after!

Oregon Blueberry Commission

P.O. Box 3366
Salem, OR 97302-0366
503-364-2944
www.oregonblueberry.com

Oregon Dungeness Crab Commission

P.O. Box 1160
Coos Bay, OR 97420-0301
541-267-5810
www.oregondungeness.org

Oregon Dukkah
Vibrant Flavors, Inc.

6327 SW Capitol Hwy.
Suite C, PMB 133
Portland, OR 97239
503-452-0456
www.vibrantflavors.com
www.vibrantflavors.blogspot.com

If you don't want to make your own dukkah mixtures, here's where you can buy a really delicious commercially made product. They have a variety of flavors to choose from. At the blog site, there is great information on additional ways to use dukkah.

Oregon Raspberry
and Blackberry Commission

4845 B SW Dresden
Corvallis, OR 97333-3915
541-456-2264
www.oregon-berries.com

Oregon Strawberry Commission

4845 B SW Dresden
Corvallis, OR 97333-3915
541-758-4043
www.oregon-strawberries.org

Pear Bureau Northwest

4382 SE International Way, Suite A
Milwaukie, OR 97222-4627
503-652-9720
www.usapears.org

Rogue Creamery

311 N. Front Street
Central Point, OR 97502
541-664-2233
www.roguecreamery.com

Producing a wide range of internationally recognized, award-winning blue cheeses.

Tillamook Creamery

4175 Highway 101 North
P.O. Box 313
Tillamook, OR 97141
503 815-1300
www.tillamookcheese.com

Oregon's largest commercial creamery, producing high quality cow's milk cheeses.

Your Northwest Stores

503-445-0279
www.yournw.com

A variety of hazelnut products ranging from raw to flavored kernels sold in their stores as well as online.

THE DRINK

OREGON WINES

Willamette Valley Wineries Association

www.willamettewines.com

This is a great source for tracking down wineries through the heart of Oregon wine country, from Portland south through Eugene, with links to each winery's website. Plus maps and touring guidelines.

Oregon Wine Advisory Board

www.oregonwine.org

A state-wide resource, broken down by regions. An excellent source for plotting a wine touring expedition.

Benton County Wineries

www.bentoncountywineries.com

Here's a little more information about the wineries I mention by name. Most of them are near my home base in the mid-Willamette Valley, with two of them representing the unique and delicious varietals grown in Southern Oregon.

Abacela

12500 Lookingglass Road
Roseburg, OR 97471
541-679-6642
www.abacela.com

Owners: Earl and Hilda Jones
Winemaker: Andrew Wenzl

This is one of my favorite Southern Oregon wineries. It produces some luscious varietals that compliment a wide range of my recipes, including Tempranilla, Syrah, Malbec, and Viognier.

Airlie Winery

15305 Dunn Forest Road
Monmouth, OR 97361
503-838-6013
www.airliewinery.com

Owner: Mary Olson
Winemaker: Elizabeth Clark

I've enjoyed peaceful wine tastings overlooking Mary's lovely little lake for years. In the summer, it's a great place to picnic and explore. She produces wonderful wine. And, she loves dogs. Riley and Rocky, the official winery canine team are usually on point, providing a tail-wagging greeting when you arrive. So if you've brought along a pooch who is well-behaved, and other guests visiting the winery have no objection, there's a good chance your 4-legged pal will have a wonderful experience as well.

Belle Vallée Cellars

804 NW Buchanan Avenue
Corvallis, OR 97330
541-757-9463
www.bellevallee.com

Owners: Steve Allen, Mike and Claire Magee, Joe Wright
Winemaker: Joe Wright

Beyond their various styles of yummy Pinot Noir, Syrah, Cabernet Sauvignon, Merlot, and their signature Pinot Port, co-owner Claire Magee brings whimsy and flair to Belle Vallée's wine labels. Each one is of her creation. She's also reproduced a limited number of the designs in her art medium of choice, fused glass. The sparkling labels, in elegant and beautiful designs crafted from vibrantly colored art glass with accents made from dichroic glass, are attached to magnum bottles containing Belle Vallée wine. What a terrific gift for a very special occasion that needs marking.

Del Rio Vineyards & Winery

52 N River Road
Gold Hill, OR 97525
541-855-2062
www.delriovineyards.com

Owners: Lee Traynham,
Rob and Jolee Wallace
Winemaker: Jean-Michel Jussiaume

Del Rio has become an impressive force within the Pacific Northwest wine industry, producing 21 varietals in the Southern Oregon appellation of the Rogue Valley. Some of those varietals include Sangiovese, Merlot, Petite Syrah, Petite Verdot, Pinot Noir, Cabernet Sauvignon, Cabernet Franc, Syrah, Pinot Gris, and Viognier. About 40 wineries in Oregon, California and Washington purchase grapes from Del Rio vineyards. Of course, Del Rio is also producing their own award-winning wines from those grapes as well.

Eola Hills Wine Cellars

501 S Pacific Highway (99W)
Rickreall, OR 97371
503-623-2405
www.eolahillswinery.com

Owner: Tom Huggins
Winemaker: Steve Anderson

Founder and general manager Tom Huggins knew that great wines could only come from great vineyards. In his former life in the world of agricultural insurance, he had located some of that precious vineyard property and acquired it. The first crop was harvested in 1986, and it's been a non-stop celebration of good wine and good food ever since.

Harris Bridge Vineyard

22937 Harris Road
Philomath, OR 97370
541-929-3053
www.harrisbridgevineyard.com

Owners: Nathan Warren and Amanda Sever
Winemakers: Ditto!

Nathan and Amanda produce small lots of luscious Pinot Noir and Pinot Gris dessert wines. You'll find reference to their creations throughout my "Sweets" chapter, in particular. In their own words: "Harris Bridge Vineyard began as a twinkle in the eye of Nathan, an urge to get back to the roots of the valley where he grew up, and an ambition to create something real and lasting. In 1998 he began establishing the vineyard and a few years later he, then joined by Amanda began making wine and building the winery. The two, now three with baby Magnolia, grow grapes, make wine, gab with guests at the tasting room, and work this little piece of land into a space for friends and family to enjoy."

Lumos Wine Company

24000 Cardwell Hill Drive
Philomath, OR 97370
541-929-3519
www.lumoswine.com

Owners: Dai Crisp and PK McCoy
Winemaker: Dai Crisp

The Lumos Wine Company was launched in 2000, but Dai was first introduced to viticulture 14 years earlier when he helped his parents plant a small, 10-acre vineyard on their farm just west of Philomath in the tiny town of Wren, Oregon. In 1990, Dai turned into a professional grape grower at Croft Vineyards where, by his own description, he honed "his own sustainable and earth and people-friendly style" of viticulture. Dai seems to have found a way to add hours to the day because, on top of his own winery dealings, he's been managing Temperance Hill Vineyard, one of the region's premier vineyards, since 1999.

If you visit their tasting room, located on the Crisp family farm in Wren, you'll be swept up into their calm and magical world the moment you step from your car and walk toward their little cabin in the woods.

Nuthatch Cellars

8792 NW Chaparral Drive
Corvallis, Oregon 97330
www.nuthatchcellars.com

Owners: John Bacon and Jane Smith
Winemaker: John Bacon

At the moment, Nuthatch Cellars is a tiny operation. But that doesn't stop it from making big and lovely full-bodied reds. Their grapes come from carefully managed vineyards ranging from the Umpqua Valley Appellation in Southern Oregon up through Northern Oregon's Columbia Valley Appellation, over to southeastern Washington's Walla Walla Appellation. You won't find their wines at any of the big box stores (yet), but if you're traveling through Pacific Northwest, keep an eye out for their label.

Pheasant Court Winery
The Wine Vault

1301 Main Street
Philomath, OR 97370
541-929-7715
www.pheasantcourtwinery.com

Owners: Charlie and Marcia Gilson
Winemaker: Charlie Gilson

The Gilson's gift to the mid-Willamette Valley is The Wine Vault in downtown Philomath, which opened in 2005. At this one-stop shop, you can taste and purchase their own wines with the Pheasant Court label, as well as a generous collection of other Benton County offerings.

Marys Peak Winery

The Wine Vault
1301 Main Street
Philomath, OR 97370
541-929-9296
www.maryspeakwinery.com

Owners: Ken Nancy Elwer
Winemaker: Ken Elwer

The Elwers moved from the Napa Valley in 2001 and jumped right into commercial wine production with the encouragement of friends and fellow winemakers. They consider themselves a boutique winery at the moment, but have dreams beyond the Cabernet Sauvignon and Chardonnay varietals they're producing right now.

Spindrift Cellars

810 Applegate
Philomath, OR 97370
541-929-6555
www.spindriftcellars.com

Owners: Matt and Tabitha Compton
Winemaker: Matt Compton

The Comptons are producing lovely, award-winning examples of Pinot Noir, Pinot Blanc, Pinot Gris, and Syrah from nearby vineyards managed by Matt's vineyard management company, West Vine Farms. Like so many other wineries in this region, they're doing it using responsible, sustainable wine grape growing practices.

Springhill Cellars

920 NW Scenic Drive
Albany, OR 97321
541-928-1009
www.springhillcellars.com

Owners: Mike and Karen McLain
Winemakers: Ditto!

The Mclains have taken great care over the years to produce lovely and award-winning Pinot Noir and Pinot Gris. That's a given.

On the social side of things, if you show up at Springhill Cellars over Thanksgiving Weekend, bring your dancing shoes. The annual Fedeweisser Festival, which has German roots, will be in full swing and you'll be treated to brats, a barn dance (it begins with oom-pah-pah music

by day, evolving into a live rock-and-roll band by night), a young and still-fermenting Riesling, plus a whole lot of really good Pinot Noir.

Tyee Wine Cellars

26335 Greenberry Road
Corvallis, OR 97333
541-753-8754
www.tyeewine.com

Owners: Margy and David Buchanan;
　　　Merrilee Buchanan Benson
Winemaker: Merrilee Buchanan Benson

Located on the historic Buchanan Family Century Farm, Margy and Dave specialize in estate grown Pinot Noir, Pinot Gris, Chardonnay, and Gewürztraminer. Tyee's winemaker and vineyard manager since 2006, Merrilee Buchanan Benson, grew up on the farm and has worked closely with her parents in the winery and vineyard for much of her life. Like her parents, she supports agricultural practices that follow Salmon-Safe Ecolabel Standards.

When Dave and Margy took over the farm in1974, they were looking for crops that could be sustainably grown. Hazelnuts and wine grapes are what they decided to move forward with. These have provided their family with a lifestyle they enjoy sharing with the community around them. For me, when out of towners arrive, a picnic at Tyee is traditional. The peace of mind achieved from even a two hour interlude, whether walking the Beaver Pond Loop nature trail or simply gazing over fields and tree lines across the valley to Mary's Peak, is a simple, priceless, pleasure.

A substantial portion of the Buchanan property has been restored to natural habitat for the benefit of native plants and wildlife. The Oregon Wildlife Society has presented the Buchanans with the Private Landowner Stewardship award "For their leadership as land stewards, conservationists and sustainable agriculture producers in the Willamette Valley."

720 Wine Cellars

P.O. Box 1641
Philomath, OR 97370
541-929-4562
www.720cellars.com

Owner: Chris Heider
Winemaker: Ditto!

As Chris states: "We make wines in our state-of-the-art, very high-tech, and extremely low-key facility that is perched high in the foothills of the Willamette Valley, Oregon, just above the tiny burg of Philomath. No tasting room on site (Chris again: "It's basically a garage, people!"). And the wine is hard to find. But I'm fond of it, so whenever I encounter it on a menu it's hard to resist. Check out the website, which is a delightful read.

SOME OF MY FAVORITE OREGON CRAFT BREWS

Any well-stocked grocery store in Oregon will boast a tempting array of regional brews. And many of these beverages are real stunners, which mirrors the strength and quality of the Oregon craft beer industry. I've tried to bring a few of the more accessible offerings into this project. By that I mean the ones that have a wide enough distribution that you'll be able to find them and enjoy them in the same spirit in which I have used them in this book. If you jump onto their websites you'll find even more tips and guidelines for enjoying these special brews.

Bend Brewing Company

1019 NW Brooks St.
Bend, OR 97701
541-383-1599
www.bendbrewingco.com

BridgePort Brewing Company

1318 NW Northrup
Portland 97209
503-241-7179
www.bridgeportbrew.com

Deschutes Brewery

901 SW Simpson
Bend, OR 97702
541-382-9242
www.deschutesbrewery.com

Full Sail Brewery and Tasting Room

506 Columbia St.
Hood River, OR 97031
541-386-2247
www.fullsailbrewing.com

Ninkasi Brewing

272 Van Buren St.
Eugene, OR 97402
541-344-2739
www.ninkasibrewing.com

Rogue Ale and Spirits

2320 OSU Drive
Newport, OR 97365
541-867-3660
www.rogue.com

Southern Oregon Brewing Company

1922 United Way
Medford, OR 97504
541-776-9898
www.southernoregonbrewing.com

Widmer Brothers

929 N Russell St.
Portland, OR 97227
503-281-2437
www.widmer.com

OTHER HELPFUL BEER CONNECTIONS

Oregon Brewers Guild

2000 NE 42nd Ave. Suite D
Portland, OR 97213
971-270-0965
www.oregonbeer.org

Oregon Hop Commission

P.O. Box 298
Hubbard, OR 97032
503-982-7600
www.oregonhops.org

Indie Hops

503-452-4677
www.indiehops.com

Hop Growers of America

www.usahops.org

THE SPIRIT

Dorris Ranch—A Living History

205 Dorris St.
Springfield, OR 97477
www.willamalane.org/pages/
parks/dorris.shtml

Experience what life was like over a century ago at Oregon's oldest working hazelnut farm. Established in 1892, this 250 acre farm welcomes visitors to tour the orchards, step back in time and experience a homesteader family's life as it was in 1852.

Oregon Tourism Information

www.traveloregon.com

Rogue River Adventures
White Water Warehouse

625 NW Starker Ave.
Corvallis, OR 97330
541-758-3150
www.whitewaterwarehouse.com

Owners: Bob Meister and Joy Henkle

Here's how to get in touch with the folks at White Water Warehouse, for whom I created the Rogue River Salad.

Watch a Hazelnut Harvest in Progress:

www.freddyguys.com

Monmouth-area hazelnut growers Barb & Fritz Foulke have chronicled the feel of the harvest on video.

Willamette Valley Visitors Association

www.oregonwinecountry.org

Epilogue

BACK IN THE KITCHEN

IT'S AN IRONY THAT DURING THE WRITING OF A COOKBOOK, I have considerably less time to cook! I'm not talking about the recipe development phase. In that world, I'm totally immersed in my cooking craft. Steaming along on all four burners. Enjoying the topic, exploring various avenues of its potential.

But engaging the writing side of my brain and putting fingers to keyboard takes a different kind of focus. And quite often it involves working through meal hours. Which isn't all bad. It's somewhat of a relief to be given a pass by family members on cranking out the evening meal.

Now the book is done and I'm back in the kitchen. But instead of moving forward with our regular fare, I've found myself continuing to hanker for all things hazelnut. It's been such a delightful ride! A ride that began over 30 years ago as a grad student at OSU when I hopped into Homer Twedt's dusty old pickup and journeyed with him through my first hazelnut orchard.

Now when I'm cruising along Highway 99W between Corvallis and Portland, I'm aware of just how many hazelnut orchards dot the landscape along the way. So many growers. So much history woven together with an abiding love of the land and a sense of stewardship for the generations to follow.

As you can see, it hasn't been easy to let go. Which is how I landed in the kitchen one day a few weeks after finishing up the manuscript.

Steve and I had been trying to resume a social life. One of our first outings was to friends Dan and Pam Bottom's house to celebrate Dan's Birthday. I was bringing a salad. A simple salad. Something with fresh greens and vegetables, but not a lot of falderal. I was far too tired to accomplish anything more elegant.

At least that's what I thought. But there I was, the afternoon of the party, seduced by ingredients still lurking in my kitchen from the recipe development work. Into my scheme went hazelnut oil, along with garlickly-toasty Hazelnut Aillade, darkly roasted hazelnuts, tempura sauce, and sweet onions. I couldn't help myself, and the salad was taking a turn for the better.

Suddenly I was back in my hazelnut element, whisking together a savory vinaigrette with the oil, Aillade, and tempura sauce. I decided that the sweet onions would be an even greater asset to the salad if they were gently caramelized, so into the skillet they went—with a little more of the hazelnut oil, of course.

I zooped them up with a dollop of Dijon and a splash of tempura sauce before taking them off the heat to cool. Cheese and crisp veggies were recruited to round things out, then off we all went to the party.

At the Bottom's house, when the salad was assembled and tossed with the vinaigrette, none of us were prepared for the experience it provided. It was a delight. And I say that unabashedly. It wasn't just Dan's Chateau du Derriere Pinot talking! It was a downright, undeniably, delicious creation. All thanks to the layering of toasty hazelnut ingredients at every level.

The lesson here is simply this: hazelnuts DO make things more wonderful. So keep them on hand in all forms of preparation. You won't be sorry. And neither will anyone you cook for, or with. If I may, I'll leave you with one more example, involving two very cute little girls and my cherished hazelnut caramels. It rather encapsulates what I have gotten from this project, and from family cooking in general.

When the book was nearing completion, I spent a morning making the caramels with my granddaughters, Anna (8 years old) and Lily (6 years old). It started out at an exuberant level. But once we got through the hauling out of bowls, the measuring of ingredients, and the negotiation of a stirring schedule ("Anna, you just stirred for 2 minutes, now it's MY turn!"), we arrived at the phase only a mature cook can have patience with: the waiting for something to happen.

You see, there was going to be a period—an interminable period by little girl standards—when the sugary mixture had to simply boil until it reached "hard ball" stage on the candy thermometer. It couldn't be rushed. And stirring couldn't be interrupted. It would take about 35 minutes. Each degree of temperature increase seemed to take forever as we watched the digital thermometer register higher, then change its mind and go backwards, then forwards after another loooong wait.

The trick to keeping the experience fresh and magical for these two little live-wires was to distract and entertain during that frustratingly slow process. Luckily, I figured out that one way to make it fun was to greet each new temperature reading with a celebration. And we did that through rhyme.

Anna and I were having great success with this ("Two eighteen...I'm a queen!"). Lily, the competitive little sister, hadn't yet developed much of a knack for rhyming, but was jumping in with both feet anyway...

ME:	TWO THIRTY-FOUR...
ANNA:	WE'RE OUT THE DOOR!
LILY:	THIS IS FUN.
ME:	TWO THIRTY-FIVE...
ANNA:	MAN ALIVE!
LILY:	HERE WE GO.
ME:	TWO THIRTY-SEVEN...
ANNA:	IT'S GONNA BE HEAVEN!
LILY:	PRETTY SOON!
ME:	TWO THIRTY-EIGHT...
ANNA:	I CAN'T WAIT!
LILY:	WE'RE MAKING CARAMELS.
ME:	TWO THIRTY-NINE...
ANNA:	THEY'RE SO FINE!
LILY:	I CAN'T RHYME!

First wide-eyed astonishment, and then a big grin appeared on Lily's face. We all burst into laughter. Brilliant! Who woulda thought? An academic milestone while making candy.

Proud of ourselves, we three Dominguez women finished making the caramels, cutting sticky morsels of sweet gold and wrapping each precious piece in a glistening square of cellophane, then sealing it with a twist. I could see how Anna and Lily were measuring the value of their delectable treasure, soon to be a memory more cherished than the sweetest caramel on earth. And so it is for me as well.

On the next page is the salad I brought to Dan's birthday dinner. It was heavenly! And it's my parting gift to you. Thanks for hanging around to the last page. Bon appetit!

JRD

August 6, 2010

1/2 cup plus 2 tablespoons hazelnut oil,
    divided

1-1/2 cups chopped sweet onion

2 teaspoons tempura sauce

2 teaspoons Dijon mustard

1/2 cup red wine vinegar

1 tablespoon Hazelnut Aillade (page 63)

1 teaspoon firmly packed brown sugar

1/2 teaspoon salt

1 head of romaine lettuce
    (or two hearts of romaine),
    torn into bite-sized pieces

1 sweet red bell pepper, seeded and sliced
    into slender 1-inch pieces

Broccoli florets

1 peeled, seeded and diced cucumber

1 cup coarsely crushed roasted and
    skinned hazelnuts

About 2/3 cup of shredded Parmesan
    cheese, divided

Celebration Salad with Fresh Greens, Sautéed Sweet Onions and Hazelnut Vinaigrette

To prepare the vinaigrette: Heat 2 tablespoons of the hazelnut oil in a medium skillet over medium heat. Add the onion and sauté slowly until it is softened and beginning to caramelize around the edges (just lightly golden on the edges), which will take about 7 minutes.

Remove from heat and stir in the tempura sauce and Dijon mustard. Let the onion mixture cool thoroughly.

Meanwhile, whisk together the vinegar, Hazelnut Aillade, brown sugar and salt. Stir in half of the cooled onions (the remaining onions will go directly into the salad when it's tossed). Whisk in the remaining 1/2 cup of hazelnut oil. This dressing can be prepared several days ahead (the onions will just get zestier, the longer they marinate in the vinaigrette).

To serve, toss together the lettuce, red pepper, broccoli, cucumber, hazelnuts, the remaining sautéed onions, and about half of the cheese. Drizzle on a portion of the vinaigrette and toss until the ingredients are evenly coated. Add the rest of the cheese and then additional vinaigrette, if necessary.

CREDITS

FOOD PHOTOGRAPHY

Karl Maasdam
Karl Maasdam Photography

Corvallis, Oregon
541-231-0679
karlmaasdam.com

FOOD STYLING

Jan Roberts-Dominguez

Corvallis, Oregon
541-758-2071
janrd.com

BOOK DESIGN

Joanne McLennan
McLennan Design

joanne.mclennan@mac.com

ILLUSTRATIONS

Here are the titles of Jan's watercolors that are featured in the book. Some of the originals are available for purchase, and most are available as prints.

Jan Roberts-Dominguez
Corvallis, Oregon
541-758-2071
janrd.com

Above the Willamette—
*   title page, back cover*
Hazelnut Sprig, page x
Late Summer at the Buchanan
*   Century Farm, page xii*
Hazelnut Catkins, page 3
Winter, page 14
Spring Orchard—Foulke orchard
*   near Monmouth, page 16*
Summer Orchard, page 18
Second Pick—Jan and Linda Wepster's
*   orchard near Yamhill, page 20*
Green Goose—
*   the Chambers' family truck, page 23*
Peaches, page 25
Mature Hazelnuts, page 39
Fresh Garlic, page 51
Red Pepper, page 58
Sweet Peppers, page 69

Oregon Pinot Noir, page 73
Oregon Craft Beer, page 74
Caesar Salad, page 93
Beet, page 98
One Pear, page 102
Winter Feast—Dungeness Crab, page 108
Lemons (detail from Caesar Salad), page 122
Comice Pear, page 133
Salmon Run, page 135
Farm to Fork, page 164
Berry Treasure—
*   Oregon Marionberries, page 191*
Homecoming—
*   Della Robbia Wreath, page 194*
Ella's Bowl, page 228
Blue Plate Special—
*   Oregon strawberries, page 230*
Apple of my Eye, page 257

ARTISTS

Since this book is a celebration of the Pacific Northwest bounty it seemed that our studio photographs ought to dress for that theme as well. So instead of diving into my own collection of food photo props—colorful platters, bowls and glassware from all over the world—I took a spin through my Rolodex, contacting a few of my favorite regional artists. Could I drop by your studio and perhaps borrow a piece or two of your art to use during our photo shoots?

Well, it was summer, high season for art festivals and so a few were on the road. One, Karen Miller, was two-thirds of the way through a 4-month tour across America, teaching along the way, to all who wanted to learn her art of Katazome (a Japanese technique of stencil dying). But each and every one arranged for access to their art.

HERE ARE THE OREGON ARTISTS WHO ENTRUSTED ME WITH THEIR ART:

Steve Aulerich
Clay With Fire

Corvallis, Oregon
541-757-3224
claywithfire.com
Salmon Bowl, page 40

Laura G. Berman
Fine Fiber Art

Philomath, Oregon
541-929-5507
lauragberman.com
Autumn orange felted wool scarf, page 167

Bruce Coblentz
Tanager Spring Turnings

Corvallis, Oregon
541-754-6849
bruce@tanagerspringturnings.com
Sweet gum bowl, page 84

Ted Ernst Pottery
Crescent Valley Pottery

Corvallis, Oregon
541-760-8729
tedernstpottery.com
Salad bowl, page 110
Heavenly bowls, pages 131,148

Linda Heisserman
Pegasus Porcelain

Bend, Oregon
541-419-1500
linheiss@msn.com
Salad plate, page 110

Lee Kitzman
Raku and Stoneware Pottery

Philomath, Oregon
503-929-5507
Hazelnuts on platter, pages 48, 72
Bruschetta platter, page 84
Romesco sauce bowl, page 56

Jan Maitland
Maitland Glass

Reverse Painting and Gilding on Glass
Corvallis, Oregon
541-753-5290
janmaitland.com
23 karat gold gilded Martini glasses,
*   page 245*

Karen Miller
Nautilus Fiberarts

Katazome—Japanese technique
of stencil dyeing
Corvallis, Oregon
541-754-1573
nautilus-fiberarts.com
Green and gold table runner, page 72
Pine cone and pine needle table runner,
    page 84

Sandy Segna
Crescent Valley Pottery

Corvallis, Oregon
541-753-9557
sjsegna@hotmail.com
Salt glazed serving tray, page 148

Deborah Shapiro and Andre Shapiro
Shapiro Porcelain

Tigard, Oregon
503-624-5780
shapiroporcelain@yahoo.com
Platter for albacore, page 178
Dinner plate with albacore, page 180

OTHER PHOTOGRAPHY

Steve Dominguez, Photographer
Summer Campfire at Tyee Winery,
Buchanan Family Century Farm,
during a special dinner event given by
Jan Roberts-Domenguez
Chapter 9, page 247

Lower Orchard at
Buchanan Family Century Farm,
Harvest 2010
Epilogue, page 265

INDEX

A

Oregon
HAZELNUTS
Indulgence in a Nutshell™

THIS BOOK WAS PUBLISHED BY: THE HAZELNUT MARKETING BOARD, (HMB), established in 1949 by the growers and handlers of hazelnuts.

We are proud to partner with B&B PRINT SOURCE to publish this book. B&B has a long history with the Oregon Hazelnut Industry. We are pleased to be working with our representative who is a fellow Nut Growers Society member and budding hazelnut grower.

THIS BOOK WAS PRINTED BY B&B PRINT SOURCE, an environmentally responsible commercial printer based in Tigard, Oregon. They emphasize printing services which include FSC (Forest Stewardship Council) certification, renewable wind energy, vegetable based inks and 100% recycled papers.

For more information, check their website at http://www.bbprintsource.com